RITUAL

RITUAL

How Seemingly Senseless Acts
Make Life Worth Living

DIMITRIS XYGALATAS

P

PROFILE BOOKS

First published in Great Britain in 2022 by
Profile Books Ltd
29 Cloth Fair
London
EC1A 7JQ
www.profilebooks.com

1 3 5 7 9 10 8 6 4 2

Typeset in Sabon by MacGuru Ltd
Printed and bound in Great Britain by
Clays Ltd, Elcograf S.p.A.

A CIP catalogue record for this book is available from the British Library.

ISBN 978 1 78816 102 2
eISBN 978 1 78283 469 4

To my parents

Contents

1

THE RITUAL PARADOX

On the tiny Greek island of Tinos, in the Aegean Sea, the daily
ferry from Piraeus shudders into the main harbour. The white-
washed cubic houses that line the waterfront stand in sharp
contrast to the rugged brown hills looming behind them. A
handful of trucks and some passenger cars trundle out of the
lower deck as tourists pour down the gangways. On the dock-
side, taxi drivers and travel agents crowd around them holding
pickup signs with hotel names, while others advertise last-
minute room-rental deals. Quickly enough, the sightseers are
spirited away, most of them to local beaches and museums. And
now the holiday atmosphere takes an odd turn.

The remaining visitors, most of them dressed in black,
move at a different pace. They seem solemn and purposeful.
Once they have assembled on the quayside, one after the other
they get on their hands and knees and begin to crawl through
the town's main street. Some of them fall on to their stom-
achs and use their elbows to pull themselves forward. Others
lie down perpendicular to the street and roll up the steep hill
in an almost Sisyphean way, twisting and turning their bodies
and pushing against their elbows to drag themselves along. A
woman slumps back while two men drag her by the hands.
There are also those who carry small children perched on their
backs while moving on all fours.

Ritual

It is midsummer. Shade is scarce, and the cobbled street bakes in the sun. As they inch their way through the steep incline, the scene begins to resemble a battlefield: bleeding knees and elbows, scorched hands and feet, bruised bodies and faces full of agony. Many collapse from the heat and exhaustion. But they push on. Accompanying family members rush to offer them water, and as soon as they regain their senses, they continue their ascent.

Their destination is the Orthodox church of Our Lady of Tinos. Towering at the top of the hill, this spectacular temple is made entirely of white marble, imported from the nearby island of Delos. From a distance its façade, draped with numerous arched porticos, carved balusters and ornate windows, looks like the finest embroidered lace. In 1823, legend has it, an ancient icon was dug up after its location appeared to a local nun in a prophetic dream. The church that was built on the same spot to host it soon became a major pilgrimage destination. People flock to Tinos every year from all corners of the world to visit this icon, which is said to work miracles.

After reaching the top of the hill on their hands and knees, the pilgrims must still drag themselves up two flocks of marble steps before paying their tribute to the icon. Carved in exquisite detail, it portrays the Annunciation. But the scene is barely visible, as the image is completely covered by jewels donated by visitors. Hundreds of silver votive offerings dangle from the ceiling above it, reminders of vows and miracles. A heart, a leg, a pair of eyes, a cradle, a ship.

Remarkable as these scenes of apparently senseless self-mortification may be, comparable ones are found all over the world. In the Middle East, Shia Muslims slash their flesh with blades to mourn the martyrdom of Imam Husayn. In the Philippines, Catholics have nails hammered through the palms of their hands and feet to commemorate the suffering of Jesus Christ. In Thailand, Taoists celebrate the Nine Emperor Gods Festival in veneration of Chinese deities by performing blood-letting and impaling their bodies with anything from knives and skewers to antlers and umbrellas. In Meso-America, the Mayans performed bloodletting ceremonies in which men pierced their penises with stingray spines. And in the Southern Appalachian states of the US today, groups of Pentecostals dance ecstatically in their churches while handling deadly snakes. Dangling by their tails, the serpents are free to strike at any time – and they often do. There have been more than a hundred documented deaths among serpent handlers. But as these practices are often secretive, the real numbers may be much higher. According to the social psychologist Ralph Hood, who has studied those communities, 'If you go to any serpent-handling church, you'll see people with atrophied hands and missing fingers. All the serpent-handling families have suffered such things.'[1]

In other parts of the world people engage in rituals that are less painful but no less costly. Tibetan monks spend decades trying to perfect their meditative practices, shutting themselves off from the world for a life of silent contemplation. Muslims around the globe deprive themselves of food and water from dawn to dusk during the month of Ramadan, and Indian wedding ceremonies can last an entire week. Preparations take several months, and hundreds or even thousands of guests are invited. The costs can be crippling for the average family. According to estimates by the Progressive Village Enterprises and Social Welfare Institute (a local NGO), over 60 per cent of all Indian households turn to moneylenders to finance their children's weddings, often at extortionate rates. Those who have no other means to guarantee these loans are often forced into servitude to pay off their debt.[2]

So far I have only mentioned religious ceremonies. Yet rituals are central to virtually all of our social institutions. Think of a judge waving a gavel or a new president taking an oath of office. They are held by militaries, governments and corporations, in initiation ceremonies, parades and costly displays of commitment. They are used by athletes who always wear the same socks in important games, and by gamblers who kiss the dice or cling on to lucky charms when the stakes are high. And in our everyday life they are practised by each and every one of us when we raise a glass to make a toast, attend a graduation ceremony or take part in a birthday celebration. The need for ritual is primeval, and, as we shall see, may have played a pivotal role in human civilisation.

But what drives us all to engage in these behaviours, which have tangible costs without any directly obvious benefits? And why are these activities often held to be so deeply meaningful, even as their purpose is so often obscure?

Several years ago, when I was living in Denmark as an exchange student, I visited the Ny Carlsberg Glyptotek, a spectacular art museum in Copenhagen. As I was wandering through the Antique collection, which included artefacts from ancient Mediterranean cultures, I came across a group of archaeology students visiting from the USA. They were gathered around their professor, a tall, energetic, middle-aged woman who was commenting on the exhibits. Her enthusiasm seemed contagious, and the students appeared attentive and interested in everything she had to say. I decided to follow them and take advantage of the free guided tour.

The professor was using what is known as the Socratic

method: rather than merely lecturing the students, she would ask them questions to probe the knowledge they already possessed and help them make new inferences. After pointing to various objects and discussing their origin and purpose, she eventually came to a strange-looking clay vessel from ancient Greece. 'What is this?' she asked. The students seemed puzzled. The object had the shape of a hollow horn, but was clearly not a drinking vessel, as it was too small and had a hole in the bottom. It was ornately carved in minute detail, but despite all the effort that clearly went into making it, it had no apparent utility. The professor turned to one student in particular. 'What do you think it does? What is it *for*?' she said. 'I don't know,' the student replied, looking embarrassed. 'We don't know,' the professor repeated. 'And what do we say when we don't know what the function is?' The student suddenly lit up. 'It's cultic!' he exclaimed. 'Yes, it's cultic!' the instructor said approvingly. 'It was probably used in the context of some ceremony.'

The professor's response struck a chord with me because it identified one the most curious aspects of human nature: ritual is a true human universal. Without a single exception, all known human societies – whether past or present – have a range of traditions that involve highly choreographed, formalised and precisely executed behaviours that mark threshold moments in people's lives. These behaviours, which we call rituals, either have no explicit purpose at all, or, even when they do, their stated goals are causally disconnected from the actions undertaken to achieve them. Performing a rain dance does not cause water to fall from the sky; stabbing a voodoo doll cannot harm people at a distance; and the only thing a Tarot card reader can reliably predict is that your wallet will be lighter after your consultation. It is this gap between means and goals that led the professor to infer that because an object which required hard labour to make had no obvious function, it probably served a ritual purpose.

Despite this puzzling discrepancy between actions and goals, rituals of all sorts have persisted for millennia. In fact, even in the most secular societies, and whether we realise it or not, ritual is just as common today as it was in the distant past. From knocking on wood to uttering prayers, and from New Year celebrations to presidential inaugurations, ritual permeates every important aspect of our private and public lives. And whether it is performed in a religious or a secular context, it is one of the most special of all human activities, deeply imbued with meaning and importance.

These features distinguish ritual from other, less special acts such as habits. Although both can be stereotypical behaviours, in that they involve fixed and repetitive patterns, in the case of habits these actions have a direct effect on the world, while in ritual they have symbolic meaning and are often performed for their own sake. When we develop the habit of brushing our teeth before going to bed, the goal of this act lies in its immediate function – it is *causally transparent*. Waving a symbolic brush in the air would not help keep our teeth clean. By turning this process into a routine, our habit allows us to perform it regularly and unreflectively.

Rituals, on the other hand, are *causally opaque*. They command focus and attention because they involve symbolic actions that must be remembered, for they must be executed precisely. By way of illustration, at a Greek Orthodox wedding the best man or woman exchange the wedding rings and place them on the fingers of the bride and groom and a pair of crowns on their heads three times; the priest must read three prayers; and the couple must drink three sips of wine from a common cup and circle the altar thrice. These actions are part of an elaborate, hour-long sequence that must be followed to the letter and requires meticulous instruction and rehearsal to ensure fidelity. As it happens, none of those actions is of any legal consequence: what makes the couple married is a different procedure, which involves the signing and stamping of a legal document. But the symbolism and pageantry of the wedding ceremony are what make the event momentous and memorable – so much so that we get the impression that it is the ritual rather than the paperwork that validates the marriage. While habits help us organise important tasks by routinising them and making them mundane, rituals imbue our lives with meaning by making certain things special.

In other words, specifically those of sociologist George C. Homans, 'ritual actions do not produce a practical result on the external world – that is one of the reasons why we call them ritual'. In fact, among many religious communities, rituals that are practised with an explicit goal in mind are often regarded as sorcery. 'But to make this statement is not to say that ritual has no function [...] it gives members of the society confidence, it dispels their anxieties, it disciplines their social organizations.'[3]

Anthropologists have explored these functions of ritual for over a century, meticulously gathering scores of fascinating observations. These scholars recognised the tremendous potential of ritual as a vehicle for personal fulfilment, empowerment and transformation, and also as a mechanism for cooperation and the maintenance of social order. They formulated insightful theories, but they were rarely able or willing to put them to the test. Cultural anthropologists start from the assumption that the social world is a complex and messy place, and some of the most meaningful things in people's lives cannot be easily quantified. They conduct ethnographic research in the field, where they observe people's ritual practices in their natural contexts. Their primary focus is on trying to understand how such customs are experienced by their practitioners in those contexts.

On the other hand, psychologists and other experimentally minded scholars acknowledge that measurement requires a high degree of control, and this control cannot be easily achieved in real-life settings. They typically work in the laboratory, where they focus on one tiny sliver of behaviour at any given time. To do this, they take people out of their normal environments and bring them into the lab, where they can isolate them from any extraneous factors that may complicate the study. In this process, much of the meaning attached to this context inevitably becomes unavailable to the experimenter.

Perhaps partly because of this difficulty in studying such meaningful activities in the laboratory, ritual never became a popular subject of research among psychologists. It was regarded either as a mundane aspect of human behaviour, a mental glitch that would eventually go away, or as an elusive topic that was all but impossible to investigate scientifically. As a result, until recently scientific knowledge on one of the most pervasive aspects of human nature was scarce and fragmentary.

In recent years this has begun to change. As anthropology came of age, ethnographers became more aware of the need to take people's claims seriously, but also of the importance of finding ways to test those claims empirically. And as psychologists began to realise that there was more to the human psyche than what their test subjects let on in the narrow confines of a college lab, they became increasingly interested in the input of culture.

In many cases, social scientists from various disciplines began working together and learning from each other. The development of new methods and technologies has allowed them to explore questions that were previously out of reach. Wearable sensors have made it possible to study what goes on in people's bodies as they take part in real-life rituals; advances in biochemistry and brain imaging have allowed researchers to peer into people's brains in the lab and in the field; innovations in the cognitive sciences have provided new ways of assessing what goes on in their minds; and increased computing power combined with new software packages have allowed statisticians to make sense of those complicated data sets. For the first time, a scientific study of ritual is in full development. We are at last able to start piecing together the solution to an age-old puzzle: what is the point of all this bizarre stuff?

Rituals have fascinated me since childhood. Growing up in Greece, I would take the bus to the city centre with my mother once a month. She would buy supplies for sewing, pay utility bills and run various errands. My reward for accompanying her was a visit to one of the city's largest bookshops. It was the only place where I could buy *National Geographic*. This was a few years before the internet became publicly available, and at the time there was no cable television in Greece. The glossy pages of *National Geographic* were my first window on to the captivating world of anthropology. They conveyed me to faraway places and introduced me to exotic cultures. I read about the massive pilgrimages of India, the folk healers of the Andes and the Voodoo rituals of Haiti; I admired striking photographs of the courtship ceremonies of the Wodaabe in Niger, the divinatory practices of the Maya in Guatemala and the painful initiations performed by various Amazonian tribes. And I learned that boys of the Maasai tribe in Kenya and Tanzania had to kill a lion as part of their coming-of-age ritual. Successful hunters earned the right to wear the lion's mane as a ceremonial headdress.

All these customs were practised in distant places, and that also made them feel removed in time: they seemed like relics of a bygone romantic era that were on their way to extinction. I didn't give much thought to the fact that rituals pervaded my own society too. Nevertheless, like all Greek schools, mine began the academic year with a sanctification ceremony. Every day we attended a morning prayer that was mandatory, as were the occasional visits to the local church. In addition to those religious rituals we had flag-raising ceremonies, sang the national anthem and marched in student parades held in every town on national holidays. But somehow those rituals seemed different. Maybe it was that they were not meaningful to me. They were imposed on me by my teachers. I participated because I had to, and always looked for an excuse to avoid them. Maybe it was because those rituals actually were different. Their repetitive, low-arousal nature was nothing like the extravagant ceremonies that featured on the pages of *National Geographic*. Or perhaps they were just so close to me that they became somehow invisible.

I was in my early teens when I saw a news report about the pilgrimage in Tinos on public television. Men and women of all ages were crawling up the hill, knees bruised and arms bleeding, to see a sacred icon. Upon reaching their destination, many of the pilgrims burst into tears, their grimaces turning into expressions of bliss. Those interviewed by the reporters stressed how important this pilgrimage was to them. Some of them had been saving up for years to make the journey. When asked why, they mentioned that it was the fulfilment of a vow they had made. Some had specific requests to the Virgin:

pleading for a pregnancy, asking for their child to pass an exam or begging for healing. For others there was no specific reason: the pilgrimage itself was the goal.

I asked my grandfather if he had heard of this practice. He was the most religious person I knew, well versed in all matters relating to Orthodox Christianity – a real 'man of the Church', as people used to say. Of course he had heard of it, he said. In fact, he could name several people in his village who had made the pilgrimage – even some I knew myself. And as he came to think of it, he brought up similar traditions found in other parts of Greece, from painful pilgrimages in the southern island of Crete to fire-walking ceremonies held in rural villages in the north. Rather than being a thing of the past or the customs of some distant and exotic tribe, these traditions existed here and now, practised by people of my own culture. But why? Why do so many strange traditions persist in the modern age of science, technology and secularisation? And what is it that pushes human beings everywhere to spend so much of their time and resources on ritual activities – time they could otherwise be spending making money, making love, socialising, taking care of their families or just living the good life?

I finally got the opportunity to explore this question a few years later, when I enrolled at the Aristotle University under the guidance of religious studies professor Panayotis Pachis. As a student, I dived into the history and the psychology of ritual, taking every course on these topics that I could find and reading any relevant books I could get my hands on. One day my professor mentioned an opportunity to study at Aarhus University in Denmark, where a new research programme in the cognitive science of religion had just been established. He didn't have to say it twice. I bought myself a warm coat, packed my luggage and boarded the first flight of my life, on my first

trip to a foreign country, on the first day of the new millennium
– a real rite of passage.

In Aarhus I became acquainted with a radically different
perspective on culture: one that used methods and theories
developed in the psychological and evolutionary sciences to
study topics that were traditionally under the purview of the
humanities. It was love at first sight. I started reading about
the latest theories from areas such as cognitive psychology, evolutionary anthropology and neuroscience. I learned about the
evolution of symbolic thought, about the way intense ordeals
are encoded in memory and about the parts of the brain
involved in certain religious experiences.

But I was still missing something crucial. If I wanted to find
my own answers to the questions I was asking, I could not do
it from my desk, the library or the lab. I would need to study
these rituals in their natural environment. This meant meeting
real people, listening to their stories and participating in their
everyday activities. In other words, I would need to become an
anthropologist.

After finishing my master's, I went to Belfast to study with
Harvey Whitehouse, an anthropologist at Queen's University
who is an expert on ritual. For my doctoral project I decided
to investigate extreme rituals. I mean extreme not in the sense
that there is anything unusual or abnormal about their practitioners – in fact, these rituals tend to be attended widely where
they occur, by people of all socio-economic backgrounds – but
extreme in much the same way as extreme sports, in that they
require extraordinary amounts of effort. In other words, if one
were to catalogue all of the world's ceremonies and measure
how much emotional stress, physical pain or energy expenditure they entail, these rituals would be at the top end of the
spectrum.

After completing the required preparatory training, I submitted my doctoral research proposal to investigate one of the rituals my grandfather had talked about: fire-walking. Various communities around the world practise ceremonies that involve walking barefoot across burning embers. To study some of these practices I would conduct fieldwork among a handful of small rural communities in Greece, Bulgaria and, later, Spain. Soon I was packing my luggage again – this time to go into the field.

Over the course of a year and a half I did what anthropologists do: I asked questions. Day after day, I entered people's homes, interviewed hundreds of individuals and attended countless ceremonies, from the routine Sunday Mass to the electrifying fire-walking rituals. I met some extraordinary individuals, had captivating conversations and heard fascinating stories. But the one question that mattered to me most was also proving the most difficult to answer. That question was the simplest and yet the most important one of all: *why*? Why do people engage in all those costly rituals? As it turned out, the answer was more complicated than I had imagined.

Alejandro was a seventy-three-year-old man from a small Spanish village called San Pedro Manrique. Ever since his teens Alejandro and most of his family had been taking part in the local fire-walking ritual. I have attended numerous fire-walking ceremonies over the years, but none of them was as fierce as the one that takes place there. Over two tons of oak are used to produce a fire hot enough to melt aluminium, and participants walk on that fire barefoot while carrying another person on their back. Many of them carry children. But not Alejandro. He carried adults who often weighed more than himself.

Alejandro took great pride in being a fire-walker. He hadn't missed the ceremony in fifty-three years. When I asked him if he would ever stop, he became thoughtful. After a long pause he said: 'I know that one day I will be too old to do it. But when that day comes, I just won't go there; I'll stay at home. Because if I am there, watching, without being able to participate, I'll jump off the bell tower and kill myself.'

The following year, a physical examination revealed that Alejandro's heart was showing signs of arrhythmia, and his doctor prohibited him from performing the ceremony. It would be too much excitement, he said, and in his condition, it was best not to take any risks. Unable to walk across the fire, the old man kept his word and decided to stay at home that night. As painful as it was for him, he was not going to watch the fire-walk if he could not take part in it.

His son Mamel, however, had other plans.

That year I had returned to San Pedro to attend the festival. I was invited to join the procession, in which the locals gather at the town hall square and then join hands, forming a human chain that rhythmically moves up the hill until it reaches the *recinto*, an open-air amphitheatre structure surrounding the flat piece of earth where the pyre burns. I was next to Mamel, our hands locked together. As we approached his father's house, he pulled me out of the chain. I was quite surprised that he would want to leave the procession. 'Where are we going?' I asked. 'You'll see,' he said.

We walked into Alejandro's house, and found him sitting by the window. He looked up, seemingly surprised to see us. Mamel stood in front of his father and announced: 'Dad, if you can't walk over the fire, then I'll carry you over the fire myself.' The old man did not speak. He just stood up and gave his son a hug, his eyes full of tears.

That night, the crowd applauded as Alejandro climbed on to Mamel's back. He looked as proud as a peacock as his son carried him across the flames in small, steady steps. The entire village cheered for them, and their family rushed to embrace them. But Alejandro hadn't finished. He waved his hand sharply, stopping everyone in their tracks. As he turned around to face the fire once more, everyone gasped. They knew exactly what his intentions were. He took two steps forward and then started stomping his feet. His smile was now gone, and his face looked more serious. He stared at the fire with such intense focus, it was almost as if he was trying to will it into submission. Without hesitation, he started walking across the glowing embers. A few moments later, he emerged triumphant from the other side of the fire pit. The crowd was now frenetic, and the other fire-walkers praised and congratulated him – except for his family, whose reluctant smiles conveyed a mix of disapproval and pride.

When I asked Alejandro why he had decided to defy his doctor's orders, he told me: 'The doctor said that if I do the fire-walking ritual, something terrible might happen to my heart. But does he know what will happen to my heart if I *don't* do the ritual?' Indeed, there seemed to be very few things Alejandro considered more important than this ceremony. He had told me so repeatedly: this was one of the most important things in his life. But when I asked him why the ceremony mattered so much to him, he seemed puzzled. He stared at me and after a long pause repeated the question, seeming at a loss for words. 'Why we do it? ... Well, I can't really say why. I guess it's something I've seen since my childhood. My father did it, and my grandfather did it, so since I was a little kid, I've always wanted to cross that fire.'

Time and again, anthropologists come across such

statements. When they ask people why they perform their ceremonies, the most typical reactions involve perplexed looks, long pauses and eventually something along the lines of the following: 'What do you mean, why do we do our rituals? We just do them. It is our tradition. It is who we are. That's what we do.'

This is the ritual paradox: people often swear on the importance of their rituals, although they are not always sure why they are so important, other than that they are time-honoured. Ritual seems pointless, yet it is experienced as something truly vital and sacred. But much like other deeply meaningful areas of human activity – think of music, art or sport – what might initially appear bizarre or futile can actually have transformative power.

In my attempt to resolve the ritual paradox I embarked on a two-decade journey to study some of the world's most extreme rituals, as well as many commonplace ones. I lived with local communities, witnessing numerous ceremonies and conducting a series of laboratory and field experiments, in order to understand the human drive for ritual. Rather than taking practitioners out of context by placing them in a laboratory, I often decided to bring the laboratory into context by moving it into the field. As a result, I spent several years visiting communities around the world and studying a panoply of ritual traditions from the mundane, such as prayer, to the extreme, like sword-climbing; and from large-scale events, like massive pilgrimages, to private and secretive black magic ceremonies. Biometric sensors and hormonal sampling allowed me to explore the neuro-physiological effects of various rituals;

behavioural measurements helped me study how these bodily processes affect the way people interact with one another; psychometric tests and surveys revealed some of the motivations behind ritual practices; and participant observation provided insights into how people experience these practices and how they find meaning in them.

My findings, as well as convergent discoveries from a variety of scientific disciplines, reveal that ritual is rooted deep in our evolutionary history. In fact, it is as ancient as our species itself – and for good reason. Although ritual actions have no direct influence on the physical world, they can transform our inner world and play a decisive role in shaping our social world. This book will take us through these scientific discoveries, which reveal the inner workings of rituals and the important functions they serve for individuals and their communities. The science of ritual can help us understand and celebrate a primordial and fundamental part of what makes us who we are. For it is only when we embrace our obsession with ritual that we will be able to harness its full potential in our lives.

2

THE RITUAL SPECIES

Every year, an ancient ceremony takes place at the shores of Lake Natron in northern Tanzania. Over a million participants travel from afar, some of them covering thousands of miles to attend the festivities. Upon their arrival, they socialise and feast together in anticipation of the main event. Dressed in flamboyant pink colours, they break off into smaller groups to perform an extraordinary dance. They gracefully move in circles, holding their heads high, bowing them down and turning them from side to side. Every once in a while, they switch partners and repeat the whole sequence. Gradually, excitement builds and the dance becomes more frantic. They start swirling, occasionally letting out excited cries and throwing their feet up in the air. In time, the entire crowd behaves like one pulsating unit. At the culmination of the ceremony, they get in formation and begin to march together in lockstep while chanting in synchrony. This is no frivolous drama – in fact, the stakes could not be higher. At the conclusion of the ceremony, young females pick their favourite male dancers, who will become their sexual partners, often for life. It is a custom that has been handed down through countless generations and remains unchanged to this day.

This mating ritual was recently studied by a group of French ornithologists: the protagonists are flamingos, and the stage for it is known as a 'lek' (a word of Swedish origin that denotes fun and games). Mating arenas like this one are found around the world, where various species of animals congregate in large numbers to engage in courtship rituals. The researchers took advantage of a pool of 3,000 tagged birds in the Camargue region of the Rhône delta in southern France, an area full of shallow lagoons that make it an ideal habitat for flamingos. The tagging system allowed them to know the sex, age and life history of each individual bird, so that they could study them at a distance without disturbing them. Over a two-year period they used high-definition video cameras to observe and record the behaviour of one hundred of those birds (fifty males and fifty females) during the mating season. They meticulously documented the type, frequency and timing of each bird's dance moves, as well as their success rates in copulating and producing offspring. What they learned is that the most skilled dancers – that is, those who had the largest repertoire and the most varied combinations of moves – had much higher chances of finding a mate.[1] The early bird may get to feed, but the groovy bird gets to breed.

The lekking behaviour of flamingos resembles some more familiar forms of ritualised courtship. If you focused on the movements of a pair of birds dancing in circles, stretching, turning and bowing their heads in synchrony, you might find it strikingly similar to a Viennese waltz. And if you zoomed out to look at the entire entranced flock dancing in unison, you might think of a rave or rock concert. Just like their avian counterparts, those human behaviours involve similar movements performed in synchrony, and they similarly often result in mating. But many social scientists will be quick to offer a word of caution here: they will insist that bird rituals are the product of hard-wired instincts. Flamingos dance because they are programmed to do so. Their brain tells them to do it, and they obey. Human ritual, in contrast, is complex and full of subtle symbolism, which is the product of our sophisticated culture.

However, as I will show in the pages that follow, rituals are part of human nature just as much as they are part of bird nature – in fact, probably even more so. They are truly universal human behaviours. If you can find a human society without any rituals, I will happily reimburse you the cost of this book. Across all cultures, rituals appear spontaneously in childhood; they are readily learned and transmitted, and are performed by religious and secular individuals alike.

Besides, not all bird rituals can be brushed away as simple automatic behaviours. Bowerbirds perform their own mating rites in elaborate love nests constructed by the males. All aspects of those ceremonies, including the dance moves, songs and the intricate details of the bower's decorative style, vary between different populations of bowerbirds and are culturally transmitted. When one bird migrates to another area, it will adapt its mating ritual to the customs of the local population.[2] Other birds, such as magpies, ravens and crows, appear to have death rituals. They flock over corpses of deceased members of their group as if standing vigil, and have been observed fetching sticks and other objects and arranging them around the corpse.[3]

Another problem with the comparison between bird and human rituals is that birds are very distant relatives, phylogenetically remote from us. If their rituals and ours are in fact related, we should find analogous behaviours among some of our closest relatives, such as other mammals, and especially other apes.

There are two possibilities here. The first is that bird and human rituals are not directly related but have evolved independently, in a process called *convergent evolution*. This means that similar traits and behaviours tend to evolve among different species whenever they need to solve comparable problems. For instance, dolphins are genetically no more closely related to sharks than gorillas are to herrings; but because both dolphins and sharks had to face similar adaptive problems associated with moving underwater at high speeds, they evolved very similar streamlined body shapes. In a similar manner, birds and humans have specific similarities that may play a crucial role in their hyper-ritualisation. Specifically, birds use vision and hearing as their primary senses, tend to be social species, engage in pair-bonding, are often monogamous, are excellent imitators and have specific proclivities related to rhythm, synchrony and vocalisation. All of these traits, as we shall see, are crucial to human rituals as well.

Another possibility is that, when it comes to ritual behaviour in animals other than birds, we simply haven't looked hard enough. Indeed, many of the traits previously thought to be uniquely human have now been found in other animals. Until recently, favourite candidates for this human uniqueness included emotions, personality, using and making tools, empathy, morality and warfare, to name a few. But as soon as scientists started studying other animals systematically in their natural environments they realised that, in one form or another, all of these traits can be found in other species. Similarly, until recently there was barely any evidence of ritual behaviour among mammals. Today there is plenty, and mounting. Dolphins engage in a form of group dance, breaching out of the water in synchrony; humpback whales perform collective songs; and various marine mammals seem to have mourning rituals, carrying their dead around for days or swimming around them in unison. Dolphins have even been observed pushing a dead calf towards a boat and waiting for the boat crew to pick up the corpse, then forming a circle around the vessel before swimming away.[4]

In addition to the air and the sea, rituals abound among land animals too. When courting, giraffes perform a love dance that resembles a tango, with the male and female walking alongside, rubbing, butting and entwining their long necks. Packs of wolves sing together, howling in unison across large distances. And elephants hold rituals to mourn for and pay tribute to their dead.

Elephants are indeed among the few animals who seem to have an understanding of death. They have often been observed trying to bury deceased members of their group by scattering dirt on them or covering them with leaves and flowers. There are even reports of elephants trying to bury other dead animals that they came across, including humans.[5] George Adamson, the wildlife conservationist whose family became the inspiration for the film *Born Free*, told the story of a woman in Kenya who fell asleep as she was resting under a tree. When she woke up, a group of elephants were standing nearby and one of them was gently poking and smelling her. The woman was petrified and decided to stay still and play dead. The pachyderms soon gathered around her and started trumpeting loudly. They collected branches and foliage from the tree and covered her body entirely with them. The next morning, local herdsmen found the woman still under the large pile of branches, too scared to move.[6]

When one of their own perishes, especially when it is an important member of the group such as a matriarch, elephants will remain with the body for days and will return to the carcass frequently. Even decades later, they travel long distances to visit the bones of their deceased relatives. When they arrive, the entire group stands in silence and they take turns to inspect the remains, gently touching, turning and smelling the bones. Adamson reported that a male elephant in Kenya was shot because he kept trespassing into the government gardens. His body was dragged half a mile away, where it was butchered and the meat distributed to the local tribespeople. That night, other elephants found the carcass, picked up the bones and carried them back to the spot where he had been killed.

Collective rites are also common among members of our own family, the *hominids*, which includes modern and extinct great apes. The primatologist Jane Goodall, who was the first scientist to systematically study non-human primates in their natural environment, described a variety of striking behaviours among apes. She spent several years living with chimpanzees in Gombe National Park in Tanzania. She noted that, when the chimps visited certain places, they engaged in some rather peculiar behaviours. For instance, when they approached a large waterfall, they often performed what Goodall called a 'waterfall dance', a spectacular display that can last for up to fifteen minutes. During this display the chimps stand upright, stamping and swaying rhythmically from foot to foot in a state of hyper-arousal, swinging from tree vines through the spray of the waterfall and hurling large rocks into the water. Once the commotion is over, they sit down and gaze quietly at the water-fall for several minutes. Chimpanzees perform similar dances 'at the onset of a very heavy rain, reaching up to sway saplings or low branches rhythmically back and forth, back and forth, then moving forward in slow motion loudly slapping the ground with their hands, stamping with their feet, and hurling rock after rock. [...] Is it not possible that these performances are stimulated by feelings akin to wonder and awe?' Goodall wondered.[7]

More recently, in a variety of locations in West Africa, chimpanzees were recorded collecting stones and carrying them to specific trees. They placed these rocks inside hollow cavities, used them to drum on the tree trunks or piled them at the base of the trees. Researchers compared these stone piles to the cairns or stone mounds that people in various cultures use to mark sacred locations.[8] Indeed, these trees seem to have some special significance for the chimps, who will often change their course when travelling in the area to visit them before resuming their trip. They then stand upright in front of a tree and start swaying back and forth, panting, hooting and jumping up and down in a state of feverish excitement. At the culmination of this performance they start drumming on the tree trunk with their feet or with rocks.

Most primates are social species, and as such they have social rituals. Some of those species live in what anthropologists call 'fission-fusion' societies, where individuals have a flexible affiliation with their group, breaking into smaller parties to forage and later merging together again. This is similar to what humans do. We divide our free time between our core and extended family, our best friends, our colleagues and various other groups based on our needs, interests and values. In species that form fission-fusion societies, individuals may split off from their group for a long time before meeting again. When they are reunited, they perform greeting rituals that help reaffirm the bonds between them. Humans shake hands, kiss or hug. Chimpanzees, bonobos and spider monkeys also do all of these things.[9] They embrace, they kiss, they groom each other and they pant-hoot (which looks a bit like a group of teenagers screaming 'Oh my God!' in excitement). Chimps perform a 'handclasp', a secret handshake that is unique to each chimpanzee group. And male baboons perform a stereotyped 'scrotum grasp', which is exactly what it sounds like and functions as a trust-building ritual.[10] The anthropologist Mervyn Meggitt observed a similar ritual among the Walbiri, an Australian tribe of aborigines who used a penis-holding ritual to defuse tensions between men. 'If the matter is serious, however, one concerning a previous killing or a death from putative sorcery, the aggrieved person may refuse to hold the visitor's penis.' Such a refusal, Meggitt reported, was a grave insult that could lead to bloodshed.[11]

The primatologist Frans de Waal has even observed chimpanzees engaging in ritualised greetings towards humans. When the chimps at the Yerkes Field Station in Georgia saw their caretakers approaching in the distance, they would burst into loud hooting. 'General pandemonium ensues, including a flurry of embracing and kissing. Friendly body contact increases one-hundred-fold, and status signals seventy-five-fold. Subordinates approach dominants, particularly the alpha male, to greet them with bows and pant-grunts. Paradoxically, the apes are confirming the hierarchy just before cancelling it, to all intents and purposes. I call this response a celebration.'[12]

These observations suggest that ritual is widespread in the animal world. But they also point to another interesting pattern: it seems that some of the most intelligent animals are also the ones that have the richest repertoire of rituals. Needless to say, measuring animal intelligence is a tricky and contentious task. There have been many attempts to come up with some kind of 'IQ of all living things' that would allow us to rank animals in terms of their mental capacity. For instance, the idea that a bigger brain means higher intelligence has intuitive appeal and has therefore been popular for a long time. But the obvious problem with this idea is that bigger organisms have bigger brain volumes, which they use to meet basic needs such as regulating body temperature and controlling large muscles. Cows have bigger brains than chimpanzees but are not generally considered to be smarter than them.

Similar problems arise when we look at other metrics, such as the number of neurons or the size of specific brain structures like the cerebral cortex or the neocortex, which are only found in mammals. And when we adjust for body size (which produces a metric called the brain-to-body mass ratio), we are now presented with new oddities: for one thing, bigger organisms typically have *smaller* brains relative to the rest of their body. A case in point: frogs have a bigger brain-to-body mass ratio than elephants. The Encephalisation Quotient (EQ) takes this into account by comparing the brain size of one species to that of other species of roughly the same size.

While these assorted metrics may be suggestive when comparing animals belonging to the same order (for example, baboons to squirrel monkeys or ravens to robins), comparisons often break down when we move between more distant species, such as elephants and caribou, or shrews and whales. And this is only half the problem: it would be no less challenging to quantify ritualisation between different species. All the same, in a general sense, when we observe ritual in the natural world, we find that it tends to be more lavish and extravagant among some of the most intelligent animals. Apes, dolphins, elephants, crows and many other stars of the animal kingdom appear to lead heavily ritualised lives.

This may seem paradoxical. Why would such intelligent creatures waste so much time and energy on apparently pointless activities when they could be finding more straightforward solutions to their problems? But this is exactly the power of ritual: it is a mental tool that allows its users to achieve a desirable outcome through obscure means. It is for this reason that intelligent organisms engage in these seemingly wasteful behaviours: not simply because they cannot help it, but because they can afford it. Those animals have the mental surplus required to engage in behaviours that function as cognitive gadgets, essentially allowing them to outwit themselves. When the situation requires it, they are able to turn their attention away from directly functional tasks, focusing instead on behaviours that are indirectly but reliably beneficial to them. This is because ritual allows those animals to deal with some of the challenges that come with having a complex psychology, such as mating and pair-bonding, coping with loss and anxiety, and achieving cooperation and social organisation. From this point of view, it should come as no surprise that the most intelligent of animals is also the most ritualised of them all.

No other animal uses ritual as extensively and compulsively as *Homo sapiens*. In fact, archaeologists often consider ritual to be one of the core defining features of behaviourally modern humans, because it is related to the capacity for symbolic thought. We humans appear to be unique in our ability to communicate complex abstract ideas and concepts, not only about the here and now but also about other times and places – even imaginary ones. We do this not just through art, narrative and myth but also through ritual. In fact, various theories on the origins of human cognition have proposed that ritual and intelligence evolved side by side.

Biological anthropologists suggest that group ceremonies could have played a key role in the transmission of cultural knowledge in prelinguistic societies. Through the symbolic re-enactment of collective narratives, ritual functioned as an embodied proto-language that provided an 'external support system' to individual cognition – a crucial step on the road towards language itself.[13] The neuroscientist Merlin Donald has argued that ritual was a mental foundation stone for the evolution of social cognition, allowing early hominids to align their minds with social conventions. By establishing a shared system of collective experiences and symbolic meanings, ritual helped to coordinate thought and memory, allowing a group of humans to function as a single organism. And because of its close connection to symbolism, rhythm and movement, as well as its role in demarcating the extraordinary from the ordinary, ritual has also been linked to the evolution of art.[14]

If these theories hold any water, ritual is a core part of who we are as a species and played a pivotal role in our evolution. Theories about the distant past are, of course, hard to test. Preliterate societies obviously did not leave any texts behind, so we know nothing about their language, beliefs, myths and narratives. But while minds do not fossilise, art and ritual can and do leave traces in the archaeological record.

The earliest evidence of ritual in our own evolutionary lineage, which separated from chimpanzees 6 to 7 million years ago, comes from burials. In the region of Atapuerca, in northern Spain, archaeologists found skeletal remains of at least twenty-eight individuals in a cave that they named Sima de los Huesos (the 'Pit of Bones'). Although the location is part of a vast cave system, all the skeletons were packed together in a small chamber far away from the entrance, and a finely carved quartzite hand axe was also deposited with them. There is no evidence of habitation anywhere in the cave, which suggests that the bodies were carried and laid there on purpose. DNA extracted from over 7,000 bones revealed that the skeletons belonged to members of *Homo heidelbergensis*, the earliest known relatives of Neanderthals, who lived 430,000 years ago.

A similar gravesite was found inside a cave in the Gauteng province of South Africa: this time the remains were from an archaic human species named *Homo naledi*. The cave contained the full skeletons of fifteen individuals. Carbon dating revealed that they had lived around a quarter of a million years ago. The site was entirely undisturbed: there was no indication of predators ever having entered the cave, such as toothmarks on the bones, and no rubble or signs of flooding. The skeletons were intact, lying in the same position as the corpses would have been. It looks as though some other *Homo naledi* carried the bodies through the cave's dark twisty passages, climbing on top of a sharp 12-metre (40-foot) rock and then descending through a narrow crevasse to enter an isolated chamber, where they laid them down to rest before securing the entrance on their way out. And this was no isolated episode. Dead bodies were deposited there again and again for generations. This seems to have been a prehistoric cemetery.

Not all scientists are convinced that this is evidence of a deliberate burial. Even as various other explanations have been ruled out, there is still no positive proof. Although quite unlikely, it is still possible that fifteen different individuals fell into the chamber and died there without breaking a bone. Perhaps the cave's topography was different then, and the bodies were swept in by flood water. Or there may be some other explanation which will be revealed by future research. It is hard to say based on a single site.

Less controversial evidence comes from our extinct close relatives the Neanderthals. Burial sites have been found in various places in Iraq, Israel, Croatia, France and elsewhere, and it is clear that these groups did not merely dump their dead. They carefully deposited the remains of their dead in graveyards, especially the bodies of young children, often placing them in the foetal position, and went to great lengths to protect those graves from scavengers. The occasional presence of bear skulls and bones, sometimes arranged in circles, has led some archaeologists to suppose that Neanderthals also practised totemism or animal worship. In the Bruniquel Cave in south-west France, for example, they broke off stalagmites and used them to construct large circular structures deep underground, which may have been meeting places for some type of collective ritual.[15]

Some remain doubtful about just how elaborate the ritual practices of the Neanderthals may have been. After all, the material evidence is limited, and we will never know what was going through their minds as they were burying their loved ones. But one thing is certain: by the time our own species appears, the evidence for ritual activity is indisputable. Anatomically modern humans (*Homo sapiens*) did not simply bury their dead. They adorned them with red ochre and placed jewellery, artwork and favourite objects and animals inside their graves. In many cases, they also practised secondary burials by charring or otherwise removing the flesh from the corpse or letting it decompose before carefully depositing the remains into a grave. They also performed a variety of other collective rituals, as suggested by numerous rock carvings and paintings, symbolic artefacts and the intentional destruction of pottery and other valuable goods.

The French sociologist Émile Durkheim noted that life in aboriginal societies alternates between two different phases.

In one phase, the population is scattered in small groups

that attend to their occupations independently. Each family lives to itself, hunting, fishing – in short, striving by all possible means to get the food it requires. In the other phase, by contrast, the population comes together, concentrating itself at specified places. [...] This concentration takes place when a clan or a portion of the tribe is summoned to come together and on that occasion [...] conducts a religious ceremony.[16]

These two different phases, Durkheim argued, constitute two very different realms: the sacred and the profane. The profane includes all those ordinary, mundane and monotonous activities of everyday existence: labouring, procuring food and going about one's daily life. In contrast, the realm of the sacred, which is created through ritual, is dedicated to those things that are deemed special. The performance of collective ceremonies allowed people to set their everyday worries aside and be transported, albeit temporarily, to a different state. And as ritual must always adhere to a rigid structure, participation in collective ceremonies established the first social conventions for early humans. By coming together to enact their ceremonies, practitioners ceased to be an assortment of individuals and became a *community* with shared norms, rules and values. This is why the anthropologist Roy Rappaport declared ritual to be 'humanity's basic social act'.[17] It is how society itself comes into being. And in fact, this may be, in a literal sense, historically true.

Göbekli Tepe is an archaeological site in south-east Turkey, just a few miles from the Syrian border. When first discovered in 1963, it was initially mistaken for a medieval cemetery and did not attract much attention. But when the German archaeologist Klaus Schmidt visited the site in 1994, he immediately realised that he had come across something far more important. What were originally thought to be Byzantine tombstones were in fact the tips of enormous T-shaped Neolithic pillars. These limestone megaliths were used to build twenty circular structures expanding across an area of 90,000 square metres (22 acres). The site is so big that several decades later only a small part of it has been fully excavated. The stones are sculpted in exceptional detail. Reliefs depict a wide assortment of wild beasts: foxes, boars, bulls, gazelles, cranes and vultures. Chiselled snakes twist around the enormous pillars, and scorpions and insects seem to crawl over them. There are also fantastical creatures, half-human and half-animal. One can only imagine how awestruck the people of the time would have been as they watched those figures come to life under the flickering light of torches and campfires. This was clearly a monumental temple of some kind.

The most astonishing aspect of this site, however, is neither its enormous size nor its elaborate artwork. It is its age. Göbekli Tepe was built more than 12,000 years ago, making it the earliest known ceremonial structure anywhere in the world. It is three times the age of the Egyptian pyramids, and more than twice as old as Stonehenge. In fact, it pre-dates every single one of the hallmarks of civilisation, including farming, writing, pottery and the wheel.

This colossal structure seems to have been used as a pilgrimage site by hunter-gatherers who travelled enormous distances to visit it – from as far as Israel, Jordan and Egypt, according to Schmidt. There does not seem to have been any permanent habitation in the area. No traces of domesticated plants or animals have been found, and the first dwellings to appear around the temple were built almost a thousand years later.

Göbekli Tepe changed everything we thought we knew about prehistoric humans. Not only did it push back the birth of civilisation by thousands of years, but it also seems at odds with the widespread idea that agriculture was the reason for permanent settlements and organised societies. For a long time the prevailing theory was that farming was the spark that ignited human civilisation. The domestication of plants, the story went, allowed humans to settle into a more sedentary life. This facilitated rapid population growth and the development of large collaborative communities that were able to produce a surplus of food and tools and to engage in new, specialised forms of labour. This in turn provided the necessary time, resources and organisation to support complex social structures, develop advanced technologies, formulate religious ideas and build monumental temples. Because of these epochal transformations, the period is often called the 'Neolithic Revolution' or the 'Agricultural Revolution'. The discovery of Göbekli Tepe poses a serious challenge to this narrative.

The very idea that agriculture suddenly propelled human societies to new levels of progress and prosperity is rather questionable, when you think about it. In today's massively interconnected world, the advantages of sedentary life seem obvious. Permanent settlement and large-scale societies make all of the great blessings of human civilisation possible: advanced science and technology, systematic education and healthcare, abundant art and leisure pursuits, high levels of safety and (arguably) greatly increased quality of life. None of these could have been enjoyed by small groups of hunter-gatherers living in scattered isolation. Yet it is also fairly clear that the comforts of our own settled lifestyle came about only thanks to the cumulative efforts and achievements of thousands of generations living before us in agrarian societies. What benefits did settlement offer them?

We now know that the so-called Agricultural Revolution in fact had a devastating impact on those first farmers. Anthropological evidence from both contemporary and ancient societies suggests that the shift from a nomadic way of life to sedentism led to a sharp decline in living conditions.[18] Hunter-gatherers exploited a wide range of environments, which ensured a relatively balanced diet and a healthy and active lifestyle. As their constant travelling precluded the hoarding of resources, those societies were strikingly egalitarian. They worked fewer hours to meet their dietary needs and enjoyed more free time.

In contrast, farming brought reliance on a much more limited diet largely restricted to a few staple crops and, in those populations which developed lactose tolerance or discovered cooking methods such as fermentation, dairy. This made the first settlers vulnerable to natural disasters and caused serious nutritional deficiencies. Farmers had to work much more to meet their basic needs, partly because agrarian life was hard and partly because the production of a food surplus required extra resources to defend that surplus from raids. The accumulation of wealth in the hands of a few elites and the formation of armies brought inequality and created the conditions for the exploitation of the masses. As people lived in close proximity to others as well as to their livestock, they became susceptible to diseases, and epidemics often wiped out entire populations. They were now having over twice as many children, but only a few of them made it to adulthood.[19]

Indeed, the decline in health and life expectancy and increase in child mortality that the advent of farming brought about is rather astonishing. The average height dropped by 10 centimetres (4 inches) and did not return to pre-Neolithic levels until the twentieth century. Agriculturalists experienced diseases, severe vitamin deficiencies and various deformities and pathologies.[20] Fossil evidence reveals that their bones decreased in density and strength and that they regularly suffered from osteoporosis, osteoarthritis and degenerative conditions. The crowns of their teeth had more pits and grooves as their enamel became thinner, which indicates nutritional deficiencies. The increased consumption of starchy plants resulted in dental caries and tooth loss. Skeletal inflammations betray the prevalence of infectious diseases such as tuberculosis, syphilis and leprosy. Their skulls became porous as a result of iron deficiency and anaemia. Excavations of Neolithic settlements show that their soil and water were heavily contaminated with animal faeces and their dwellings infested with parasites.[21] And so the Neolithic Revolution was not accompanied by any immediate population increase, or the flourishing of big cities and advanced civilisations. For thousands of years the life of the early farmers looks to all appearances as though it was simply worse than that of hunter-gatherers.

What was the motive, then, for permanent settlement? Obviously, Neolithic people did not decide to exchange a comfortable subsistence for the back-breaking toil of agriculture so that their descendants could reap the benefits of their sacrifice thousands of years later. The forces of natural selection, whether biological or cultural, have no foresight: unless a behaviour has some immediate utility, it will not spread, whatever benefits it might have for future generations.

The discovery of sites such as Göbekli Tepe offers one intriguing explanation: the driving force behind this transition was a social rather than an economic one. People were coming together from various places in order to perform large collective rituals that were held in massive temples. But the building of those temples would have necessitated cooperation on a scale that was entirely unprecedented at that point in human history. Some of the stones used in the construction of Göbekli Tepe, carved out of a nearby quarry, are over 6 metres (20 feet) tall and weigh as much as 15 tons. Extracting, carrying, sculpting and placing those monoliths without any sophisticated technology would have required large groups of individuals working together for years, laying the foundation for the development of complex societies. Once completed, the temple would have provided an incentive to start farming in order to provide for a permanent priesthood and the large numbers of visiting pilgrims. Sure enough, genetic evidence shows that within 500 years of the construction of Göbekli Tepe, the world's oldest domesticated strains of wheat are found not too far from that location. A few centuries after that, people had also begun corralling livestock in the area. In Schmidt's words, 'First came the temple, then the city.'

This is a profoundly radical proposition. For centuries the prevailing idea has been that civilisation was driven by material forces. Some archaeologists attribute the social changes that occurred during the Neolithic era to demographic pressures that forced humans to find ways of increasing food production. Others believe it was climatic changes that pushed them to search for fertile lands that could support more game animals. Or perhaps the opposite occurred: it was precisely those groups stuck in marginal environments that were forced to innovate with new means of subsistence in order to survive. There are also those who argue that the shift was the result of technological advances that provided better ways of harnessing calories. Or maybe it was the alpha males of those early societies who convinced or coerced them to scale up so that they could satisfy their thirst for political power.

Philosophers and political theorists have long engaged in fierce disagreements about whether the transition from foraging to a settled life was a good idea. There are those, like Thomas Hobbes, who see it as a pivotal moment that elevated the human race to a more moral and meaningful existence. For others, such as Jean-Jacques Rousseau or Karl Marx, it was a terrible mistake that led to the corruption of human nature and paved the way for the exploitation of the masses. But all of them agree that it was the material base, the conditions relating to the means of economic production, that gave birth to the emergence of a *superstructure*, a society's norms, religious beliefs, artistic endeavours and ritual practices. Schmidt's interpretation turns this orthodoxy on its head. If it is true, then a major chapter in the history of our species needs to be revised. What if the irresistible drive that created the first great civilisations was not hunger for food but the urge for ritual?

○

Humans are obsessed with ceremony. In some cases this fixation can even become pathological. Obsessive–Compulsive Disorder (OCD) is a condition characterised by intrusive thoughts and fears and the urge to perform highly ritualised actions in order to alleviate those worries. These actions have some of the core attributes of cultural rituals: they are characterised by rigidity, repetition and redundancy, and they have no obvious purpose. Nonetheless, those who suffer from OCD feel the compulsion to perform them and become intensely anxious if they are unable to do so.

The anthropologist Alan Fiske and his colleagues examined historical and ethnographic records from numerous cultures, ranging from ancient states to contemporary hunter-gatherers and industrial peoples. They found that, across those cultures, the content and form of OCD-related actions were similar to those of the locally prevalent rituals.[22] Both revolved around precautionary behaviours such as acts of cleansing and purification (dealing with contamination), repetition and redundancy (checking for dangers) and rigidity (aversion to novelty and emphasis on precision).

These similarities have led some scholars to propose that ritual behaviour is an evolutionary accident, a mental glitch without any adaptive value. For instance, Pascal Boyer and Pierre Liénard have attributed the human preoccupation with ritual to the misfiring of mental systems that serve to detect danger in our environment.[23] This 'hazard precaution system' evolved to make inferences about the potential presence of threats such as predators, contaminants and social exclusion, and to trigger relevant protective actions. According to Boyer and Liénard, ritualisation is so compelling because it mimics the inputs of that system, even when there is no actual danger.

Although the mental glitch hypothesis is worth considering, on closer examination it seems rather unlikely. Evolution is not wasteful: behaviours that are impractical or maladaptive do not tend to stick around forever. To be sure, evolutionary glitches are not uncommon, especially when environmental conditions change too fast for natural selection to catch up. Our craving for junk food is a good case in point. Before processed foods became available, sugar, salt and fat were sought-after scarcities that were essential to our ancestors' survival. In that environment, if you found a honeycomb, you'd better gobble all of it up in one sitting, because there was no telling when you would get another opportunity. Today, sugar, salt and fat are for most of us very easy to find, often in the same dish, but our brains are still inclined to obey the same age-old urge to overindulge.

Ritual, however, is not like junk food. Throughout history it has served some of the same functions for our ancestors as it does for us today. And the more we study it scientifically, the more evidence we find that these functions are important enough to outweigh the costs. Rather than ritual being the accidental misfiring of an adaptive system, Fiske argues, it is the other way around: OCD is simply an exaggerated, pathological manifestation of the basic human capacity to perform and be moved by rituals.[24] According to this theory, our species has an innate proclivity to invent, enact and transmit rituals. This deepseated need for ceremony is evident in the myriad ways in which human cultures around the world celebrate the most important moments of their members' personal and public lives.

Why on earth should ritual matter so much? A clue may be discovered in the importance we gave it not only at the dawn of civilisation but also at the beginning of each of our own lives.[25] From around the age of two, children typically develop a variety of rules and routines that they follow compulsively. They may insist, for instance, on fixed household schedules, often requiring specific mealtime and bedtime rituals such as listening to the same story every night, kissing their favourite toy or saying goodnight to the moon. They become attached to specific toys and other objects that are treated as special – and seem to have their 'favourite' version of everything. They develop rigid food preferences and like to eat their meals in particular ways. They are obsessed with repetition, acting out the same things over and over again. They like arranging and reordering objects in specific patterns. And they require strict adherence to rules, never satisfied until an action has been performed in just the right way.[26]

Remarkably, children also appear to believe that rituals have a causal influence on the external world: studies of pre-school children in Israel and the USA, for example, found that they often believe that having birthday parties actually causes people to grow a year older.[27] Children were told a story about a little girl who had a party on her first and second birthdays, but a year later her parents were not able to organise a celebration for her. When asked how old the girl was, many of them said that she was still two. When they were told a similar story about a girl who had two birthday parties on turning three, many of them said that she would be four years old. And when the researchers asked them why we celebrate birthdays, many of them used causal language: we have birthday parties *so that we can grow older*. Why should this be so?

To become functioning members of society, children must quickly learn to adhere to the norms and conventions of their social groups.[28] For this reason, they eagerly adopt normative rules and prescriptions and are quick to protest when social norms are violated.[29] They imitate the behaviours of other people, especially members of their own social groups. In fact, they are so good at copying behaviours faithfully that they are willing to do it even when those behaviours are not relevant to the task at hand.

A group of psychologists at the University of St Andrews compared imitative behaviour in children and young chimpanzees.[30] They built a puzzle box that released a gummy bear when solved – a reward that both children and chimps coveted. The researchers demonstrated the solution, which involved four steps: 1) opening a bolt to reveal a hole at the top of the box; 2) inserting a stick into the hole and tapping it three times; 3) sliding a door at the front of the box to reveal a second hole; and 4) using a metallic rod to pull the treat out of the hole. Then they offered the box to the participants.

In half of the cases the puzzle box was opaque, so participants could not see exactly how each action affected the outcome. In this case, both chimps and children copied the actions precisely and got the reward. The other half of the participants saw exactly the same demonstration, except that the box was now made of transparent acrylic glass. This revealed that the first two steps in the process were in fact irrelevant to the goal: the top of the box had a false ceiling and therefore inserting the stick through the top hole had no impact on the subsequent steps. When they realised this, the shrewd chimps cut to the chase. They skipped the unnecessary actions and immediately jumped to the final steps, which were all that was needed to get to the treat. When it comes to food, there is no room for etiquette. The children, by contrast, still copied the whole sequence faithfully, including the steps that were irrelevant to the end goal. Other studies found that even when children are specifically told to copy only the actions that are relevant to the task, they still imitate the entire procedure faithfully, including the non-functional actions.[31]

So it appears that apes do not mindlessly ape, but that human children do. In fact, a follow-up study found that children's tendency to over-imitate actually increased with age.[32] The researchers expected that, as they became more cognitively developed and better able to understand causality, children would be more selective about which actions they copied. The results showed just the opposite: while all children imitated the actions with a high degree of fidelity, three-year-olds often omitted some of the irrelevant tasks rather than carrying them out. Five-year-olds, on the other hand, copied the demonstration to the letter, including the non-causal actions.

There is, however, a wrinkle here that deserves note. It seems that increased maturity may have allowed the five-year-olds to appreciate that those steps were *intentional* and needed to be carried out with precision. Indeed, research shows that children copy intentional actions even if they don't make much sense, but they do not copy mistakes. When researchers indicated that some of the actions where unintended by saying 'Whoops!' as they executed them, children in those experiments omitted those actions from the sequence.[33]

This over-imitation is thought to be an adaptive strategy that humans evolved to facilitate social learning.[34] Because we rely on cultural knowledge more than any other animal, copying the behaviours of those around us can be a very convenient strategy, even when we don't fully understand their meaning. We may often not know why people do things the way they do, but the fact that they do feels like sufficient justification. After all, when it comes to learning a craft, no amount of theory can take the place of experiential learning through apprentice-ship. For the same reasons, neither do we bother to question each step of the process. When we follow a recipe or traditional remedy, we copy the entire sequence. We don't know why it is important to use arborio rather than basmati rice or to cook the pasta in a pot that is only half-filled with water, but we trust that there is a reason, and we do as instructed.

Even as adults, most of what we need to know is based on understanding social convention rather than any deep grasp of causation. Imitation therefore continues to play important social roles for us throughout our lives. We are, nonetheless, rather picky about who we imitate. Children and adults alike are more prone to copying their fellow group members and those who look like themselves. For example, they prefer to learn from those who share their own language, accent or ethnicity. Studies show, for example, that when minority college students are taught by instructors who have similar backgrounds to their own, they get better grades and are more likely to graduate.[35]

In an experiment conducted at the Evolution, Variation, and Ontogeny of Learning Laboratory at the University of Texas, researchers recruited five- and six-year-old children to examine how they would behave when they felt socially excluded.[36] The children were told that there were two groups of people in the experiment, the yellow group and the green group, and that they would be part of the yellow group. They were given yellow hats, shirts and wristbands to wear as their insignia. Then they played a virtual game that involved tossing around a ball with other players, who were members of either the yellow or the green group. Studies show that players who do not receive the ball in this game feel excluded and ostracised. But the children acted out more frustration and reported more anxiety when they were being excluded from their own group.

After the game the children watched an adult from either the yellow or the green group arrange certain objects on a table by using an arbitrary sequence of actions, such as tapping on a cube twice before moving it, touching it to their forehead or placing their hand under their chin. They were simply told that 'this is how this group does it', and after the demonstration was over, they were told: 'Now it's your turn.' Children who had been excluded by their in-group in the game imitated the demonstration with higher fidelity than the children who had been included. They also showed higher fidelity than those who had been excluded by the out-group. It was specifically being shunned by one's own group that led to the most faithful adherence to the group's norms. Other experiments found that even watching a cartoon about characters who were ostracised by their in-group led children to engage in over-imitation.[37] This suggests that young children may use behavioural imitation as a means of strengthening important social bonds.

◠

The special appeal of ritualisation goes far beyond early child-hood. It remains a key part of our lives that persists throughout development and well into adulthood, and is honed into the myriad ways in which human beings in every culture celebrate the most important moments of their personal and public lives. In fact, ritual is one of the most predictable features of every human society. The anthropologist Donald Brown compiled a list of human universals. 'What do all people, all societies, all cultures, and all languages have in common?' he asked. He pro-vided the answer in the form of a description of what he called the Universal People. 'Theirs is a description of every people, or of people in general.' The list includes language, cooking, kinship, music, dancing, art and many other aspects of human expression for which there are no known exceptions. It also includes numerous ceremonial acts: marriage rites, childbirth customs, burials, oaths and more: 'The Universal People have rituals, and these include rites of passage that demarcate the transfer of an individual from one status to another.'

Ritual scholars use the term 'rites of passage' to describe ceremonies that mark major life stages and changes. The anthropologist Arnold van Gennep was the first to note that all rites of passage follow a similar structure and play similar roles. Such rituals involve three stages. First, initiates are sym-bolically separated from their previous way of life and begin moving towards a new identity and status. For example, cutting or shaving one's hair is a common part of many rites of passage (think of initiation into the army or a religious community), which symbolises leaving part of oneself behind in order to become a new person. The second phase (often called 'liminal') is the transitional period between the other two stages, where initiates have left their former status behind but have not yet acquired their new status. During that period the adolescent is neither a boy nor a man; the bride is neither single nor married; the deceased is neither part of this world nor part of the after-life. They are betwixt and between. In the third and final stage the transition is complete and the initiate is reintegrated into society as a new person. At the end of a graduation ceremony the pupil has become an expert; a military initiation turns civilians into soldiers; a funeral helps the deceased become an ancestor. Rites of passage do not merely celebrate the transition to a new state – they *create* this new state in the eyes of society.

These practices start at the very beginning. In every culture the birth of a child is surrounded by ritual. Common customs include shaving the baby's first hair, performing cleansing rites or using protective amulets. In Bali babies are not allowed to touch the ground for the first three months of their lives. Other birth rituals can be more eccentric. In the Spanish village of Castrillo de Murcia, newborns are placed on mattresses in the street and men dressed as the devil jump over them. And in the Indian town of Solapur babies are tossed from the rooftop of the Baba Umer Dargah shrine, with the hope that the people holding a bedsheet 50 feet below will manage to catch them.

University of Nevada anthropologists Sharon Young and Daniel Benyshek examined 179 societies and found that most of them had specific rituals for disposing of the placenta after childbirth, including burying it, burning it, hanging it on a tree and ingesting it.[38] Similar traditions dictate the handling, storage or disposal of the umbilical cord after birth. By intro-ducing special forms of cleansing and protection, those rituals are meant to assuage the fear of danger and contamination that parents experience after childbirth. They are our first rites of passage.

However, birth alone is not always adequate for acceptance into a social group. In many societies an infant is not considered a full person and has no social status until a naming ceremony has taken place. As our ancestors faced much higher infant mortality rates, birth was no guarantee of survival. Therefore, delaying name-giving by several days, months or even years after birth provided a psychological mechanism for dealing with a potential loss by postponing emotional investment until the likelihood of death was lower. Indeed, research shows that infant mortality rates correlate with the time elapsed before the naming ceremony: the higher the chance of a premature death, the later the ceremony takes place.[39]

Adulthood is also widely celebrated by rituals that are meant to help turn boys into men and girls into women. In West Africa, girls of the Fula tribe are ushered into womanhood by enduring painful facial tattoos, while the boys' initiation involves a fierce flogging from their peers. But not all coming-of-age ceremonies are as frightening. Bar Mitzvahs, confirmations, *quinceañeras* and 'sweet sixteen' parties are only some of the many festive ways to mark the transition to adult life.

Coming of age means becoming eligible for marriage. Every society has wedding ceremonies, which tend to be among the most lavish of all rites of passage. In 1981 the wedding of Prince Charles and Lady Diana Spencer in England cost more than the entire annual GDP of some of the world's poorest countries. And while royalty can bill the taxpayers for such luxuries, people around the world deplete their own savings and even get into years' worth of debt to organise extravagant marriage ceremonies. Indian weddings can last up to a week and have hundreds or even thousands of guests. In a traditional Jamaican wedding the entire village is invited. And in Swaziland the groom must pay the bride's family eighteen cows – quite a hefty price by local standards. Those who cannot afford these expenses often resort to borrowing money to fulfil their ritual obligations.

All major life transitions are marked by ritual, and so is the ultimate one. In Indonesia, the Toraja people have a remarkable tradition that involves keeping the bodies of their dead relatives in their homes for months or even years until they prepare an elaborate funeral for them. During that time the corpses dry and become mummified but the relatives treat them as if they were still living. They keep them on a bed, change their clothes, offer them food and drinks and have daily conversations with them. When all the preparations have been completed, a large public gathering is attended by the entire community and the corpse is finally laid to rest. But the interactions with the deceased do not end with the funeral. Each year the mummified body is exhumed, dressed up and paraded around town.

The practices of the Toraja may seem unusual, but similar traditions abound around the world. Many cultures practise what is called a 'second burial', which involves exhuming the remains and interring them again in a second ceremony. And in many societies people build monumental architecture for their dead even when they cannot afford the same standards for the living. I have visited parts of Madagascar where the locals dwelled in tiny windowless reed or adobe huts, vulnerable to predators, cyclones and other disasters, while their deceased ancestors inhabited the only safe, spacious and robust brick-and-mortar buildings in the area. And anyone who has seen the ancient city of Petra in Jordan will marvel to recall that the countless palatial structures carved directly into the rock were used as tombs. As the dead rested in these architectural masterpieces, the local Nabataean people dwelled in goatskin tents.

This preoccupation with the dead is truly mystifying. From

our perspective, as creatures that mourn our dead, it may seem natural. But why would evolution create a creature that goes to such lengths to mourn its dead – or indeed that mourns them at all? As ultra-social animals, we have a number of adaptations for social living. These include particularly strong forms of attachment and bonding, which start with the core family but also extend to more distant relatives, sexual partners and social companions and friends. When young children are separated from their parents, they often experience an acute stress reaction known as separation anxiety, as do parents who lose track of their offspring. This is because our brains trigger the release of stress hormones that serve an obvious adaptive function: they motivate parents and offspring to stay close to each other. Lovers may experience similar stress after a break-up, and so can good friends that have had a falling out. This stress incentivises them to seek reconciliation in order to keep their social networks from disintegrating.[40] But when death occurs, the anxiety of separation cannot serve its intended purpose, as reunion is no longer possible, which only exacerbates the pain. This view seems to be supported by the fact that all those non-human animals that appear to mourn their dead, such as elephants and chimps, are also highly social creatures.

From this perspective, the *capacity* for grief may stem from evolutionary adaptations shaped by natural selection, although grief itself may not be adaptive. The reason it persists is that separation occurs much more frequently than death, and so the cumulative benefits of this anxiety are greater than the cost of grief. To cope with such debilitating emotions as the experience of loss and the fear of mortality, all human cultures have developed death rituals.

Death is not the only domain in which this happens. As we will see, there is rather a more general pattern: rituals can help us deal with intensely worrying prospects that only a certain level of social sophistication can make us aware of in the first place. Across various areas in which our evolved mechanisms are somewhat ill fitted to the challenges of life, rituals may serve as mental tools that help us to overcome those challenges by bypassing or recalibrating those mechanisms. Thanks to this utility, the thirst for ritual runs deep in the human psyche. We are drawn to perform them not merely because we like to, but because we need to.

3

ORDER

In 1914 a young Polish student undertook a journey that would transform the discipline of anthropology. His name was Broni-slaw Malinowski, and his destination was the Oceanic island of New Guinea. Malinowski's scholarly career was shaped by serendipity in more ways than one.[1] As a child he was frail and sickly, suffering from respiratory problems and poor eyesight. On his doctor's advice, his mother took him on lengthy trips to warmer climates. They travelled to the Mediterranean, north Africa, Asia Minor, Madeira and the Canary Islands, often for many months at a time. Living in these exotic places left an indelible impression and sparked his interest in foreign peoples and customs. He marvelled at the medieval palaces of Venice and the picturesque fishing villages of the Dalmatian coast. In Tenerife he allowed himself to be carried away by the exuber-ance of a fortnight-long Carnival celebration, breaking with his usual ascetic lifestyle. As he was recovering from his illness, his mother would read books to him for hours. Years later he singled out the influence of one book in particular: James Fraz-er's *The Golden Bough*, the first extensive study of the world's myths and rituals.

Despite his illness, Malinowski was a bright and accom-plished student. He was awarded a doctorate in the philosophy of science from the Jagiellonian University in Kraków. His thesis was so well received, in fact, that it won him the most prestigious award: the *Sub auspiciis Imperatoris,* which was presented to him in a special ceremony by none other than the emperor Franz Josef himself, who bestowed him with a gold and diamond ring. This extraordinary distinction opened many doors for Malinowski, who found he was free to research more or less whatever he wanted. He chose to pursue the passion for anthropology that he had acquired through his mother's readings. He went on to study with some of the most prominent scholars of his time, receiving training from Wilhelm Wundt, one of the founders of modern psychology, and Karl Bücher, a renowned economist and father of journalism, before eventually undertaking postdoctoral work in anthropology at the famed London School of Economics under the guidance of two heavyweights of the discipline, Charles Seligman and Edvard Westermarck.

For his research Malinowski planned to do fieldwork in Sudan. He started reading the relevant literature and learning Arabic, but he was eventually not able to secure the funding, as the department's administrators felt that they had sponsored too many projects in Africa. Instead, Seligman managed to obtain a grant to send him to New Guinea, where he had done his own fieldwork some years earlier. Malinowski jumped at the opportunity. But things did not start off very well.

On his way to his field site the First World War broke out. At the time, the area was under the jurisdiction of Australia, a colonial dominion of the British Empire, and though Malinowski was from Poland and lived in England, he had an Austro-Hungarian passport. This technically made him an enemy subject, and as such he was barred from returning to Europe until the war was over. His exile was to last four years. Malinowski's wanderings during that period allowed him time to explore various options for his research, eventually landing on the Trobriand Islands, an archipelago of small coral atolls off the east coast of New Guinea. It was there that he carried out his most pioneering fieldwork – pioneering, that is, because it *was* fieldwork.

In those early days of the discipline, cultural anthropology was to a surprising degree an armchair venture. The prototypical anthropologist of the time was a bearded old man who sat comfortably in his study somewhere in Britain, smoking his pipe and reading reports sent by travellers, missionaries and colonial administrators about the inhabitants of exotic lands. The practices described in those narratives were often exaggerated by the observers, who judged them to be irrational, primitive or pagan, by the prudish and ethnocentric standards of Victorian society.

Based on such descriptions, these peoples' customs would have surely seemed radically different from those of British upper-class intellectuals, who readily concluded that this was due to inherent biological factors. They proposed that there was a natural hierarchy, with their own civilisation at the top and those 'primitive' cultures at the bottom. Their racist views were exacerbated by the fact that they never met the people they studied. Nowadays those scholars are often referred to as 'armchair anthropologists'. As a famous anecdote has it, when Sir James Frazer, one of the most prominent anthropologists of the nineteenth century, was asked whether he had actually ever encountered in the flesh the people he wrote about, he replied: 'Heaven forbid!'[2]

By the beginning of the twentieth century anthropologists had begun leaving their armchairs and travelling in order to learn about the cultures they studied. But their interactions with the locals remained limited. Upon their arrival, they would usually take up residence in a missionary compound or a mansion owned by some colonial governor, where everything was provided for them. The stereotypical anthropologists of this era would spend their days socialising with diplomats, missionaries, military attachés and other colonial compatriots, and reading administrative records and reports. Most of their interactions with the natives consisted of observing the local servants while sipping tea at the mansion's front porch. Occasionally they would summon some of those servants to ask them questions with the help of an interpreter. This era has been christened 'veranda anthropology'.

Malinowski was one of the first anthropologists to step off the veranda and live among the people he was studying. Although he had the opportunity to stay in the house of a British trader in the Trobriands, he decided to give up the comforts of the mansion and pitch a tent in the forest, where he could live among the natives and get first-hand experience of their culture and demeanour. The anthropologist, he wrote with a dose of literary flair,

> must relinquish his comfortable position in the long chair on the verandah of the missionary compound, Government station, or planter's bungalow, where, armed with pencil and notebook and at times with a whisky and soda, he has been accustomed to collect statements from informants, write down stories, and fill out sheets of paper with savage texts. He must go out into the villages, and see the natives at work in gardens, on the beach, in the jungle; he must sail with them to distant sandbanks and to foreign tribes, and observe them in fishing, trading, and

ceremonial overseas expeditions. Information must come to him full-flavored from his own observations of native life, and not be squeezed out of reluctant informants as a trickle of talk.[3]

He called this approach 'open-air anthropology', a radical deviation from the 'hearsay note-taking' that was the common method of the time.

During his time with them, Malinowski meticulously documented the Trobrianders' family structures, their trading systems, their morals, their sexual practices and various other aspects of their daily lives. In the process he realised that, far from being the irrational fools that armchair anthropologists had portrayed them to be, those people had extensive knowledge of their environment and a firm grasp of the natural forces and principles related to their livelihood. Despite their lack of any advanced technology, farmers had all the necessary botanical, geological and meteorological knowledge to produce not only enough to feed the local population but indeed a surplus that they could trade with other tribes. Fishermen knew how to use celestial bodies, winds and sea currents to navigate. Canoe makers had all the necessary (even if unarticulated) understanding of structural mechanics and hydrodynamics to build a solid vessel. Each builder, Malinowski wrote approvingly,

has a whole array of component parts, and he must make them fit together with a considerable degree of precision, and that without having any exact means of measurement. By a rough appreciation based on long experience and great skill, he estimates the relative shapes and sizes of the planks, the angles and dimensions of the ribs, and the lengths of the various poles.[4]

But Trobrianders did not rely on these skills alone. To be on the safe side, they also used what Malinowski referred to as 'magical rites'. These were rituals that were practised only under specific circumstances. For example, the local fishermen performed elaborate ceremonies before fishing in the open sea, but they never bothered with such details before fishing in the lagoon. Malinowski noted that the two activities were equally vital to the subsistence and economic life of the community, but they were very different in their nature. Protected by the coral reef, the shallow waters of the lagoon made navigation safe all year round. Fishing in the lagoon consisted in picking up molluscs or using a poisonous root extract to stun small fish and then drive them into fishing nets. As the experienced fishermen had knowledge of the habits of the lagoon fish, an easy catch was essentially guaranteed.

In contrast, deep-sea fishing was risky business. It involved spear-fishing sharks or searching for shoals of fish that were never certain to arrive, while battling the dangerous waves, the fragile canoes at the mercy of unpredictable tropical weather. There was no guarantee the fishermen would come back with a good catch, or come back at all. So treacherous were these waters, in fact, that young sailors would be cautioned by their seniors through the telling of scary stories about sea monsters, jumping rocks, petrified canoes and other legendary misfortunes.

Before setting out on such a dangerous journey, sailors engaged in laborious preparations. They observed taboos, kept vigils, used special herbs, sacrificed pigs, covered their canoes with plaited mats and made offerings to the spirits. Once on board, they rubbed the canoes with mint, beat them with banana leaves, tied pandanus streamers to their masts and recited spells. They used special body paint, blew on conch shells, chanted in synchrony and used a stale potato to remove the heaviness of the canoe. Special sets of rites were associated with departing, sailing, arriving at their destination, making the final approach, returning home and keeping safe.

Ritual also permeated the construction of the vessels. Before felling the tree chosen for the canoe, magical spells and food offerings were used to exorcise the *tokway*, evil wood spirits that dwell in trees. During transportation the log was twice beaten with a bunch of dry grass, which was meant to make it lighter. When the log at last arrived at the village, a public ceremony was held to signal the beginning of construction. The creeper used to transport the log was cut with an axe whose blade had been wrapped in herbs. On the same evening, herbs were also placed between the canoe and the transversal logs on which it laid. Scooping out the log was preceded by the recitation of a special formula over the *kavilali*, the tool that would be used to carve it. When the carving was complete, a spell was recited over a bundle of leaves soaked in coconut oil that was placed inside the canoe and struck with an axe. Meanwhile, the various other parts of the canoe – the ribs, the sail, the rafter, the planks that formed the gunwale and so on – were prepared, each accompanied by its own set of rituals. When all those components were finally pieced together, another ceremony was used before the placement of the ornamental parts of the canoe, which were hammered with a sacred stone and covered with mint sprigs. Numerous additional rites ensued in relation to caulking, painting and other parts of the process. When the construction had finally been completed, an elaborate naming and launching ceremony was held, including public singing, dancing and communal meals.

In striking contrast to this obsessive ritualisation of the canoes used in Oceanic expeditions, those boats that were used for fishing in the safe waters of the lagoon or for transporting goods along the shore did not require any special ceremonies. Similarly, crafts such as house building, which were just as laborious and technically complicated as the construction of those deep-sea canoes, did not require any rituals either.

After surveying various other domains of life in the Trobriand Islands, Malinowski began to discern a clear pattern. In general, rituals were largely absent from domains that had predictable outcomes but abundant in areas associated with danger and uncontrollable circumstances such as warfare, illness, love and natural phenomena. They were, for example, indispensable when planting garden vegetables that were vulnerable to diseases or bad weather but unnecessary when tending to hardier plants such as fruit trees. 'We find magic wherever the elements of chance and accident, and the emotional play between hope and fear, have a wide and extensive range,' he wrote. 'We do not find magic wherever the pursuit is certain, reliable, and well under control of rational methods and technological processes.'[5]

Based on these observations, Malinowski proposed that magical rituals served an important psychological function in the life of Trobrianders. Ritual, he argued, stems from the same deep-seated need to control our world that leads us to pursue scientific discoveries. This need motivates us to perceive causal relationships between phenomena in the world and to seek ways to influence those relationships. In the case of ritual, the causal links may be illusory, but the action may still have therapeutic value:

It enables man to carry out with confidence his important tasks, to maintain his poise and his mental integrity in fits of anger, in the throes of hate, of unrequited love, of despair and anxiety. The function of magic is to ritualise man's optimism, to enhance his faith in the victory of hope over fear. Magic expresses the greater value for man of confidence over doubt, of steadfastness over vacillation, of optimism over pessimism.[6]

And this, he realised, was not very different from what we find in our own societies. Although the content of our beliefs and practices may vary widely across cultures, people all over the world think and behave in fundamentally similar ways, and members of all cultures use ritual to cope with the stresses and uncertainties of life.

○

Sure enough, when we examine our own societies, we find that areas of life involving lots of stress and anxiety also tend to be ritualised and surrounded by superstition. If we want to observe the spontaneous birth of personal rituals, a good place to start would be those areas associated with high stakes, high uncertainty and limited control: think of casinos, sports stadiums or war zones.

Gamblers are notoriously superstitious. When you walk into a casino, you surrender all control at the door. By its very nature, gambling is a game of chance, so players have limited or no control of their fate, and this can be anxiety-provoking. To cope with this anxiety, gamblers develop all sorts of personalised rituals.[7] They may close their eyes while the roulette is spinning; they may talk to the slot machines; or blow on the dice before rolling them. And it's not just that gamblers are more superstitious than non-gamblers: the more time they spend gambling, the more rituals and superstitions they enact.[8]

The sociologist James Henslin studied the rituals of craps

players in St Louis, Missouri. He observed that players developed specific ways of throwing the dice depending on the desired outcomes.[9] 'It is believed as a principle', he noted, 'that a hard throw produces a large number, and a soft or easy throw produces a low number.' By establishing a metaphorical similarity between the values on the dice and the speed of movement, players attempted to influence one by manipulating the other. Other gamblers would try to get their luck from another player by touching or rubbing their dice on someone who was having a winning streak. Here the intuition is that physical contact will enable luck to be transferred (to rub off) from one person to another.

These behaviours fit James Frazer's definition of sympathetic magic.[10] The related actions, he argued, rest on two main principles: similarity and contagion. The law of similarity is the idea that 'like causes like', or that physical resemblance also implies similar functions. This is why in some parts of the world people believe that a rhinoceros horn can help a man get an erection, and why others believe that stabbing a voodoo doll can harm an enemy. This is also the basic idea behind homeopathy, which is based on the premise that 'like cures like'.

The law of contagion is the idea that things carry immutable essences that can be transmitted through contact. Psychological studies show that this type of magical thinking is very common. For example, experiments have found that people are reluctant to wear a sweater that has been worn by a mass murderer, even if it has been thoroughly washed and disinfected, although they may be happy to wear an identical sweater that has not been in contact with the killer.[11] Of course, participants in those studies responded to hypothetical scenarios. But these results are corroborated by real-life data. When an unnatural death occurs in a house (a murder, suicide or fatal accident), the property's value decreases by as much as 25 per cent, and even neighbouring units generally lose part of their value.[12]

Positive essences can be transmitted too. Some years ago I was invited to give a lecture at Oxford University. My former doctoral adviser had recently been appointed to the chair of the anthropology department there, and naturally I paid him a visit. His office was not what I had expected. It had old furniture and seemed in need of some renovation. I sat on a red couch that was pretty uncomfortable and felt broken. Surely, I thought, being at one of the most prestigious academic institutions in the world, he could afford a better sofa. I can't have done a good job concealing my surprise, for my host remarked that the couch was indeed broken. The reason he did not want a new couch, he explained, was that this one used to belong to the famed anthropologist Sir Edward Evans-Pritchard, who once occupied his position.

All of us engage in some form of magical thinking. This is why John Lennon's piano sold for over $2 million, and why concert-goers often try to touch the star performers, hoping (whether consciously or unconsciously) that some of their charisma will rub off. A more startling example of this kind of thinking occurred when Pope Francis addressed the US Congress in 2015. After the pope had finished his speech, Congressman Bob Brady rushed to the podium and snatched His Holiness's water glass. He sneaked it into his office, where he had a sip and shared some of it with his wife and staff. He then took the rest of the papal water home and sprinkled it on his grandchildren. When asked about it by the press, he stated: 'I'm considering it as holy water [...] I mean, the Pope drank out of it, the Pope handled it [...] I'm sure it's blessed if the Pope drank out of it.' From a theological perspective, Brady's claim is incorrect: for water to become holy water, a special ritual is required that involves salt, an exorcism and a blessing. Be that as it may, his intuition is a very common one. Indeed, it bears a resemblance to certain passages from the New Testament, where Jesus's followers try to touch him with the belief that this will heal them of various illnesses. In fact, it is reported in Mark 5:29 that Jesus realised that a woman had touched his garment, because he felt some of his power being drawn away.

Like gambling, athletic competitions can also entail high stakes and high uncertainty, and to cope with it – wouldn't you guess it? – sports people are prone to ritualisation. Surveys show that athletes have more rituals and superstitions than non-athletes. But much like the magical practices of the Trobriand Islanders, sports rituals are not performed indiscriminately. The anthropologist George Gmelch studied baseball players, a group known for their many superstitions. He found that their rituals were overwhelmingly related to the most uncertain actions in the game, such as pitching and hitting, but not actions like fielding, which have less to do with chance.[13] Similar observations have been made in numerous other sports, including basketball, football, volleyball and hockey, as well as among golfers, track and field athletes, tennis players and fencers. What is more, ritual behaviour among athletes also seems to increase when they face tougher opponents or compete in higher-level competitions.[14]

One might expect that top athletes would rely more on their skill and less on superstition. In fact, we see the opposite. As elite athletes face higher stakes, they engage in *more* superstitious behaviours than average athletes.[15] Sports people often develop elaborate routines that they enact before and during games. Take, for example, Rafael Nadal, one of the greatest tennis players of all time. He has an elaborate repertoire of rituals that is reminiscent of that of OCD patients. Before each match he always takes a freezing-cold shower. When he arrives at the stadium, he enters the court holding a racket in his hand, taking great care never to step on the lines and always crossing each line right-foot first. He then places his bag on the bench and turns his tournament ID face up. His chair must be perfectly perpendicular to the sideline. As he prepares for his warm-up, he always makes the game officials wait for him. During the warm-up routine, which must be performed facing the crowd, he removes his jacket while jumping up and down. He takes an energy gel, opens it and consumes it, always in the exact same way: folding it once and squeezing it four times. He checks his socks to make sure they are perfectly even on his calves. During the coin toss he faces the net and starts jumping until the coin falls down, then immediately runs to the baseline, where he drags his foot across the entire line in a single sweeping motion before hitting each shoe with his racket. When the game begins, he starts performing repetitive hand gestures that resemble those of Catholics crossing themselves. With his right hand he touches the back and front of his shorts, then his left shoulder, then the right, then his nose, left ear, nose again, right ear and finally his right thigh. This sequence is repeated before every serve. After each point he goes to the towel. At each changeover he picks up two towels. He waits for the other player to cross the line, and then he crosses right-foot first to take his seat. He carefully folds one towel and puts it behind him without using it. Then he folds the second towel and places it on his lap. He takes one sip from a bottle of water, then another sip from a second bottle. Very carefully, he returns the two bottles to the exact same position, the labels facing the same way. When the game resumes, he gives one towel to a ball boy and then crosses over to the other side to give the second towel to another ball boy. This sequence is repeated throughout the match.

The top female tennis player Serena Williams washes her hands thoroughly before each match. Throughout each tournament she insists on always using the same shower and wearing the same pair of socks, which will not be washed until she loses. She makes sure to tie her shoelaces in exactly the same way and always walks into the court while listening to the song 'Flashdance … What a Feeling', by Irene Cara. The golf legend Tiger Woods always wears a red shirt on Sundays at golf tournaments. And Michael Jordan, the greatest basketball player of all time, reportedly wore his University of North Carolina shorts under his Chicago Bulls uniform during games throughout his entire NBA career.

Strangely enough, the athletes who become obsessed with such rituals often do not see themselves as superstitious.[16] In his autobiography, Nadal wrote: 'Some call it superstition, but it's not. If it were superstition, why would I keep doing the same thing over and over whether I win or lose? It's a way of placing myself in a match, ordering my surroundings to match the order I seek in my head.'[17]

Like many others, Nadal rejects the term 'superstition', which has negative connotations. The word commonly refers to beliefs and behaviours that are similar to those we call religious but which are frowned upon by the religious establishment. Whether a belief or a behaviour is superstitious therefore depends on one's cultural framework and point of view. In any case, Nadal's actions constitute what we call ritualised behaviour: they are stereotypical actions that are seen as indispensable (they *must* be performed), although they have no clear causal outcome.

Athletic competitions can cause a lot of stress, but few situations are more stressful than war. Several studies on ritual and anxiety have been conducted in Israel, a country that has been in a perpetual state of warfare since its inception in 1948. During the Gulf War (1990–91), the psychologist Giora Keinan surveyed 174 Israelis about a variety of superstitious beliefs and behaviours. She compared people who lived closer to the Iraqi border, and were thus more vulnerable to missile attacks, with those living outside the range of the missiles.[18] She found that those who lived in the high-stress areas were over 30 per cent more likely to enact superstitions such as tearing up photos of their enemies or entering a bunker right foot first during a missile attack. One decade later, during the second Palestinian uprising (Intifada), from 2000 to 2005, Israelis again lived under the constant fear of attack. The anthropologist Richard Sosis interviewed 367 Israeli women and found that those who were exposed to more war-related stressors (for example, those who had lost someone in the war or suffered financial damage) engaged more frequently in the recitation of psalms.[19]

These observations confirm that rituals abound in those areas of life that are stressful and uncertain. But all these findings are *correlational*: they tell us that two things tend to occur around the same time. They don't tell us whether one of those things causes the other to happen. Take the following example: ice cream sales correlate with the number of deaths by drowning, such that there are more deaths on days when more ice cream is consumed. Does this mean that eating ice cream *causes* people to drown? Clearly, this is not the most plausible explanation. It is far more likely that there is some third factor that affects both of these variables independently – in this case, temperature. On warmer days people are more likely to eat ice cream but also more likely to swim, and therefore more likely to drown. So how can we be certain that this is not also the case with ritual? For example, in many sports, some of the most stressful and uncertain moments are related to periods of physical inactivity, such as a timeout called in the final moments of a basketball game or the prolonged break before a penalty kick in football. Might such moments of anticipation both accentuate anxiety and give players more idle time during which to perform their rituals? Or perhaps consider this: in the context of warfare there could be socio-economic or personality factors that result in more anxiety as well as more ritualisation. For example, isn't it possible that more conservative individuals are more likely to have family members who serve in the military, meaning that they face a greater risk of losing someone in war, and also that they are more likely to practise religious rituals?

To avoid this problem of spurious correlation, scientists conduct controlled experiments, where they can manipulate what they suspect to be the causal factors and see whether these manipulations have the predicted outcomes. In one such experiment conducted in 2002, Giora Keinan asked two groups of people different kinds of questions and then observed their behaviour. The first group were asked questions that were intended to make them anxious, such as 'Has anyone in your immediate family suffered from lung cancer?' or 'Have you ever been involved in a fatal road accident?' People in the second group were asked more neutral kinds of questions, such as 'What is your favourite TV programme?' Respondents then completed survey scales that assessed their stress levels. Keinan found that those in the first group, who had been exposed to the stressful questions, were more likely to knock on wood during the interview than those who were asked the more neutral ones. Overall, those who reported feeling more anxious were also more likely to knock on wood.[20]

Of course, knocking on wood is a very specific cultural practice, and people across different societies may use any number of ritualised behaviours to overcome stress. But are there any universal features of ritualisation that we can measure experimentally? A few years ago I joined my colleagues at the Laboratory for the Experimental Research of Religion at Brno, in the Czech Republic, and together we designed an experiment to do just that.

Anthropologists have long been aware that even rituals that seem very different and that take place in entirely unrelated domains can still have remarkable similarities. It's not just that they involve causally opaque actions with no obvious relation to a specific outcome. The daily routines of little children, the superstitions enacted by gamblers and athletes, the prayers directed at various deities, religious and secular collective rituals, and even the pathological hyper-ritualisation of those who suffer from Obsessive–Compulsive Disorder, all seem to share some key structural elements.[21]

First of all, ritualisation is characterised by *rigidity*: ritual actions must always be performed in the same way (the *right* way). Fidelity is crucial; deviations from the script are not acceptable. In most contexts, drinking tea can be done in any number of ways. All you need is some tea leaves and some means of boiling water. But a Japanese tea ceremony must be choreographed precisely. A strict protocol defines when guests should arrive, how they will be greeted and where they must be seated. The tea room must be square, with an alcove at one end, a hearth and a hanging scroll with a floral arrangement on the wall. The hosts wear special clothes. Preparation requires specific utensils that must be handled with exquisite care: they are often only to be touched with a gloved hand and must be purified before and after each use. Guests too must be pure: they remove their shoes, bow silently and perform ablutions. A bell rings to mark the various stages of the ceremony. The tea is served on the floor. It must be picked up with the right hand, placed on the palm of the left hand, turned clockwise twice and bowed to. Myriad other rules prescribe even the minutest details, from how to hand a towel to the way the lid must be placed on the kettle. As a result, the tea ceremony can last up to four hours.

The social importance of adhering to the script became apparent during the inauguration of US President Barack Obama in 2009. Chief Justice John G. Roberts Jr made the tiniest of mistakes when administering the oath to the president. The wording mandated in the US Constitution reads: 'I do solemnly swear that I will faithfully execute the office of President of the United States ...' Roberts, who was reciting the oath from memory, said '... that I will execute the office of President to the United States faithfully'. Obama realised the mistake and paused, giving the chief justice a chance to recite the oath again. Roberts once more stumbled over the words, and Obama finally declared, 'I will execute the office of President of the United States faithfully.' Although all three sentences carried identical meaning, it is the letter, not the spirit, that matters in ritual. Public controversy arose after the inauguration, which led some to question the very legitimacy of the presidency. The constitutional lawyer Jack Beermann stated that 'it's an open question whether he is president until he takes the proper oath', and other legal scholars expressed similar worries. Although Obama initially dismissed these concerns, he eventually met Roberts at the White House, where the president retook the oath. Members of the press were invited to document the event, which, according to the White House, was done out of 'an abundance of caution'.

The mistake in Obama's oath was discovered immediately,

and he got off cheaply. But for Revd Matthew Hood things were a bit more complicated. He had been serving as a pastor at the St Lawrence parish in Utica, Michigan. In 2020 he was going through his father's collection of family videos and found an old tape of his baptism from when he was an infant. When he played it, he noticed that the deacon who performed the baptism had used the words 'we baptise you' instead of 'I baptise you', which Hood was accustomed to. Alarmed, he went to the arch-diocese of Detroit. 'We talked to some theologians and canon lawyers, and we thought it was probably valid,' he said. But a statement from the Vatican said otherwise. The deviation from the script meant that Hood had never been baptised. As a con-sequence, his confirmation was not valid either, which meant that his ordination as deacon was void, and therefore his ordi-nation as priest as well.

To return to his job, Hood would have to be baptised anew, then confirmed, made a deacon and ordained priest all over again. He did all this within a week, but there was more to the story. The mistake meant that he had not been a real priest before, and therefore any sacraments he administered during his ministry were also rendered null. His church had to contact thousands of people with some unexpected news: those who had been confirmed by Father Hood were informed that they were not full members of the Catholic Church. Those who had been ordained by him found out that they were not legitimate clergy. Those who went to confession before him learned that their sins had not been absolved. People who attended Holy Communion were told that they had not received the Eucharist, as they thought. As for the marriages at which he officiated, things were unclear, because in some cases non-ordained Cath-olics are allowed to perform weddings. Ironically, those who were baptised by him had no reason to worry: when it comes to baptism, it does not matter who administers it, as long as they use the right formula.

A second hallmark of ritualisation is *repetition*. A mantra might be repeated 108 times; Orthodox Christians cross themselves three times; and those who knock on wood always do so more than once. In addition to this internal repetition, in most cases the ritual itself is reproduced regularly. The Book of Psalms contains phrases like 'Evening, and morning, and at noon, will I pray' (55:17), or 'Seven times a day do I praise you' (119:164). Similarly, Muslims pray five times a day, soldiers raise and lower the flag daily and schools hold yearly leaving ceremonies.

Finally, another characteristic of ritualisation is that it involves *redundancy*. That is, even when ritual actions can be said to have a direct causal effect, they often go above and beyond what might be normally expected for practical purposes. Washing your hands for twenty seconds might be enough to ensure proper hygiene, but a cleansing ritual may go on for hours. In my fieldwork I have attended Hindu ceremonies that lasted up to a week and involved countless ritual actions. Similarly, the professor of Indian philosophy Fritz Staal documented the *Agni*, a Vedic ritual performed in India, which continued for twelve days and included a total of eighty hours of collective recitations and chanting.

Observing the frequency and duration of a ceremony is fairly straightforward. But how can we measure things like rigidity and redundancy, and what counts as repetition? The traditional way of doing this would be to observe or film people's behaviour and make a note each time a new movement or sequence of movements occurred. But this requires great effort, constant attention and many subjective decisions, so there is a lot of room for error. Luckily, technological advances now allow us to automate this process. In our study, we used motion-capture technology to measure ritualisation in people's actions.[22] Our hypothesis was that, as people got more stressed, their movements would become more repetitive (think of tapping, waving, scratching, etc.), rigid (following predictable action patterns) and redundant (lasting longer than necessary).

To evaluate this hypothesis, we first needed to induce anxiety – in other words, to create a stressful situation. With that in mind, we brought people into a lab, showed them a decorative object and gave them some questions about it. Half of the study participants were told that they had three minutes to think about the answers and then discuss them with the experimenter. This was not a particularly stressful task. But the other half of the participants had a very different experience. They were told that they would have to present their answers in the form of a public speech delivered in front of a panel of expert art critics who were waiting in the next room. To prepare that speech, they would only get three minutes. People dread being put on the spot, especially when they are unprepared and the audience is made up of experts. Such is our fear of public speaking that there is a special word for it: glossophobia. And since the study participants were also wearing heart-rate monitors, we were able to verify that their experience was indeed stressful.

Before they made their presentations we asked our participants to clean the artefact with a piece of cloth, although it was already clean when they entered the room. This was the time during which we used our motion sensors to analyse their actions. We found that those who were more stressed displayed more ritualised behaviour: their hand movements became more repetitive and predictable, engaging in the same action patterns again and again. And the more anxious people felt during the experiment, the more time they spent cleaning the object. Under the stress of the situation they began to clean obsessively even when there was nothing left to clean.

Ritualisation, then, seems to come as a natural response to anxiety. And in fact, we are not the only species for which this holds true.

In 1948 the famed Harvard psychologist B. F. Skinner published an article with the peculiar title 'Superstition in the Pigeon', in which he reported the results of a rather unusual experiment. Skinner had concocted an apparatus called an 'operant conditioning chamber' (now more commonly known as the 'Skinner box'), which he used to conduct various studies with animals. It was a highly controlled environment in which he could vary one element at a time and observe what changes it wrought on the animal's behaviour. Skinner was interested in how organisms learn, and especially in 'operant conditioning', a form of learning that occurs through rewards and punishments for a given behaviour. In one experiment an electrical current ran through the floor of the box, but a lever on the wall of the box could be pressed to stop the current. When a rat was placed in the box, it would feel pain and start to move around. Sooner or later it would stumble on the lever, and the current would stop. The rat would quickly learn to press the lever each time it was placed into the box, even when the floor was not electrified. Another experiment was designed to look at positive reinforcement. The lever delivered a reward in the form of a food pellet. Once the animal discovered this, it would start associating it with the reward and within a few trials it would immediately rush to the lever as soon as it was let into the box.

Then Skinner decided to introduce some uncertainty and

see what happened. He placed a hungry pigeon inside the box and programmed the release mechanism to deliver the food pellets randomly, no matter what the bird did. The results astounded him: much like gamblers and athletes, the birds began to develop elaborate rituals. Skinner wrote:

> One bird was conditioned to turn counter-clockwise about the cage, making two or three turns between reinforcements. Another repeatedly thrusted its head into one of the upper corners of the cage. A third developed a 'tossing' response, as if placing its head beneath an invisible bar and lifting it repeatedly. Two birds developed a pendulum motion of the head and body, in which the head was extended forward and swung from right to left with a sharp movement followed by a somewhat slower return. The body generally followed the movement and a few steps might be taken when it was extensive. Another bird was conditioned to make incomplete pecking or brushing movements directed toward but not touching the floor.[23]

The same kinds of response that Skinner observed in pigeons were later documented in children. In what sounds like a rather unsettling experiment, Gregory Wagner and Edward Morris placed children in a room with a mechanical clown that dispensed marble balls from its mouth; the children could later exchange these for toys. Just like Skinner's avian subjects, the children started enacting various ritualised behaviours to get the clown to release the reward. Some of them started touching the clown's face, pressing their nose against his or kissing him. Others made grimaces or begging gestures, and some started swinging, swirling or jumping, performing a sort of 'rain dance'.[24]

In adults, too, ritualisation seems to trigger intuitive biases related to causal reasoning. A study conducted in Brazil and the USA found that structural aspects of rituals such as repetition and redundancy make these rituals seem more efficient. Research subjects were asked to evaluate the efficacy of *simpatias*, formulaic magical spells used in parts of Brazil to address all manner of practical problems, from finding love to curing toothache. The spells varied across a number of characteristics, such as how many steps they involved, how many times those steps had to be executed and how strict and specific they were. The researchers found that rituals that were more repetitive, rigid and strictly defined were also perceived to be more effective in dealing with everyday problems.[25]

Another study of *simpatias* conducted by the same researchers found that introducing uncertainty increased people's expectations of ritual efficacy. They presented two groups of subjects with a cognitive task consisting of sorting out a series of scrambled sentences. The first group was given sentences that were meant to prime them with randomness, such as 'the committee is chaotic' or 'he chose the orange at random'. Participants in the second group unscrambled similar sentences containing neutral or other negative words, such as 'the committee is lazy' or 'the door is green'. Following this task, all subjects were shown the same list of *simpatias*. The group that had been primed with randomness judged those spells to be more likely to work than the other two groups.[26]

One interpretation of these findings may be that people's intuitions about those rituals are dependent on cultural notions of supernatural agency. After all, magic spells are typically meant to invoke the powers of some spirit, deity or karmic force to bring about the desired outcome. This is certainly true of many cultural rituals. But does ritualisation trigger intuitions about causality independently of those cultural beliefs? To find out, my team and I conducted a study in my lab at the University of Connecticut.[27]

Using recordings of college basketball games, we showed people videos of players shooting free-throws. After the ball left their hands, we paused the video and asked them to predict the success of each shot. Half of the time the players in those videos performed pre-shot rituals, such as spinning, bouncing or kissing the ball, or touching the soles of their shoes. These behaviours are common among basketball players. The other half of the time no rituals were enacted before the shot. In reality, participants saw exactly the same shots in both conditions, but we manipulated the camera angle to either reveal or obscure the ritualised actions. We found that participants expected the ritualised shots to be over 30 per cent more successful. This perceptual bias was consistent no matter what their level of expertise: people with no knowledge of the sport, fans who regularly watched basketball and even basketball players were equally susceptible. Moreover, this effect became stronger when the game score was more negative. The more they were losing – in other words, the less control players had over the game – the more our study participants expected the rituals to work.

These findings suggest that ritualisation is a natural way to try to control the world around us. We spontaneously engage in ritualised behaviours when we face stressful and uncertain situations, and we intuitively expect those ritualised actions to have an effect. But if this sense of control is illusory, what could possibly be the benefit of it? Why would this cognitive glitch persist rather than being weeded out by natural selection?

Stress is a survival mechanism that serves an obvious evolutionary function. When we are anxious, our autonomic nervous system releases a cascade of chemicals (stress hormones), which give our body instructions on how to prepare to face danger. Our heart beats faster to pump more blood to the muscles, and our breathing becomes heavier to provide us with more oxygen. Muscles tense up to protect us from injury and to facilitate fighting or running. Sweating helps cool the body down. Our attention increases, and our reflexes become sharper, keeping us alert. Stress acts as motivation, helping us to focus on our goals and rise to meet our challenges, whether those involve studying for an exam, flying a fighter jet or scoring that match-winning goal. In short, stress serves a purpose.

The problem, however, is that beyond a certain threshold stress ceases to be useful. The Yerkes–Dodson law, named after the two psychologists who first described it at the beginning of the twentieth century, postulates that there is an inverse U relationship between stress and cognitive functioning.[28] Up to a point, stress helps boost performance. But once it crosses a certain threshold, it becomes detrimental. Some anxiety before an important job interview can help you focus and motivate you to prepare and perform better. But if the stress becomes extreme, you may have difficulty breathing, start feeling chest pain or have cold sweat running down your neck. You become passive and your reactions slow. You feel dizzy, weak, detached from reality. You experience a panic attack. Over time these effects can add up and take a heavy toll on your health. Long-term stress weakens your immune system and can cause hypertension and cardiovascular disease. It can impair memory and concentration and lead to withdrawal, depression and sleep disorders. This type of stress is not adaptive. In fact, it can be devastating to our normal functioning, health and well-being.

But why is it that a common biological response would be so prone to misfiring?

Evolutionary analyses suggest that stress is not what it used to be.[29] For most of human history our ancestors lived in physical and social environments that were very different from what most of us experience today. Life in those environments imposed a set of selection pressures that shaped our species's genome and behaviour, leading to the evolution of anatomically modern humans. Although it is not entirely clear where exactly one should draw the line between them and more archaic forms, paleoanthropologists agree that by at least 50,000 years ago our ancestors were fully human. Yet a much bigger kind of change was still brewing.

The transition from a foraging to a sedentary way of life appears to have begun no earlier than 12,000 years ago. In evolutionary time this is the mere blink of an eye. Although some minor genetic changes have occurred since then (for example, those responsible for blue eyes and lactose tolerance), our physical and mental capacities have remained virtually unaltered. If an infant from that era could be transported in time and adopted by a contemporary family, we would not expect that child to stand out as an adult in any way at all. But while our brains have not changed in the last few millennia, everything else has. The sluggish pace of biological evolution has not been able to keep up with our ongoing explosion of cultural and technological innovation. As a result, many of the biological adaptations that helped our ancestors navigate their world no longer serve us in our radically different circumstances. This is known as an evolutionary *mismatch*.

To be sure, our hunter-gatherer ancestors did not live a stress-free life. They were vulnerable to predators, natural elements and often food insecurity. But they also had ways of mitigating chronic anxiety. They lived in small, egalitarian groups of closely related individuals who comprised strong social support networks. They worked relatively little to meet their needs and had ample leisure time. And their flexible mode of subsistence allowed them to adapt to changes in their environment and engage in regular physical activity.

The transition to agriculture and sedentism, as we saw, resulted in a far more stressful way of life. It created social inequality and oppression, back-breaking working conditions and exposed us to new diseases and the constant fear of raids and warfare. Modern industrialised societies have managed to alleviate some of the anxieties of agrarian life, thanks to social progress and the advances of modern medicine. But at the same time, they have introduced many new stressors. Life rhythms are dizzyingly fast compared with any other point in history; nuclear and extended families, traditionally a major buffer of anxiety, may now be scattered thousands of miles apart; new technologies allow bad news to spread instantly and hijack our brains, resulting in new forms of addiction. These are just some of the ways in which our evolved stress responses no longer serve us well in our current environment.

In light of this mismatch between our brain and our lifestyle, effective stress-management techniques can have a major impact on our overall fitness and quality of life. This raises the intriguing possibility that ritual serves as a mental technology that helps us live outside our ecological niche. What may have started as a bug has been turned into a feature – yet another testament to our behavioural flexibility, which has allowed us to transform our way of life, engineer our environment and dominate the planet.

But perhaps we are getting ahead of ourselves. Thus far, we have seen evidence that there is a link between ritual and anxiety, in that people turn to ritual when they are stressed. But is ritual really an effective stress-management strategy? Or is it simply a waste of time or, worse, a dangerous distraction from our real problems?

C

Field observations suggest that ritual may indeed help people cope with anxiety. In yet another study conducted in Israel, researchers interviewed local women during the Lebanon War of 2006. They found that among those women who lived in war zones and thus experienced the stress of war, reciting psalms was associated with lower overall stress levels.[30] No similar association was found for women living outside the war zones. While participants in this study were the judges of their own anxiety, similar effects were found at the physiological level. In my lab at the University of Connecticut my colleagues and I observed a group of students during the mid-term exams, one of the most stressful periods of the year. In addition to surveys, we collected hair and saliva samples, which we used to measure levels of cortisol, a hormone associated with stress. Salivary cortisol changes over the course of a few minutes, so it can be used to measure stress around a specific activity. But traces of the hormone also accumulate in our hair, and they can be used to track long-term anxiety. We found that students who participated in more rituals had lower anxiety across all of these measures.

Once again, however, these are correlational findings. They help us point to an association but cannot establish a causal relationship. For that, we need to turn to experimental studies. Fortunately, a number of experiments have been conducted on this topic in recent years. In one of these studies Matthew

Anastasi and Andrew Newberg randomly assigned Catholic college students to either reciting the Rosary (a set of repetitive prayers) or watching a religious film, and measured anxiety levels before and after those tasks. They found that those who recited the Rosary experienced a greater decrease in anxiety.[31] Alison Brooks and her colleagues found similar results when they asked participants to enact an artificial ritual that resembled a magical spell. As it turned out, performing this ritual helped people engaged in various stressful tasks such as taking a maths test or participating in public karaoke to cope with anxiety.[32] In another study, Michael Norton and Francesca Gino asked participants to think about a loss they had experienced – someone who had passed away, a broken relationship or even a monetary loss. They found that, when they asked some of them to perform a ritual, they were better able to cope with the anxiety caused by the loss.[33]

Moving from the lab into the real world, my colleagues and I designed a field experiment on the Indian Ocean island of Mauritius.[34] To see whether some of the traditional local rituals helped people reduce anxiety, we measured a property of the autonomic nervous system known as heart-rate variability. A healthy heart does not beat evenly like a metronome. When we have a heart rate of sixty beats per minute, this does not mean that our heart ticks exactly once every second. Rather, it means that all the slightly different periods between each two successive beats average out as one second. This variance in the timing between beats is known as heart-rate variability. When it is high, the nervous system is more balanced and the body is better able to respond to changing circumstances. But when we are stressed, this balance is disrupted and the heart beats in a more rigid way – it has low variability. As a result, the body maintains a state of high alert, which is experienced as anxiety.

Our study took place in a small fishing village called La Gaulette. As is often the case with such villages, most public life took place near the coast. All restaurants, shops and other commercial activities were arranged alongside the coastal road, and so were all public services, including a police station and two places of worship: a Catholic church near the south entrance, and a Marathi Hindu temple on the north side. Sitting at the café each morning, we could see many of the local Hindu women, dressed in colourful saris, walk to the temple to perform religious prayers. Those prayers involved making offerings to the statues of various Hindu deities and executing circular movements with an incense burner or incense stick. These were just the kind of repetitive action patterns that we were interested in and, importantly, ones that were culturally scripted rather than dictated by the experiment.

We recruited seventy-five of these women and split them into two groups. We asked those in the first group to meet our team at the temple. The second group arrived at a makeshift lab we had set up in a non-religious building of similar size and arrangement to the temple. This would be our control group. Participants wore a small monitor that recorded their heart beats before being invited to engage in a task that was designed to be stressful: we asked them to write an essay describing the kinds of precautions they would take when faced with an impending flood or cyclone. Such natural disasters regularly plague the island, often with catastrophic consequences, and are therefore a constant source of anxiety for the locals. To create additional stress, we also told them that their essay would be evaluated by a group of public safety experts. After the stressor task, those who were in the temple were asked to go to the prayer room and perform their rituals in the same way as they always did. They entered the room in privacy, lit the incense and made their offerings to the deities. Those in the control group went through the exact same procedure but performed no rituals. Instead, they were told to sit and relax.

As we predicted, the ritual had beneficial results. Reflecting on natural disasters caused a rise in anxiety for both groups. But those who performed the ritual were faster to recover from that anxiety. Their heart-rate variability increased by 30 per cent, suggesting that they were better able to cope with the stress. This was also consistent with how they felt: subjective ratings of anxiety were twice as high for those who had not performed the ritual. These are no trivial differences: clinical studies have documented effects of similar magnitude between healthy individuals and people suffering from major depression.[35] Ritual, it turns out, can be as effective in reducing stress as some of our best anxiety medications. How can we explain these findings?

C

Rituals are highly structured. They require rigidity (they must always be performed the 'correct' way), repetition (the same actions performed again and again) and redundancy (they can go on for a long time). In other words, they are predictable. This predictability imposes order on the chaos of everyday life, which provides us with a sense of control over uncontrollable situations. Studies show that, when people experience uncertainty and lack of control, they are more likely to see patterns or regularities where there are none. These patterns can range from visual illusions (such as seeing faces in the clouds) to seeing causality in random events and forming conspiracy theories.[36] Under these circumstances people are also more likely to turn to ritualised behaviours. This is known as the *compensatory control model*: we compensate for lack of control in one domain by seeking it in another.[37] Whether this sense of control is illusory is of little importance. What matters is that ritual can be an efficient coping mechanism, and this is why those domains of life that involve high stakes and uncertain outcomes are rife with rituals.

In the experiments conducted by Alison Brooks and her colleagues, engaging in rituals helped participants to perform better in mathematics contests and sing more accurately in karaoke competitions. And in Israel the women who recited more psalms felt less need to take other precautions, which might have impeded them from going about their normal life. In contrast, those who did not perform as many rituals seemed overcome by anxiety. This led them to avoid public places, buses, restaurants and large crowds after rocket attacks. This sounds very sensible until you learn that, even at the height of the conflict, the chances of getting killed in a terrorist attack in Israel were lower than those of dying in a car accident. Living in fear could do more harm than good, and rituals helped those women deal with their fears and live a normal life in the face of the conflict.

Similar effects extend to a variety of other domains. For instance, a group of German psychologists found that people who used lucky charms and rituals such as keeping their fingers crossed performed better in an assortment of skill games and puzzles.[38] And other studies have found that ritualisation may help athletes perform better. For example, basketball and golf players are more successful after performing pre-shot rituals.[39] Stopping them from performing these rituals can be detrimental to their performance, leading them to miss more shots.[40] The reason for these remarkable effects appears to be that these rituals allow the athletes to ease their own anxiety, regaining a sense of control.

In recent years philosophers, psychologists and neuro-scientists have revised their models of the human mind. The long-standing classical view was that our cognitive apparatus functions as a data-processing device: it receives input from the environment and reacts by producing the appropriate responses. But evidence has been mounting that our brain is much more sophisticated than that. It is a *predictive* device. Rather than passively absorbing information about the state of the world, it actively works to make inferences (predictions) about what types of stimuli it is most likely to encounter at any given situation. Those predictions are based on information derived from our prior experience and socialisation, our surroundings, as well as hard-wired knowledge.

Take, for example, the blind spot in our vision. The optic nerve, a bundle of nerve fibres that carry information from the eye to the brain, passes through the retina itself. As a consequence, the spot where the optic nerve enters the eyeball has no photoreceptor cells to detect light. This is why it is called a blind spot: whatever part of our visual field falls on to that spot becomes invisible to us. If you had never noticed that you have a blind spot, that is because your brain makes up the missing part of the image by using information from the surrounding environment to fill in the gap.

Our brain makes similar types of inferences in all sorts of other domains. Imagine that you live at the outskirts of San Francisco, and as you wake up you feel your bed shake. Fearing it might be an earthquake, your immediate response might be to try to get out of the building as quickly as possible. But now imagine that you live in New York, which does not experience many earthquakes, and that an elevated train line runs alongside your building. Perhaps the first time that you wake up to the vibration you rush to the door, only to embarrass yourself as you run down the hallway in your underwear. But once you know what to expect when you feel the shake, it will no longer cause you to panic. As your brain has now updated its prior knowledge, it can predict with greater confidence that the shaking will not cause the roof to fall on your head. The situation is no longer stressful. In fact, over the years, the familiar sensation of the train going by at regular intervals may even start to feel comforting.

Because our brain never stops making these kinds of predictions, we tend to look for patterns and statistical regularities everywhere around us. This is extremely important, because any computational device (and the human brain is no exception) becomes dramatically more efficient when it can build on prior knowledge. This way, we do not have to learn everything from scratch. But one consequence of this cognitive architecture is that when our predictive potential is limited – that is, when there is high uncertainty – we experience anxiety. Our predictive brain does not like unpredictability. This is where ritual comes in.

The repetitive action patterns found in ritual function as cognitive gadgets that help us cope with stress. By embedding these gadgets into our cultures, all human societies capitalise on their potential. Religious prayers that are used in times of anxiety commonly involve repetitive utterances or actions. *Japa* is a meditative technique found in many Asian religions. It involves repeating the name of a god or a mantra hundreds or even thousands of times. The chant may be spoken, whispered or simply recited in the practitioner's mind. Initially, meditators may use a string of beads known as a *japa mala* to count the repetitions. As they become more skilled, they are able to recite the mantra while performing other activities. Expert meditators can accumulate so much practice that they are said to reach *ajapajapam,* a state of constant awareness of the mantra.

A variety of mystical traditions use similar techniques. In Greece and Cyprus the prayer bead, initially used by meditating monks, evolved into a widely popular version called the *komboloi* (also known as a 'worry bead'). Several ways of handling the *komboloi* developed, all of which consisted in repeating the same motion sequence over and over again. This was said to produce a calming effect, which is why the *komboloi* was often used in stressful situations. Today, football coaches in Greece can still be seen fidgeting with it during important games.

Malinowski's time among the Trobrianders made him realise that they were not so different from Europeans after all. By immersing himself into their world, he began to see his own world with new eyes. That world too was full of ritual. Like the Trobrianders, British fishermen had numerous superstitions, as did those who went to war or suffered from illness. And, like people everywhere, they had rites of passage and other ceremonies that marked the most important moments of their lives. To an outsider those rituals too would seem irrational. But our cognition did not evolve to be rational; it evolved to be efficient in dealing with the kinds of problems that our ancestors faced in their environment. Rituals are found in every human culture because they help solve some of those problems and satisfy some of our basic human needs. We rely on time-honoured traditions and practices not because they are logical but because they work for us. Even if these ritualised practices cannot directly manipulate our environment, they can bring changes in ourselves, and those changes can have real and important effects on our world.

4

GLUE

Ritual comes naturally to us. It appears early in our childhood and stays with us for the rest of our lives, reliably surging when we need it the most. It helps us soothe our anxieties and get a sense of order in an otherwise chaotic world. But we humans are social creatures, and most of our ceremonies take place in social contexts. It is in those contexts that the full potential of ritual reveals itself.

The anthropologist Megan Biesele spent three years living with the !Kung people of the Kalahari Desert. Genetic analyses have found that these hunter-gatherers belong to a group carrying one of the most ancient maternal DNA lineages, suggesting that they may be one the world's oldest living populations. Anthropological evidence suggests that many aspects of their culture have also remained unchanged for long periods of time, and these are thus often thought to be representative of the earliest known human practices. The keystone of those customs is a ritual dance that has been passed down the generations for millennia – it is already depicted in prehistoric rock paintings found throughout the area. At dawn the community gathers around a campfire. The women sing and clap rhythmically as the men begin to dance in a circle around them to the sounds of rattles, long strings of dried moth cocoons containing seeds or stones and worn around their legs. They take small steps in synchrony to the music, stamping each foot on the ground twice or thrice before moving the other, and occasionally hopping on both feet. Over the course of the night the dance slowly builds up to a frenzied pace until everyone joins in, many of them in a state of trance.

The dance is said to drive away evil spirits and cure illness and misfortune. Nonetheless, it is performed regularly, every one or two weeks, even when no malady is known to exist among the group. This led Biesele to argue that the true utility of this ritual lies in its social function: 'The fact that all members of a group participate personally in this effort accounts for much of its psychic and emotional efficacy. The dance is perhaps the central unifying force in bushman life, binding people together in very deep ways which we do not fully understand.' [1] Biesele is not alone; anthropologists have long described collective ceremonies as the glue that holds society together, although the ways in which this glue operates have been elusive. How do collective rituals help boost group solidarity? What are the ingredients that make this glue work, and how do they combine to give it its bonding properties?

There is no single recipe to the ritual glue. Cultural rituals are diverse and complicated phenomena, which work in diverse ways. But this variability is not infinite, and those ways need not be mysterious. A handful of psychological mechanisms provide a set of basic ingredients that each tradition can combine, resulting in varying types and degrees of social adhesion. To understand those different versions of the recipe, scientists who study ritual apply a fractionating approach, examining one ingredient at a time.[2]

By their very nature, rituals are *causally opaque*: there is no obvious causal connection between the specific actions they involve and their purported end goal. As we have seen, many rituals are also *goal-demoted*, lacking an external goal altogether: performing the rite is the goal itself. But even if the end goal of a ritual is known, its content cannot be inferred or predicted on the basis of that goal. A purification ceremony may require pouring water, sprinkling salt, smearing dirt, burning incense, blowing in the wind, ringing a bell, chanting or any other of a myriad of symbolic actions. To an observer it is unclear how these actions might bring about purity. This gap between behaviour, intention and outcome is why rituals often seem puzzling, pointless or even comical to outsiders. But while causal opacity may look like a bug, it is in fact essential to ritual's ability to create special and meaningful experiences.

Unlike ordinary actions, which are linked to specific cause-and-effect relationships, ritual actions are not bound by such expectations. As a result, their inner workings remain a mystery. Crucially, this is not the same kind of mystery that may also be involved in certain instrumental actions. When we press a button on the remote to switch on the TV, when we use a microwave oven or when we type things into a search engine, we are initiating a chain of events of which we probably have a very limited understanding. When hard pressed, we might vaguely say something about light entering the camera lens, signals travelling through cables or radio waves, pixels on a screen or electricity going into the television set. In reality, our understanding of those things is likely to be very superficial, and many of the steps in the process are entirely mysterious to us. Even so, we expect that each of those steps is linked to the outcome of the action in ordinary, mechanistic ways that can, with effort, be known and understood. By contrast, the links between ritual actions and their outcomes are in principle unknowable. We do not expect an explanation for why immuring a rooster in the foundation of a house during construction may ensure the stability of the building or the prosperity of its occupants. It just does.

This peculiar quality turns out to have a major impact on the way we perceive ritual actions.[3] Generally speaking, the human perceptual system analyses and interprets people's actions rapidly and automatically, allowing us to make intuitive inferences about their goals and intentions.[4] This ability is fundamental to our social functioning, because it helps us understand other people's motivations and predict their behaviour, often with minimal input. If I see Mary open the fridge, take out some meat and vegetables and begin to slice them, I do not need to be told that she is hungry or that she is about to cook and eat a meal. I can infer all that from what she is doing. Nor do I need to pay attention to every single one of her gestures, because many of these movements can be predicted in the context of a larger goal-driven sequence in which each step is necessary in order for the next step to occur. Our brain can therefore easily fill in the gaps, even if we haven't observed all of the actions in the sequence. For example, we expect that Mary peeled the onion before chopping it and that she seasoned the vegetables after washing them rather than the other way around. Moreover, the fine details of her motions are of little importance, as long as they get the job done: it doesn't matter whether she wielded the knife ten or twelve times to chop the onion, or whether she used her left or her right hand to open the fridge.

Ritual actions, on the other hand, do not lend themselves to interpretation in this way. Because their various steps do not have any obvious causal relationship, our mind cannot make the same kinds of inferences. Consider an example from the *Greek Magical Papyri*, a collection of ancient texts produced in Egypt during the Graeco-Roman era, each containing a list of spells and rituals of the time. One of those texts, known by its serial name as *PGM IV. 3172–3208*, provides the instructions for a rite meant to invoke dreams. To achieve that goal, practitioners must do the following:

> Pick up three reeds before sunset. After sunset, raise the first reed while facing East, and say three times: '*Maskelli Maskello Phnoukentabao Oreobazagra, Rhexikhthon, Ippokhton, Puripeganyx*', followed by the vowels of the alphabet, and then the words '*Lepetan Azarakhtharo: I pick you so that you might bring me a dream.*' Raise the second reed to the south and repeat the formula, replacing the last part with the word '*Throbeia*'. Hold the reed and spin around; turn north, then west, and repeat the second formula three times. Then raise the third reed and say the same words, adding the following: '*Ie Ie,* I pick you for such a deed.' Inscribe these words onto each reed: on the first, '*Azarakhtharo*'; on the second, '*Throbeia*'; on the third, '*Ie Ie*'. Then take a lamp that is not painted red and fill it with olive oil; take a clean strip of cloth and write down all the names; utter these words to the lamp seven times. Let the lamp be facing east, next to a censer in which you must burn uncut frankincense. Then use the fibres of a date palm to bind the reeds together into a tripod, and place the lamp on it. Your head must be crowned with olive branches.

Faced with this set of actions, it is not possible to make the same kinds of predictions as we can with an instrumental procedure.

Save for the verbal invocation of dreams, none of the behaviours in this sequence provides any clue about their purpose whatsoever. There is no obvious reason for using a reed rather than a rock, or a lamp that is not red rather than a chalice that is gold. In addition, there is no discernible logic to the ordering of these actions: if we saw practitioners hold the reed and spin around, we would not infer that this must have been preceded by reciting a formula or that it should be followed by turning to the north. Finally, since we are unaware of their inner workings, we do not expect that the specific actions can be substituted or altered in any way. The formula must be recited three times – not four, nor two.

Indeed, experiments show that ritual actions are not processed in the same way as ordinary actions. When non-instrumental (ritualistic) behaviours are observed, each step is treated as a unique action rather than as the logical consequence of a previous action. Studies of perception show that when people are presented with ritualised behaviours, they actually see a greater number of distinct actions taking place.[5] While chopping vegetables in the context of cooking might be perceived as a single overarching event, cutting fruit in the context of a Hindu prayer might be perceived as a series of distinct actions: for example, moving the knife back and forth seven times. As a consequence, rituals command more attention and are described in greater detail.[6] In other words, compared with ordinary actions, ritual actions are intuitively perceived to be *special*.

This was demonstrated by Rohan Kapitány and Mark Nielsen, who examined how people judge the significance of various actions.[7] The two researchers presented 474 subjects with videos of a man pouring a drink into a glass. In one version of the video, the man's actions appeared ordinary:

picking up the glass, cleaning it with a cloth, pouring the drink and inspecting the glass before setting it on a table. In the other version, the event was ritualised. Although the man essentially performed the same task and used almost identical movements, some of his actions were causally opaque: after picking up the glass, he waved the cloth at it without touching it, raised the drink high up before pouring it and bowed to the glass before setting it on the table.

When the researchers asked participants whether the two glasses were the same in terms of their physical qualities, they overwhelmingly agreed that there was no difference between the two glasses. But despite that, when asked whether one of the beverages was special, they pointed to the ritual drink. This is hardly surprising. The most important occasions in our lives are accompanied by ritual. It is therefore natural to infer that, when a ritual is being performed, it marks something of value. Sure enough, when presented with the choice of which beverage they would prefer to have, participants were three times more likely to pick the special drink. Even though people said that the actions had not changed the object, an important change did occur: their perception of the actions changed, and this in turn changed their behaviour towards the object. What is more, these effects became even stronger when the researchers explicitly described the actions as rituals. On being told that the gestures were part of a traditional ceremony practised in some faraway place such as Gabon, Fiji or Ecuador, participants were twice as likely to select the special drink.

Kapitány and Nielsen's findings highlight an important connection between ritual's psychological and social effects. Developmental research suggests that from an early age humans are adept at learning both instrumental skills and cultural conventions, thanks to their ability to pursue two distinct strategies of acquiring information. Psychologists have called these two learning mechanisms the *instrumental* and the *ritual* stance.[8] Using the instrumental stance is what allows us to recognise and interpret actions that rely on physical causation to achieve specific goals, such as using a broom to clean the floor, chopping vegetables to make a meal or working together to build a boat. The ritual stance, on the other hand, allows us to recognise and assimilate cultural conventions, such as burning incense to purify a room, chopping fruit to make a sacrifice or coming together to perform a collective prayer.

The causally opaque nature of conventional behaviours signals that these behaviours are normative, and thus socially meaningful.[9] We intuitively expect that people who engage in the same ordinary actions simply have the same goals: when a group of people work together to build a fishing boat, it is presumably because each of them is motivated by the same individual desire to catch fish. Their actions are simply the means of achieving that goal. But when the actions themselves are the goal, such as when the same people work together to build a ceremonial pyre, this is probably because they are bound by the same cultural norms and values.

Psychological experiments have documented the ritual stance even in toddlers. In one study, sixteen-month-old children viewed videos of two people performing ritualised actions together. Those actions consisted of causally opaque sequences such as moving a box back and forth on a table and repeatedly touching it with their heads and elbows while saying 'Oh!' In half of those videos the pair seemed to get along after performing the ritual, facing each other and smiling. In the other half they seemed inimical, facing away, crossing their hands and frowning. The researchers tracked the children's gaze to determine their reactions to the videos. This is a common method in developmental research, because babies will look longer when they see something unexpected or startling. As it turned out, the children expected people who performed the same rituals (but not those who performed different rituals) to be socially affiliated, and indicated surprise by staring longer when these people appeared to be socially disengaged in the videos.[10]

As we saw in Chapter 2, children are excellent imitators. Developmental studies conducted in Australia, in the USA and among communities of hunter-gatherers in South Africa show that children imitate their group's ritual actions more willingly and more precisely than they do instrumental actions.[11] This is especially true when these actions are goal-demoted – that is, when they lack an explicit purpose.[12] Children also expect others to perform normative actions accurately, and zealously protest when they don't.[13] For some reason, it seems that we are cognitively and culturally prepared to adopt the rituals of those around us.[14] But why?

When Hindus attend a ceremony, they may receive a *tilak* (or *tilaka*), a mark on the forehead made by using ash from a sacrificial fire, vermilion or some other powder. To the familiar eye, the particular type of *tilak* on someone's forehead may signal their affiliation to a particular Hindu denomination, or even a specific temple. Similarly, members of some Christian denominations have their foreheads smudged with ashes in the shape of a cross to mark the beginning of Lent and the rituals associated with Easter. Other rituals involve more permanent markers. When the boys of the Chambri tribe in Papua New Guinea are initiated into manhood, for instance, their skin is cut with bamboo blades, leaving scars that are meant to resemble crocodile scales. Sharing and brandishing these symbolic markers not only allows participants to express their group identity but in fact actively shapes it, thanks to ritual's ability to exploit some of our most basic social propensities.

The social psychologist Henri Tajfel knew all too well how groupish humans can be. During the Second World War he joined the French army as a volunteer and was taken prisoner by the Nazis. His fluency in French allowed him to conceal his Polish-Jewish heritage and he was thus able to survive by passing as French, but when he returned to France, he discovered that his entire family had been killed in the Holocaust. Formerly a chemistry student, he was influenced by this experience to turn to psychology, where he made his mark in the study of prejudice.

Tajfel knew that a core part of who we are as individuals is defined by the various social groups to which we belong. Our membership of these groups plays a fundamental role in moulding our personal identity and self-image. But, rather than focusing on the individual in the group, Tajfel thought it was more interesting to study the group in the individual: the very idea that one is part of a group, no matter how insignificant that group might be. In the early 1970s he launched a research programme aimed at testing the limits of this inbuilt need to belong. He wanted to establish the minimal conditions that may be sufficient to trigger a sense of belonging. For this reason, this methodology has become known as the *minimal group paradigm*.

The members of some groups have meaningful similarities. The players of a basketball team may have similar skills, physique and goals; Japanese citizens may share a similar culture and genetics; and a group of vegans may be similar in not just their dietary preferences but also other aspects of their lifestyle.

But what about groups that are not made up of any homogeneous membership? People who own purple shirts? People whose name begins with the letter E? Or those who were born on 21 April? What does it take to produce the idea of a group in those people's minds? As it turns out, not much.

In a series of experiments, Tajfel and his colleagues found that even the most arbitrary group markers may be sufficient to make people feel that they have more in common with other group members than with outsiders. In one study children were shown abstract paintings created by Paul Klee and Wassily Kandinsky and told to pick the ones they liked the most. There are substantial stylistic similarities between the two artists, but the children were not familiar with their work. After stating their choices, they were separated into two groups, the Kandinsky group and the Klee group. In reality these groups had been assigned by the experimenters at random without any relation to their aesthetic preferences (after all, the children didn't know which name belonged to which artist). When the children were later asked to distribute monetary rewards to other participants, they preferred to give money to members of their own group rather than those in the other group. Similar results were obtained when people were assigned into groups based on other meaningless characteristics: those who saw more dots on a screen versus those who saw fewer dots; those who wore the same colour shirt; and even people who had been assigned to a particular group based on a coin toss. All of these studies led to the same conclusion: the minimal requirement to feel attached to one's group is the existence of the group itself.[15]

It is easy to see why the conditions for group identification are so minimal in humans. As hyper-social animals, we are embedded in multiple social networks on which we rely for our survival and well-being. Some of these networks are narrowly defined and their members easy to discern. We know our relatives because we grew up with them, because we use special kinship terms to refer to them and because we are assured by other family members that they are related to us. Similarly, we know our friends because we spend time with them and we share common interests. But some of our social networks are so extensive that their full membership is never known to us in its entirety: our nation, our ethnic group or those who share the same religious or political convictions. Even so, identifying those members can be of paramount importance.

In his book *The World Until Yesterday*, the geographer Jared Diamond explains how recognising group membership can, in some cases, even be a matter of life and death. In New Guinea, where he conducted fieldwork, the numerous local bands and villages were connected through references to common ancestors, whether real or mythical, into groups forming large tribes. Rival tribes were engaged in perpetual warfare, so that chance encounters between strangers could be fatal unless they were able to establish some tribal link. Often, unacquainted individuals who bumped into each other in the forest would spend hours naming all their relatives and explaining how they were related to them in an effort to find a shared ancestor and thus avoid bloodshed.

Even in the absence of tribal warfare, those belonging to the same groups would preferentially want to trade, associate and cooperate with fellow group members. Short of personal knowledge or direct information about a particular individual, the best way to identify one's own is by paying attention to their appearance and behaviour, a strategy known as *phenotypic matching*: like other animals with complex social arrangements, humans have evolved mechanisms for recognising related individuals by generating inferences on the basis of their similarity to themselves and their group. This can be a very useful heuristic, because genotypic and phenotypic traits tend to be correlated: those who share similarities in their genetic make-up (their genotype) also tend to be more similar in some of their observable characteristics, such as their appearance and behaviour (their phenotype). For this reason, it can often be reasonable to assume that a person who looks like you is more likely to be related to you than someone who looks rather different.

Studies show that we frequently make use of such cues when making decisions about who we interact with and how. For example, parents, especially fathers, tend to favour children who look more like themselves. Even among strangers, people rate unrelated individuals more favourably and are more willing to help them when their facial features are more similar to their own.[16] This phenotypic matching also extends to symbolic similarities. In an experiment conducted in Mauritius we found that people trusted anonymous strangers more when they were wearing symbolic markers of in-group membership. For example, when Christians saw other Christians wearing a cross, and when Hindus saw other Hindus sporting a *tilak*, they rated them as more trustworthy and gave them more money in an economic game.[17] By contrast, when they saw members of their own community wearing out-group markers, such as Hindus wearing crosses, they trusted them less.

While we are not the only animal that employs phenotypic matching to discern potential allies, the unparalleled richness of human culture makes it possible to extend this strategy in unique ways. Each human society has distinct forms of expression that range from languages and accents to dress codes and make-up to art and, of course, rituals. Because these expressions are culturally specific, they are very effective indicators of group affiliation: all groups have communal meals, but our group may require reciting a particular chant before sharing food; everyone is preoccupied with cleanliness, but our group may stand out by using blue paint to ensure purity. While these cues can vary in endless ways, rituals are uniquely potent markers because they involve not just abstract but also embodied symbols, enacted in behaviour. Rituals thus provide cues about people's *behavioural* type, signalling that those who act similarly in one domain are also likely to share other important similarities.[18]

C

Have you ever wondered why soldiers in every army spend so much time doing drill – that is, simply marching up and down? In ancient times, marching drills may have helped army units practise tactical manoeuvres used in the battlefield. But in modern warfare, dominated by long-range projectile weapons, a large group marching in formation across an open field would look like a suicide mission. Besides, even military branches, such as the air force, that do not engage in ground combat practise marching regularly. Why is it then that even the world's most advanced armies keep using this antiquated training regime? In his 1995 book *Keeping Together in Time*, the historian William H. McNeill proposed an answer to this puzzle: engaging in coordinated rhythmic activity creates shared feelings that help create bonding between soldiers.

McNeill was no outsider to the topic. He was a Second World War veteran who had enlisted in the US army and served in the artillery for three years. During his basic training in Texas he was often frustrated at the lack of practical training. His battalion was short on supplies and possessed a single anti-aircraft gun, which was broken. In the absence of anything else to do, the officers had them march up and down for hours. Marching became an end in itself, dictated by tradition rather than necessity. 'A more useless exercise would be hard to imagine,' McNeill wrote. Soon, however, he realised that despite the apparent futility of the exercise, the soldiers did not mind strutting around in unison. Neither did he. In fact, he described the rhythmic ritual as bringing about a feeling of exaltation and a sense of personal enlargement shared by all participants. 'Obviously, something visceral was at work; something, I later concluded, far older than language and critically important in human history, because the emotion it arouses constitutes an indefinitely expansible basis for social cohesion among any and every group that keeps together in time, moving big muscles together and chanting, singing, or shouting rhythmically.' McNeill called this visceral feeling 'muscular bonding', an emotional response that allows an assortment of individuals to feel like a unified group: those who move together bond together. Long before the formation of modern armies and other formal institutions, our ancestors used drill, music, dance and ritual as the foundations of social solidarity, and the utility of those social technologies is as relevant to us today as it was to them.

In recent years researchers across various fields have found support for McNeill's claims. A number of studies have shown that the coordination of movement increases interpersonal rapport and promotes bonding. In one experiment, Stanford professors Scott Wiltermuth and Chip Heath organised a series of group walks across campus. Half of the groups walked in step while the other half walked casually. The researchers found that those who marched in synchrony reported feeling more connected with their counterparts, trusted them more and behaved more cooperatively.[19] Other studies showed that performing synchronous activities such as chanting and dancing, and even trivial tasks like finger-tapping to the same beat, can have similar outcomes.[20]

In a laboratory experiment in the Czech Republic my colleagues and I explored some of the mechanisms that might be responsible for these effects. We randomly divided 124 participants into three groups and asked them to perform a sequence of choreographed hand movements in response to the beat of a drum.[21] Those in the first group performed this task alone, while those in the other two groups were paired with a partner located in another room via a live-streamed video – or so they were told. In reality, the 'interaction partner' was an actor trained to perform the sequence, and the video stream was not live but had been pre-recorded. This allowed us to introduce a crucial difference between the two types of pairs: in one group (we called this the 'high-sync' condition) the actor performed the movements at a steady speed without making any errors, which more faithfully tracked the motions of the participant. In the other group (the 'low-sync' condition) the movements were distorted, in that the actor's reactions to the beat were often delayed or out of sync and he sometimes made the wrong moves. You can imagine this as trying to dance the salsa with someone who has a poor sense of rhythm and sometimes forgets the steps. Just to be sure, we used motion sensors to confirm that the movements between pairs in the high-sync condition were truly more synchronous than those in the low-sync condition – which they were.

After each session we used an algometer, a device that records a person's pain threshold by applying mechanical pressure until they feel pain. We found that people in the high-sync group were better able to tolerate pain, suggesting that their bodies had ramped up the production of endorphins. Those neurohormones are part of the endogenous opioid system, which plays an important role in regulating motivation by elevating mood, reducing discomfort and anxiety, boosting self-esteem and alleviating pain. Crucially, endorphins are also associated with social bonding by creating feelings of safety, trust and rapport when we are around other people. This is why they surge during some of the most intimate interpersonal interactions, including physical contact, sex, laughter, gossip and, in our primate relatives, grooming.[22]

Sure enough, these neurological differences were related to social outcomes. The high-sync group felt more connection with their interaction partners and considered that they had more in common with them; they perceived their interactions to be more successful and mutually cooperative; and they reported more willingness to work with their partner in future tasks. These convictions were also reflected in their behaviour. We used what is known as the Trust Game to put participants in a situation in which they had to decide whether to put their faith in another person by giving them their own money in the hope that they would reciprocate. In a very real sense this task allowed us to see whether they would put their money where their mouth was. They did: the high-sync group was more trusting, endowing their partners with 30 per cent more money in the economic game than the other two groups. Synchrony had a profound impact at the biological, the psychological and, most importantly, the behavioural level.

Owing to our social nature, we are hard-wired to become attuned to other people's actions, especially those who are close to us.[23] When we observe individuals who mimic each other's behaviour, we usually expect that they share some social bond.[24] Friends smile and laugh in tandem, while enemies may respond to their competitor's smile with a frown. A team of players may move in the same direction while their opponents try to go the opposite way. Our brain is so adept at discerning those patterns of affection and cooperation that it extends those inferences to our own behaviours. When we act like others, we perceive ourselves as being more similar to them, and as a result we like them more. This is why dancing, music, chanting and moving in tandem are such common parts of collective rituals.

Ritual is of course a common method of socialising children in every society, and we now have some intriguing experimental insights about how it works. The psychologists Nicole Wen, Patricia Herrmann and Cristine Legare at the University of Texas randomly divided seventy-one children into groups and gave them distinct insignia to instil a sense of membership.[25] Each group met six times over a two-week period, during which they engaged in a necklace-beading activity. For half of the groups this activity was presented in the form of a ritual: the procedure involved several scripted and redundant steps, such as touching the beads to their foreheads, clapping their hands and using specific colour sequences. The other half of the groups, who served as the control condition, were simply handed the beads and string and told that they were going to build some necklaces. Both the ritual and the control groups were told that this was a special way of playing: 'the way this group does it!' But when the researchers probed the children's affiliation with their groups, they found that those who had engaged in the ceremonial way of necklace-beading felt stronger in-group sentiments than the ones who performed the same activity in the absence of a ritual. In particular, those in the ritual conditions were less willing to part with their group's insignia and more likely to pick fellow group members to be their partners in unrelated tasks. Further experiments using the same paradigm found that children who took part in group rituals became wary of outsiders and monitored their behaviour more.[26]

This reveals a crucial point: collective ceremonies involve some of the oldest tricks in the book when it comes to building affiliation, such as the use of symbolic group markers and the alignment of behaviours. Those elements are ubiquitous in various domains of social life. Athletes, firefighters, nurses and schoolchildren wear the same uniforms and coordinate their actions to achieve their collective goals. Such conditions foster a sense of group identity and cohesion. Rituals are therefore not unique in harnessing their benefits. But thanks to their causally opaque, symbolic and normative character, the team-building effects of ritual go above and beyond those mechanisms, amplifying group affiliation in ways that instrumental actions alone do not. Ritual is the ultimate minimal group paradigm.

Still, minimal groups are just that: minimal. Wearing the same insignia may provide a sense of similarity and connection, but in the absence of additional reinforcement this connection will not be enough to motivate extended cooperation between group members.

Then again, the power of ritual is just getting started.

Denis Dutton was an American philosopher known for his provocative views on art. He argued that all humans have an innate appreciation for art and criticised elitist and pretentious forms of expression. As editor of the journal *Philosophy and Literature*, he established the Bad Writing Contest, which presented awards for the most stylistically atrocious, pseudo-profound gibberish written by pretentious scholars. In 1984 he moved to New Zealand to teach at the University of Canterbury. There he developed a fascination with Oceanic art, and especially the tribal carvings of nearby New Guinea. Having read descriptions and analyses of these artefacts written by European art scholars, he began to wonder how their evaluations would compare to those of the people who actually made the objects. He therefore travelled to New Guinea to conduct ethnographic work in the village of Yentchenmangua, a small settlement on the Sepik River where carving traditions were still thriving.

Dutton spent most of his nights in Yentchenmangua socialising in the men's house, a large communal hut where males in some tribal societies congregate to discuss important matters and perform ceremonies. One night he noticed that the collective spirits were low and everyone seemed preoccupied. He asked what was going on. His hosts explained that some of the nearby areas occasionally received visits from tourists, which provided a welcome means of supplementing their meagre income. But no one visited Yentchenmangua. This was why everybody was disheartened. What could they possibly do to attract more visitors? After some discussion they turned to Dutton and asked him if he had any wisdom to impart on the matter.

Unable to think of anything else, Dutton said the first thing that came to his mind. He remembered an event he had witnessed performed by motivational trainers in New Zealand. 'I don't know. Why don't you try … fire-walking?' he said, jokingly. 'What do you mean?' the locals asked curiously. He doubled down: 'Light a big fire and walk across it barefoot. This will certainly get the tourists' attention!' He expected the men to react to this proposal with laughter, which would lighten the otherwise gloomy mood of the night. To his dismay the villagers were rather intrigued. In fact, everyone seemed to think that this was an excellent idea. 'Can you teach us?' they asked, their eyes wide open. Dutton was now realising that he might have taken things too far. 'Well … maybe. We'll see,' he said, hoping to change the conversation. But it was too late for that. 'OK, tomorrow then!' the men decided.

Early the following day the whole village gathered and formed a circle around him, awaiting his instructions. As a sceptic, Dutton had often remarked that, contrary to the claims of New Zealand spiritual healers, there was a physical explanation for fire-walking: coal is a poor conductor of heat, which means that it takes slightly longer for that heat to transfer to skin upon contact with coal compared to something like metal. It is therefore possible to walk on burning embers without getting burned. But theory is one thing; walking on fire is another. Besides, he had seen enough fire-walks to know that they often do lead to serious injury. As he helped the group prepare the pyre and spread the coals, and as he led the way through the fire himself, he was terrified. Could this possibly work? What if someone got hurt? What if *he* got hurt?

Despite his worst fears, everything went smoothly and no one was badly injured. The fire-walk was deemed a great success. News of the ritual spread quickly around the area. The next time it was held, people from the nearby villages also came to watch. The locals did not allow them to participate and hurried to put out the fire with water, lest the outsiders attempted to copy their practice. This was *their* ritual now.

When the time came to return home, Dutton asked the people of Yentchenmangua: 'So, what if some anthropologist visits your village in the future, inquiring about the origin of the fire-walking ritual? What are you going to say?' 'Oh, easy,' they replied. 'We'll say that we've always done it this way. Our fathers did it, and their fathers before them, and ultimately our ancestors learned how to do it from a white god.'

What the people of Yentchenmangua evidently understood is that cultural rituals draw their authority from *tradition*. This is peculiar, because not all age-old things are considered to be better. If I told you that my mobile phone was twenty years old, you would not conclude that it must therefore be a very good phone. For some things, old and unchanged means antiquated and obsolete. But, unlike electronics, cultural technologies are time-honoured. A ritual that has existed since time immemorial has been performed by countless generations and has served them well. Like fine wine, these customs only improve with age. This is why practitioners so often insist that their rituals are unchanged and unchangeable – even as they undergo revisions and modifications. Among every community that I have studied, people told me that their traditions had been passed down the generations unaltered. Even when I mentioned this or that aspect of the ritual that was known to be different, people would readily dismiss it as a rare and insignificant exception. 'True, we used to sacrifice buffalo and now we sacrifice sheep. But that's just because there are no buffaloes around here any more,' a woman told me in Greece. This continuity is important. Performing a ritual in the same way as it has always been done makes us part of something not only greater than ourselves but greater even than our entire social world, connecting us to a society of fellows that transcends place and time.

Although this transcendental aspect of group membership can be conveyed with words, it can be felt at a deeper level through participation in communal rituals. This is what Abraham Maslow came to realise. Maslow was an American psychologist best known for his theory of motivation, based

on what he called the human 'hierarchy of needs'. He visual-
ised this hierarchy as a pyramid, with the most basic needs at
the bottom: food, water, air, sleep, sex – the bare minimum
our species needs to survive. At higher levels people seek things
like material security, safety, love, family, social connection, the
respect of others and self-esteem. When we are able to cover
all those needs, we are content. But to lead a truly fulfilling
life or, in Maslow's term, to reach self-actualisation, we also
need to meet higher needs. The upper levels of the pyramid
include some of the most noble pursuits: arts, music, sports,
parenting, creativity – the kinds of things we tend to consider
as deeply meaningful. At the very top of that upper triangle
Maslow placed the human need for transcendence. In one of
his lectures he chronicled how he came to grasp the role of
ritual in fulfilling those transcendental needs.

As a university professor, Maslow avoided ceremonial gatherings, which he considered a mere waste of time. But when he
became chair of his department, he had to attend the yearly
graduation ceremonies. Dressed in academic regalia, surrounded by his peers and students and shrouded in decorum
and symbolism, he began to see those rituals with new eyes. It
dawned on him that participating made him part of an endless
procession. The sociologist Robert Bellah, who attended
Maslow's lecture, reported on his words: 'Far, far ahead, at the
very beginning of the procession, was Socrates. Quite a way
back but still well ahead [...] was Spinoza. Then just ahead
of him was Freud followed by his own teachers and himself.
Behind him stretching endlessly were his students and his students' students, generation after generation as yet unborn.'[27]

Later, Bellah reflected on how Maslow's experience allowed
him to apprehend the 'true' nature of the university as a sacred
community of learning that transcends time and space.

For the real university is neither a wholesale knowledge outlet for the consumer society nor an instrument in the class struggle, though the actual university is a bit of both. But if the university does not have a fundamental symbolic reference point that transcends the pragmatic considerations of the world of working and is in tension with those considerations, then it has lost its raison d'être.[28]

While traditions in general are considered important, rituals have a special status. In a series of studies led by Daniel Stein at Berkeley University, a group of researchers examined how people react when traditions are altered.[29] They found that such alterations provoke moral indignation because they are perceived as an affront to sacred group values. For example, fraternity members said that it was wrong to neglect group rituals such as saying the Creed or reciting the founders' names, and they expressed anger and frustration at new members who skipped them. On the other hand, they did not feel as upset at violations of less ritualistic traditions, such as missing registration day or study hours. When they ranked those events in terms of how ritualised they were – for instance, how much repetition, redundancy and rigidity they involved – the researchers found that the rankings corresponded to participants' moral judgements: the more ritualised the event, the more upsetting people found its omission.

In another study the researchers asked people in the USA how they felt about the possibility of a public holiday being altered. Participants were told to imagine that the government decided to 'move celebrations for the holiday one week forward'. This is not unheard of. In 1939 President Franklin

Delano Roosevelt issued a Presidential Proclamation moving Thanksgiving one week earlier so that consumers would spend more money during the prolonged Christmas shopping season. This caused uproar. The majority of Americans strongly disapproved of the change, which became known as Franksgiving, and many states refused to enforce it. It is thus unsurprising that the participants in this study expressed similar condemnation at the thought of such alterations. But not all holidays were equal. Whether religious or secular, holidays associated with rituals – for example Christmas, Thanksgiving and New Year's Day – elicited about twice as much outrage as less ritualised holidays such as Columbus Day, Labor Day or George Washington's birthday. People did not merely find these alterations annoying or inconvenient: they judged them to be morally appalling. Further studies and measures showed that even minor alterations, such as changing a single ingredient of a sacred meal, are enough to elicit condemnation, to the point where people are motivated to punish other members of their in-group for failing to uphold the group's ritual traditions.

C

By using symbolic markers of group membership, evoking notions of continuity, coordinating ideas and actions and creating meaningful experiences, rituals generate feelings of unity that can transform individuals into communities. But as these feelings are tied to specific actions and events, their effects can be fleeting. On their own, these ingredients may not be enough to form the social glue to secure strong and lasting bonds. To cement those bonds, rituals need to recruit additional mechanisms.

In 2011 the psychologist Quentin Atkinson and the

anthropologist Harvey Whitehouse scoured the anthropological record to examine some of the patterns underlying the great variation in the world's ritual practices. Using the Human Relations Area Files (HRAF), the world's largest ethnographic archive, based at Yale University, they compiled systematic data on 645 rituals from seventy-four cultures. The files encompassed a broad range of practices, from the divinatory rites of the Azande in Africa to the bloody initiation ceremonies of the Blackfoot tribes of North America.[30] Yet a closer look revealed that this diversity was not boundless. As it turns out, most of the world's rituals primarily rely on one of two basic strategies to increase their efficacy.

On the one hand, there are rituals that are performed with high frequency – monthly, weekly or even several times a day. These rituals are typically not very spectacular or exciting. On the other, there are those ceremonies that are performed less frequently (once a year, once a generation or even once in a lifetime) but which are emotionally intense and extravagant.[31] There seem to be two diametrically opposite cultural attractors: one centred around repetition and the other relying on arousal. While new rituals are born every day, most of them are quickly forgotten. But those rituals that live long enough to become tradition tend to fall into one of these two groups.[32]

This distribution is in accordance with what Whitehouse described as the two basic modes of collective ritual, which he called *doctrinal* and *imagistic*. Each ritual mode produces a fundamentally different kind of experience and provides a distinct pathway to social cohesion.

One way to secure the durability of the bond is through frequent applications of the social glue. This allows any cracks to be sealed, and the addition of each new layer helps fortify the connection. Whether it is Sunday Mass for Christians, Friday prayer for Muslims or the Shabbat for Jews, all major religions stipulate the performance of periodic collective worship. And the practice of regular ceremonies extends just as much to the secular world. In the USA most schoolchildren start their day by reciting the Pledge of Allegiance and sporting events open with the singing of the national anthem. In the army soldiers begin and end each day with the ceremonial raising and lowering of the flag. And many companies hold end-of-week celebrations such as Friday bar. These are the kinds of ritual that constitute Whitehouse's doctrinal mode. Such routinisation is particularly important for groups that emphasise shared identity and ideological coherence. The regular displays of collective symbols (a cross, a flag, a corporate logo or company swag) act as recurrent reminders of similarity and unity that help weld the group's social identity. The habitual re-enactment of the group's customs and retelling of its ideas allow its members to internalise the collective norms and ensure that the group's core values will be faithfully remembered and transmitted.

What is more, such recurrent rituals make it easy to identify true members and spot deviations from the orthodoxy. Ritual actions are characterised by rigidity: they must be performed with the utmost precision. Consequently, knowledge of how to perform an elaborate ritual can come only through recurrent practice. Thanks to their frequent performance, the motions of those rituals become second nature to seasoned participants, who execute them almost automatically, while remaining mysterious to outsiders – who can easily be spotted. Simply following other people's lead is not enough. If you have ever attended a religious service of a foreign culture for the first time, you have probably felt at a loss as to how you should behave. Everyone else around you goes through the motions effortlessly, knowing exactly where to sit, when to kneel, stand, bow or chant, how to interact with other members and when each part of the ceremony will begin and end. If this has happened to you, it probably made you feel uncomfortable, because it was obvious to everyone present that you did not fit in. And that, in a sense, is the point.

Another way to make the ritual glue stronger is by introducing a catalyst, an element that interacts with the other ingredients to amplify their power, resulting in a more robust fastening – a sort of superglue. This is why, in place of frequency, some rituals rely on grandeur and intensity to generate feelings of excitement and momentousness among their performers.[33]

Take, for example, the State Opening of Parliament, an annual ritual that marks the beginning of each yearly session of the British Parliament. This elaborate ceremony involves the Queen departing from Buckingham Palace in a golden carriage escorted by the Household Cavalry to arrive at the House of Lords at Westminster. The Queen's crown travels in its own carriage, drawn by a different set of horses. It is placed on a cushion and entrusted to hereditary state officials along with an ancient sword and a hat. The Prince of Wales arrives in a separate procession, and so do the Queen's two golden maces. Several hundred officials dressed in colourful clothes earn their day's pay by standing, marching and on occasion bowing. After those officials have waved around numerous white sticks, black rods, silver swords and golden maces, the Queen appears in her royal attire. This includes the Robe of State, an 18-foot-long red velvet cape whose tail is carried by four children, and jewellery with an estimated value of over $5 billion. The Queen takes her place on a golden throne and is greeted by the members of the House of Lords dressed in ceremonial robes and judges of the High Court of Justice sporting wigs. Her speech is placed in a special silk bag and presented to her by the Lord Chancellor on bended knee. It is only after this speech has been delivered that the Members of Parliament can get to discussing public business.

It is not only state rituals that are loaded with splendour. In our personal lives too we make sure to mark some of our most important moments with flamboyant ceremonies. From personal milestones such as coming of age and getting married to family gatherings like Thanksgiving, Christmas or Hanukkah, the rituals associated with these occasions are bursting with pageantry. Sensory stimulation is an elemental ingredient. The exuberance and theatricality involved in such events take the mundane and ordinary and transform it into something extraordinary by arousing all of our senses. They involve lights and colours, music, singing and dancing, the smell of food and incense, and often literal bells and whistles. All these elements activate psychological processes related to how we appraise and appreciate things and situations. When we attend a ritual loaded with pageantry, it is as though a little voice inside our brain is telling us: 'Pay attention, remember this moment, because something important and meaningful is happening.' The more important the moment, the more extravagant the ritual. It is as though those moments were engineered to provide a sense of significance. This is why leaders who lack direct popular legitimacy tend to hold more flamboyant public ceremonies than their democratically elected counterparts. Massive rallies and military parades are most common under tyrannical regimes, and even in countries where kings and queens are powerless, as happens in parts of Europe, their enthronement is celebrated with far more splendour than the inauguration of the prime ministers or presidents who hold the actual power.

Extravagant rituals arouse all the senses to create special moments. Pageantry can even be awe-inspiring. But certain ceremonies raise the bar even higher.

If you ask a Catholic what it is like to attend Mass, they will probably describe what *usually* happens in the Mass, rather than any particular Mass they attended. Sure enough, they might be able to recount the ceremonial procedures in great detail. This is the perk of frequent repetition: it gives us what are known as *semantic* memories. But although practice makes perfect, arousal makes special. Participation in imagistic rituals creates unforgettable experiences that become a core part of the autobiographical self. These are the kind of personally meaningful memories known as *episodic*.

To understand the distinction between semantic and episodic memory, imagine that you are walking across a field of tall grass. With each step you take, the grass is depressed under your feet, leaving visible tracks behind you. If you wanted to find your way back at the end of your stroll, you could probably retrace your footsteps. But as soon as you walk away, the grass slowly begins to bounce back and recover. A few days later your tracks will be all but impossible to trace. However, if you follow exactly the same route every day, walking over the same steps again and again, you will begin to carve a more durable track. Given enough time, your recurrent actions will create a well-defined path through the field. As this path is the result of cumulative foot traffic, it will not bear evidence of any particular walk you took. Semantic memories are formed in a similar way. Every experience triggers a specific neural pattern in our brains. Most of the time this pattern is short-lived. But each time the experience is repeated, the pattern becomes more durable. Neurons that fire together wire together.

Now imagine that you are crossing the same field, except this time, rather than walking, you are driving a bulldozer.

Scarring and compressing the soil and uprooting all plants in its path, the bulldozer carves a deep trench through the field, leaving a long-lasting path that will be traceable for decades, even after the vegetation has grown back. This is similar to the effect that truly exceptional experiences have on our brain. A single incident can create a neural pattern so strong that it can be activated in detail for years to come. Rather than generic schemas, extreme rituals are recalled as vivid images – hence the term 'imagistic'.

Episodic memories are related to exceptional and emotionally arousing, often even traumatic events: a near-death experience, the birth of your child or the time you watched your house burn to the ground. These are transformative experiences because they shape our narrative self, our very sense of who we are as individuals.

From the fire-walking traditions of Greece and Spain to the body-piercing ceremonies performed by Hindus, and from the hazing ordeals of US college fraternities to the arduous initiations practised among military and paramilitary groups around the world, extreme rituals can produce transformational experiences that serve to bind group members into cohesive teams. It is primarily these rituals that are characteristic of Whitehouse's imagistic type. Since those personally meaningful experiences are shared with other participants, their memories are at once private and communal, and as a result the boundaries between oneself and one's group become blurred. By creating an exclusive experience that can only be understood by those who have undergone the ordeal, imagistic rituals forge an inner circle of initiates who share powerful bonds. Whitehouse describes this as a form of kinship: family members often go through the hardships of life together, and those shared tribulations play a crucial role in bringing them closer. Going through a traumatic ritual may have similar effects by creating shared experiences that trigger psychological notions of kinship. This may also be reflected in the language people use in reference to their fellow participants, whom they often refer to as 'brothers' and 'sisters'.

Imagistic ceremonies produce unique experiences for the people who undertake them and have far-reaching consequences for the groups who practise them. But, owing to their intense nature, they also pose unique challenges as objects of scientific study. While anthropologists have long conjectured about their cohesive potential, this potential has eluded scientific confirmation. As a result, our understanding of one of the most ancient and efficient social technologies, and therefore our potential to harness its power, has long remained limited. But this situation has changed swiftly as interdisciplinary work across the human sciences has allowed us to study these rituals in new ways, resulting in fascinating insights into their nature.

5

EFFERVESCENCE

I was about eight years old when my father took me to my first football game. Not the American version. I am talking about the King of Sports. At a global level, no other sport comes close to football in terms of popularity or financial and social impact.

We arrived two hours early in order to get a good spot. My city's most popular team were on their way to winning the championship that year, and we knew the stadium was going to be packed. At the time there was no assigned seating. In fact, there were no seats at all – just rows of concrete terraces, occupied on a first-come, first-served basis. For a few drachmas street vendors sold rectangular pieces of polystyrene that served as cushions. To my surprise, it appeared that the cushions were to be used only before the game. As soon as the home team entered the pitch, people jumped up, simultaneously threw their cushions in the air and never sat down again. For most of the game my father kept trying to lift me up so that I could watch the action. But that didn't matter much to me. The most interesting part was what was happening in the terraces.

Uniformly dressed in black and white, 40,000 fans put up an extraordinary spectacle. As soon as the referee blew the first whistle, it was as though a jolt of electricity had run through the stadium. Thousands of burning flares appeared, seemingly out of nowhere, waved by ecstatic fans who jumped up and down, chanting in unison. Covered in a thick red cloud, the stadium looked like a volcano putting on a spectacular lava show. A mere few seconds after it had started, the game had to be paused for several minutes until the smoke had cleared. For the ninety minutes that followed, the fans never stopped chanting. Everyone knew the words. They did not merely sing the songs – they lived them. As if led by some invisible conductor, they jumped up and down in extraordinary synchrony and shouted at the top of their lungs. It was as though the crowd had become a single entity with a life of its own. That day I became a lifelong fan.

Similar scenes take place every weekend in thousands of stadiums around the world. In many respects they resemble some of the most primordial human ceremonies. The anthropological literature is replete with similar observations. There is something about high-arousal rituals that seems to thrill groups of individuals and transform them into something greater than the sum of their parts. The sociologist Émile Durkheim, whom we met in Chapter 2, argued that collective ceremonies can produce unique experiences by triggering the alignment of emotional states, a phenomenon he called 'collective effervescence'. In his 1912 book *The Elementary Forms of the Religious Life*, he described the special feeling of exhilaration and togetherness experienced by those who take part in highly arousing collective rituals:

> The very act of congregating is an exceptionally powerful stimulant. Once the individuals are gathered together, a sort of electricity is generated from their closeness and quickly launches them to an extraordinary height of exaltation. Every emotion expressed resonates without interference in consciousnesses that are wide open to external impressions, each one echoing the others. The

initial impulse is thereby amplified each time it is echoed, like an avalanche that grows as it goes along.

This is something many of us may have experienced. If you have ever got goosebumps while dancing together with thousands of people at a concert, that was collective effervescence. And if you have ever felt awestruck, inspired or even moved to tears by a massive crowd of demonstrators chanting in unison, that was the kind of feeling Durkheim had in mind. As for me, I never miss an opportunity to return to that stadium when I visit my home country, and each time I go I still feel the hairs on the back of my neck stand up as I join the chorus.

In the course of my ethnographic research I saw how the communities I studied became energised during important collective events. Yet the participants often found their experience strangely difficult to describe. 'Words cannot do it justice,' one young man told me. I can attest to this: if you have not been to my home team's stadium, I cannot possibly convey its atmosphere to you. This problem of description makes such feelings notoriously challenging to study scientifically, very relatable though they may be. For how does one go about studying an inner state that is also shared by everyone else in the crowd? How can we measure such things as emotional alignment or the sense of togetherness?

The human need to congregate is primeval. From pre-historic hunter-gatherers to contemporary city-dwellers, individuals across all societies are on various occasions compelled to assemble in large crowds and engage in communal expressions that allow them to transcend their ordinary existence and feel as one. It is this same primordial urge that drove our ancestors to walk for weeks on end to visit Göbekli Tepe 12,000 years ago. Given that no cities existed at the time, those pilgrims would have constituted the largest congregation of human beings in prehistory. And thus since the dawn of civilisation the greatest gatherings have always been ceremonial.

In 1953 an estimated 3 million people attended the coronation of Queen Elizabeth II in London. In 1995 some 5 million Catholics gathered in Luneta Park in Manila, in the Philippines, to attend a Mass officiated by Pope John Paul II during World Youth Day. And in Tehran in 1989 more than 10 million people attended the funeral of the founder of the Islamic Republic of Iran, Ayatollah Khomeini. Still, even those gatherings are dwarfed by the world's largest religious pilgrimages. In Iraq over 30 million Shia Muslims flock to Imam Husayn's shrine in Karbala to commemorate his martyrdom. And in India the Hindu pilgrimage of Kumbh Mela, held every twelve years on the banks of four sacred rivers, draws massive crowds. In 2019 an estimated 150 million devotees attended the festivities in Allahabad, in the Indian state of Uttar Pradesh, making this the largest congregation of human beings in history. There is barely anything about the experience of attending such events that could be replicated in a lab.

However, it is not just a matter of scale. Another thing that makes collective rituals particularly hard to study in the laboratory is that they are typically tied to particular contexts. They unfold over predetermined periods of time and they occur in special locations, from wayside shrines to the Wailing Wall in Jerusalem or the River Ganges in India. They require the presence of specific people, whether they officiate or attend as participants, or of specific material objects.

Finally, collective rituals can often involve insense emotional arousal, as well as painful, stressful or even dangerous activities, including self-mutilation, exhaustion or hazing. Consider the land-diving ceremonies performed by the men of Pentecost Island in the Pacific Ocean nation of Vanuatu. Often regarded as the precursor to bungee-jumping, this ritual involves jumping off wooden towers up to 30 metres (100 feet) high and plunging head-first to the ground. The only thing protecting the divers from a fatal crash are two tree vines wrapped around their ankles. The vines must be measured precisely to allow each diver to just brush the soil as he falls without breaking his neck. Land diving is a fertility ritual meant to ensure a bountiful yam harvest, but since only males are allowed to take part, it is also regarded as a coming-of-age ceremony for young boys, who practise it from as early as seven years of age. You can't try stuff like this in the lab.

To be sure, individual components of ritual can be replicated in experiments, and it is often very useful to do so. For example, researchers have examined the effects of repetitive behaviours, synchronous movement, symbolic markers or physiological arousal. Each of those elements may contribute something unique to the ritual experience, and all of them have measurable outcomes that can be studied in controlled settings. But although we can learn a lot by studying the properties of flour, water or yeast, if we are interested in understanding bread-making, this cannot be done unless we pay attention to the interaction of those ingredients in the oven.

How, then, are we to study collective rituals, given all those limitations? Perhaps we need to think outside the box. Both laboratory and field methods have a lot to offer, but it is often their combination that can yield the most powerful insights. The idea is simple: rather than taking participants out of context and moving them into a sterile lab, why not move the lab *into* context by bringing it into the field?

My first foray into this mixed methodology took place in the Spanish village of San Pedro Manrique. More commonly referred to by the locals simply as San Pedro, it is a small farming community located in the autonomous community of Castilla y León in north-east Spain. The village has been populated since ancient times, when Celtiberian tribes roamed its land. Although the region has seen many conquerors over the years, San Pedro has enjoyed independence throughout its history, owing to its remote location and its inhospitable rugged terrain, suitable for little more than sheep herding. But precisely thanks to the sheep and wool trade, it rose to prosperity during the Middle Ages, when it came to form part of the powerful association of livestock owners known as the *Mesta*. At its apogee, it was home to four parishes and over 4,000 inhabitants. The ruins of a medieval wall, a castle and various churches stand as reminders of that bygone glory, but a lot has changed since then.

The province of Soria is now one of the least populated areas of Europe. Within that province, San Pedro's 600 residents make up one of the smallest municipalities. Its narrow cobbled streets, surrounded by stone houses crowned by red tile roofs, are mostly empty during the day, when most of its inhabitants work in neighbouring towns or at the local ham factory. On weeknights, a handful of bars and restaurants situated around the main square compete for the occasional customer, though their activity is somewhat boosted when the local youth who study in nearby towns come home for the weekend. Other than that and a municipal sports centre, there is not much going on in the surrounding area. Yet once a year San Pedro becomes the centre of attention for the entire region.

Held every June, the festival of San Juan lasts a full week. Three young girls called the *móndidas* are selected by lottery to be the focal figures of the festival. They and their families lead processions, recite poems and host meals and receptions. The festival also includes concerts, dances, public speeches, religious services and a horse race across the main square. But a single event stands out as one of the most spectacular rituals found anywhere in Europe. On the summer solstice this small village is flooded by thousands of visitors, who gather to watch a group of local men and women walk barefoot across fire.

The origins of this festival are lost in time. Some believe that the fire-walk is a relic of ancient Celtiberian rites or that the *móndidas* represent pagan priestesses of Ceres, the Roman goddess of agriculture and fertility. Others think that the *móndidas* commemorate the end of a tragic period in the region's history. According to legend, the Christians of northern Spain were forced to pay an annual tribute of one hundred virgins to the Moors of the Islamic emirate of Córdoba in exchange for their independence. Each year San Pedro contributed three girls to this tribute, until the mythical Battle of Clavijo in 844, when the king of Asturias, Ramiro I, defeated the Moors and ended the dreadful toll. It's a legend, and no one knows for sure whether there is any truth to it, but the locals are fond of it.

I first visited San Pedro as a graduate student. For my doctoral thesis I had been studying fire-walking in Greece and Bulgaria, so when I found out that a similar tradition existed in Spain I had to investigate. Although a handful of Spanish folklorists had written about it in obscure local magazines, at the time there was barely any information available on San Pedro and its rituals. That being the case, I wasn't really sure what to expect. Was the fire-walk still a big deal, or was it one of those disappearing traditions that are only practised by a handful of elders, like the fire-walking rituals of Bulgaria? Would anyone even know about it?

It quickly became apparent that it was indeed a big deal. The village's flag and seal featured a fire-walker and three *cestaños*, decorated baskets carried by the *móndidas* in the processions. Several of the local businesses had names like *Paso del fuego*, which is Spanish for 'fire-walk', or *La Hoguera*, which means 'bonfire'. Shops and bars featured posters and calendars with images of the ceremony, and people's living rooms were decorated with framed photographs of their own participation. In a village of no more than 600 inhabitants, a stone amphitheatre large enough to seat 3,000 spectators had been built specifically to host this ceremony once a year. The locals called this structure *el recinto,* which simply means 'the venue'. Clearly there was no need to clarify what the venue was for. The dirt floor at its centre, separated from the stone terraces by a metallic fence, was covered by dark scorch marks.

As soon as I brought up the topic of fire-walking, San Pedrans eagerly told me stories of past performances. Although the ritual was the same every year, some years had special significance for each individual: their first time, the time they got burned or when they carried someone special over the coals. The local mayor, who was about to retire after being in office for over two decades, called his forthcoming participation in that year's ceremony the highlight of his career. 'Not only because I get to oversee the preparations for the last time,' he said, 'but because this year I'll get to carry my daughter across the fire.' Everyone stressed the tremendous importance of this tradition. Participating made them feel 'very San Pedran', they told me time and again, and San Pedro would never be San Pedro without this ritual. They talked about the sense of pride that came with being the custodians of this tradition and expressed their great anticipation at attending the ceremony again the next year, and the one after that. When asked just how important this ritual was in his life, a man told me: 'On a scale of one to ten, this would be a twenty.' Several others went as far as to say that it was the single most important occasion in their lives.

Preparations for the festival started months in advance. Anticipation would slowly build to an explosion of joy and excitement. Once it was over, the buzz would last a few weeks longer, during which every little detail of the festival would become the topic of discussion and scrutiny. And then came the bittersweet feeling of nostalgia. Over the following months people relished their memories of the celebration, yearning to relive those moments. Talk of the fire-walk would often be accompanied by sighs, dreamy eyes and melancholy smiles.

When I asked San Pedrans what it was like to walk on the burning embers, people described an exhilarating – ecstatic, even – feeling of energy permeating them, and a sense of oneness with the crowd of spectators. 'It is a feeling that cannot be expressed in words. There are thousands of people there, but you feel like one,' they would say. And although no one seemed to be able to articulate exactly why the ritual was performed, other than that it was the custom, their comments frequently spoke to its ramifications: 'You feel part of the village, it's a sense of belonging, being one with the group,' a woman told me.

It sounded very much like the phenomenon that Durkheim had called 'collective effervescence': the electrifying feeling that is shared between participants in the context of high-arousal rituals, resulting in the alignment of their affective states and the creation of strong social bonds between them. But although anthropologists had been talking, writing and teaching about this concept for one century, no one had been able to demonstrate it. For how *does* one measure such things as emotional alignment and togetherness in the midst of a fire-walking ritual?

C

After completing my doctorate I was offered a research position at Aarhus University in the context of a cognitive science institute called the MINDLab. There I started discussing my ethnographic work with another young researcher, Uffe Schjødt, who had just received his doctorate in the psychology of religion. Having done his research using brain imaging techniques to study prayer, Uffe was very receptive to the idea that, if collective rituals resulted in emotional alignment, it should be possible to detect this alignment in people's physiology. At the same institute we later met graduate student Ivana Konvalinka, a bioengineer who was working on measuring the coordination of movement between pairs of people in the lab and was interested in testing some of her methods in a real-life setting. Together we assembled a team of people and designed a study to do just that. Our plan was to focus on the activation of the autonomic nervous system, which plays a critical role in producing subjective emotional experiences.

As we saw in Chapter 3, the autonomic system provides the body with an emotional thermostat, releasing hormones that allow it to regulate arousal. Its sympathetic division is involved in raising alertness and pumping the body up for action, while the parasympathetic division is engaged to cool things down and help the body relax. Together these two divisions control changes in a number of involuntary body functions such as heartbeat, blood flow, breathing and sweating. If you are interested in bodily markers of emotional arousal, this is a good place to start.

In the past, it would have been impossible to measure the activity of the autonomic system during an event such as a fire-walk without causing a major disruption to the ceremony. Luckily for us, recent developments in wearable sensors had made it possible to record physiological responses in real-life settings without having to follow people around with bulky devices and cables trailing all over the place. Heart-rate monitors were now light and unobtrusive and could be worn comfortably under the clothes, invisible to any observers. Nowadays this technology is widely accessible and affordable; in fact, there is a good chance you even have something like it on your wrist as you are reading the book, as I do on mine as I am typing it. But at the time this was a high-end market, mostly used by professional sports teams or the military, and certainly above our pay grade. The fact that we were planning on using these monitors in an environment hotter than an industrial oven meant that renting or borrowing them from another institution was not an option either.

We sought the help of Armin Geertz, who was the leader of a research group called the Religion, Cognition and Culture unit, and Andreas Roepstorff, one of the directors of the MINDLab. We laid out the plan: going to San Pedro and placing heart-rate monitors on people as they walked barefoot across fire. Andreas listened carefully and took a long pause. 'This is the craziest research idea I've ever heard,' he said. After a short pause he added: 'Let's do it.'

When the time finally arrived, San Pedro was looking festive. Buildings had been repainted, balconies decorated with flags, and flowers planted. Three large trees were chopped from the nearby forest and ceremonially transported to the village, each in its own procession. Adorned with ribbons, balloons and lanterns, they were placed in enormous planters and used to mark the houses of the *móndidas*. The doors to these houses remained open all day, and passers-by were invited to drop in for a treat. Bursting with pride, the girls and their families tended to the scores of people that flowed in and out of their homes throughout the day. They served seemingly endless quantities of Spanish ham and red wine, two of the area's signature products. I had eaten earlier in the day, which was a mistake, as the hosts insisted that I had to sample everything – and watched closely as I did so. I was scolded for removing the white fatty portion of the ham. That, I was informed, was the best part – and healthy too. I obliged.

The cobbled streets of the village were swarming. San Pedrans who now lived in urban areas had taken days off to attend the festivities. Visitors had come from all over the country, and even from abroad. In that sparsely populated region, accommodation within a radius of several miles had long been sold out, so many were in town just for the day. The bus from nearby Soria, which normally operated six times a week, now ran every few hours. Parked cars stretched far outside the village. The bulk of the activity was concentrated around the village's two squares and the narrow, winding street connecting them. Bars and restaurants were overflowing with patrons and mobile cantinas offered options to those who were not able to find a table. Vendors had set up a variety of booths and tables, selling hats and sunglasses, religious icons and souvenirs.

The evening began with a parade led by the *móndidas* and

accompanied by the municipal band and town officials. The procession carried the icons of San Pedro and the Virgin Mary from the main church to a small chapel called the Humilladero. Meanwhile, a group of men were starting to prepare the pyre. Using over two tons of oak wood, they created a heap the size of a small room. Once lit, it produced a column of flames over 15 metres (50 feet) high. The caretakers relied on their experience to time the blaze precisely, as it would take many hours for the logs to burn down to a bed of coals ready for the stroke of midnight.

As for us, conducting a study in the midst of this feverish activity was not easy, to put it mildly. Things were stressful, and everything that could go wrong did. But such is the nature of real-life experiments. Thankfully, things eventually fell into place, and we managed to use up all of our heart-rate monitors, which were worn by fire-walkers as well as spectators of the event. In fact, in the end we did not have enough devices for all the volunteers.

Back in the village a crowd started congregating around the town hall. A band was playing and everyone was dressed up. Those who were going to walk on the fire were wearing a red handkerchief around their necks. As the time approached, one could see the anticipation building in their faces. They had been waiting for this night all year, and only a few more hours separated them from the crescendo.

When the time came, one of my local friends grabbed me by the hand and another took my other. I was now part of a long human chain that was starting to move. I knew that it was crucial to stay in that chain, because it would lead me straight into the enclosure. I had called my colleagues who were already there to make sure they found a good spot from which to film the ceremony, so I knew that the venue was already packed. The locals knew this too and made sure to arrive early, but many of the visitors didn't manage to get in.

The chain moved quickly up the hill, followed by the crowd. A few minutes later we were crossing the gates of the *recinto*. There was something stirring about walking into the centre of this arena to the tunes of the band, greeted by thousands of spectators. It must have been nearly overwhelming for the fire-walkers, who knew that all eyes were on them. A long fire pit of glowing coals radiated heat across the arena. Just looking at it felt like sticking your face into an oven. Our pyrometer (an instrument used to measure extreme temperatures) marked 677 °C (1250 °F) on the surface of the coals, before it started melting. I had seen numerous fire-walking rituals around the world but none over a fire as ferocious as this one. As the crowd got more and more animated, the fire-walkers became more solemn. No wonder: they were about to walk barefoot across a surface hot enough to melt aluminium.

As the coals are so hot, many assume that some trick is involved. In fact, there is no special preparation for the fire-walk. No ointments or drugs, no secrets. In the past, some argued that the locals had unusually calloused feet from working barefoot in the fields. Even if this dubious claim were once true, it is certainly not the case today. Most San Pedrans do not walk barefoot any more than the average city-dweller does. Others have speculated that their feet are protected by sweat or water which keeps them moist. But the floor of the *recinto* is made of compacted dirt, which gets thoroughly dry as it is baked by the fire. Besides, getting your feet wet in this situation would actually be a bad idea, as the embers could stick to your soles and cause severe damage. It is the poor conductivity of coal and the short time of exposure that make it possible to walk on fire without getting burned.

But *possible* does not mean that anyone is guaranteed to come through unscathed. Even the slightest protrusion or imperfection in the surface of the coals can cause the feet to blister. A small rock, a piece of metal or any other foreign object in the fire would also pose great danger. If you move too slowly, your feet will begin to roast. But walk too fast and you will push deeper into the embers, making things even worse. This is why those who panic and try to run usually end up getting burned. Concentration is key: the slightest misstep or hesitation can lead to serious injury, not to mention humiliation in the eyes of the entire community.

When the music stopped, the fire-walkers removed their shoes and gathered around one last time to discuss the order in which they would cross. Going through the burning embers, each of them would carry another person on their back, typically someone very dear to them. The three *móndidas* would be the first to be carried. Exactly at midnight the raucous sound of a trumpet signalled that it was time. Silence descended.

Alejandro, the oldest and most experienced of all the fire-walkers, would have the honour of going first. He stood up and walked towards one of the *móndidas,* his own granddaughter. Alejandro was seventy-five years old, and the girl was a full head taller than him. As she climbed on to his back, he seemed for a moment to be struggling to stay upright, as if trying to balance a top-heavy Jenga tower. Everyone held their breath. A few men came closer to check if he needed help, but he dismissed them with a sharp gesture.

The trumpet sounded again. The moment had arrived. The arena fell silent. Alejandro turned to the girl perched on his back and asked her to hold tight. He took a long breath and stared at the fire for a few seconds, concentrating. Then he looked up, summoning his courage, and took the first step.

He walked across the burning embers with unwavering determination. His head held high, he looked defiant and fervent, like a warrior in the heat of battle. When he reached the other end of the coal bed, a roar erupted among the crowd. The girl dismounted, and they barely had time to embrace before their families proudly joined them in a group hug.

One after the other, a few dozen pairs traversed the coals that night. They stomped their feet hard, almost as if trying to put out the ferocious fire, raising a small cloud of sparks and flares behind them with each step. People often describe this as an attempt to dominate the fire and show that they have no fear. Perhaps they are showing this to the crowd, but importantly, they are also showing it to themselves. Looking at that same fire and feeling its mightiness from a much greater distance than they were, I could only wonder how intimidating it must be. To cope with the anticipation, the walkers often cross themselves, hold lucky charms, meditate or pray and try to clear their mind of everything else. The walk only lasts a few seconds but it feels like an eternity. Fire-walkers say that it is like moving in slow motion, being in a kind of flow that allows them to be aware of every step and every movement. At that moment, they say, there is nothing else in the world, no other thought in your mind. There is just you and the fire. And then it is over, and it's time to celebrate.

With each successful walk, the initial fear and anxiety gave way to a burst of relief, joy and pride, as friends and family rushed to hug the pair of walker and rider. Experienced men led the way, carrying adults on their back: spouses, parents, offspring or other beloved ones. Women and novice walkers followed, some carrying children and some walking alone. The village priest also crossed the fire; the crowd liked that. A young man named Fernando was planning to carry his girlfriend that night, but they had had a falling out a few days earlier and she didn't come. It looked like it was going to be just him. But when his turn came, he turned to his father and gave him his hand. The man glowed with pride and delight. As Fernando braved the fire wearing a stern expression, his father smiled blissfully.[1] As soon as the short ride was over and the father got down off his son's back, the two men engaged in a tight embrace.

After the last fire-walker crossed over the coals, the crowd flooded the enclosure and everyone mingled together. The band struck up again and they began to move downhill. It was already two o'clock in the morning, but they were much too excited to go home. The party that was going to follow was of the kind that only Spaniards know how to throw. People danced and sang together in the streets until dawn. Beer and wine flowed in bountiful quantities from barrels that had been stored in people's garages for the occasion. In all this excitement, most of our participants seemed to have forgotten that they were wearing our heart-rate monitors.

As soon as we saw the first analyses, we knew we had found something truly remarkable.[2] First, our data revealed an extraordinary level of synchrony among people's heart-rate patterns during the fire-walk. This was striking, because they were doing very different things. Had they all been dancing to the same tune, engaging in identical movements, we would have expected such coordination to be reflected in their bodies. But only one of them was walking at any given time, while the others were standing and waiting for their turn, seated in the terraces or moving about after finishing their own walk. And yet the synchrony was much stronger during the ritual than any other part of the day, stronger even than the times when every-one had been marching together or dancing in tandem.

This kind of physiological synchrony is often observed at the brain level in what is known as the 'mirror neuron system'. Watching someone else use a hammer activates the same brain areas that fire up when we use a hammer ourselves. Could it be that we were seeing some version of this phenomenon reflected in people's heart rates? If we had looked only at the biometric data, we might have thought so. But examining the social context revealed a crucial detail: this affective synchrony was not indiscriminate. The effect was strong among fire-walkers, and even extended to the local spectators. In contrast, we found no such synchrony between locals and outsiders. For the scores of curious visitors who had come to the village from elsewhere, this was just a spectacle. For the locals, it was an event of monumental importance.

This social component became even more apparent when we mapped our participants' social networks – the list of each participant's family and friends – and their perceived strength of those relationships. We discovered that the greater the social proximity between two individuals, the more their arousal patterns synchronised during the ritual – so much that one would be able to predict the type of social relationship between two people just by looking at how closely their heart rates matched.[3] Pairs of friends and relatives showed marked similarities in their arousal patterns that were clearly visible in the graphs, even before applying any statistical analysis. A pair of twins in our sample showed nearly identical heart rates, even when one of them was seated and the other was walking through fire. Local spectators and fire-walkers were closely aligned too. By contrast, the arousal patterns of unrelated spectators – the outsiders – showed nothing comparable to this. This was not simply a case of an automatic empathic response in people's brains – it was a fundamentally social phenomenon.

C

This social dimension of ritual emotional arousal has also been documented by neuroscientific research. Paul Zak is an economist and neuroscientist at Claremont Graduate University, where he specialises in the neurochemistry of human bonding. This has earned him the nickname 'Dr Love'. In his lab in Southern California, Zak and his colleagues found that when people displayed trust and trustworthiness (for example, when transferring money to someone with the expectation of reciprocating), their brain produced larger quantities of oxytocin, a neurohormone that plays a critical role in social bonding. It is released in large quantities during childbirth and breastfeeding, creating a state of calm and focused attention that helps mothers bond with their infants. It also shoots up during sexual intercourse, which helps to make sex pleasurable but also facilitates pair-bonding by increasing empathy and affection.

When Zak and his team gave people infusions of oxytocin through a nasal spray, they became more generous and trusting of others. Couples who received oxytocin engaged in more eye contact, displayed more agreement and found each other's presence more reassuring. Having established these effects in the lab, Zak was eager to investigate how they would hold up in real-life situations. He got his chance in the form of a wedding invitation.

Linda Geddes is a British science writer, best known for her writings on pregnancy and child-rearing. She published several articles about the impact of oxytocin on bonding between romantic partners as well as between parents and their children.

This led her to wonder about the role of this 'cuddle molecule', as she called it, in the context of emotional cultural practices such as wedding ceremonies. As no such research was available at the time, she decided to volunteer herself as a guinea pig. And what better occasion to do that than her own wedding day?

Geddes contacted Zak, whose work she had been reporting for years, and asked him if he was interested in drawing blood samples from attendees at her wedding. Of course, Zak was interested in drawing blood: there is a reason people often refer to his line of research as 'vampire economics'. He packed a suit, a centrifuge, a hefty supply of dry ice and lots of syringes, blood tubes and adhesive bandages (a typical suitcase, if you are Paul Zak) and flew to Devon. There he took two blood samples from a cross section of friends and relatives attending the wedding, one before the ceremony and one immediately after the exchange of vows. This allowed him to measure the impact of this highly emotional ritual on oxytocin levels.

When the results of the tests came in, they confirmed what Zak had expected: the ceremony had caused a spike in oxytocin levels, but this spike was not the same for everyone. Just like in our study of the Spanish fire-walkers, levels of oxytocin could be predicted on the basis of social relatedness, with the bride recording the largest increase, followed by the couple's parents, the groom, then other close friends and relatives, and finally some of their less intimate friends. According to Zak, 'the increase in oxytocin was in direct proportion to the likely intensity of emotional engagement in the event'.[4] These effects may be the reason why wedding ceremonies are one of the most ancient of all rituals, as they help bind the couple to their in-laws and their new extended family, creating kinship bonds not only symbolically but at the very molecular level. As Durkheim had already pointed out when he theorised on the existence of collective effervescence, its function lies in 'not merely generating emotions, but bringing those who share them into a more intimate and more dynamic relationship'.[5]

When I showed the people of San Pedro their own data, they were both intrigued and surprised. The day after the ritual, I had asked them to estimate their level of arousal during various parts of the ceremony. Without exception, they all claimed that the time they went through the fire was the calmest they had been during the day. In fact, some of them offered to bet money that this would be visible in our data. Having already glanced at the data, it would have been unfair to take that bet, for I knew that they all had extremely elevated arousal levels during their fire-walk, even compared with activities like dancing or jogging up the hill during the procession. Their heart rate often exceeded 200 beats per minute. For most of them, that was beyond the medically recommended safe level of arousal: the fire-walk was stressful enough to give them a heart attack.

This opens up some intriguing questions. What *is* the personal experience of a fire-walker who feels (or, more precisely, remembers) being blissfully calm, while in reality their heart is pounding 200 times per minute? The truth is that we don't know. But this sharp discrepancy between physiology (the inner workings of our bodies) and phenomenology (our lived experience) shows that when we rely on one method alone, we risk missing the big picture. It is only by using a combination of methods that we can even become aware of puzzles like this. If these different methods all point to the same conclusion, then we can be more confident about our findings. And if not, we will be able to ask new and more interesting questions. This is how scientific knowledge progresses.

On the other hand, the synchrony data seemed to make perfect sense to the people of San Pedro. A few months later, once we had the first analyses of that data in our hands, I shared with them some simple line graphs that showed how closely their heart rates aligned with those of their loved ones during the ritual. Looking at those images, people nodded in agreement. Many used the word 'resonance' (*resonancia*) to describe what those images represented to them. I found that very interesting, because this was the same technical term used by a group of physicists we had consulted in order to analyse our biometric data. One fire-walker pointed to the graphs and said: 'I told you it was hard to express the feelings that I experience during this ritual. *This* is how I feel. Our hearts become one.'

A substantial portion of my anthropological research has focused on fire-walking rituals. I studied them in various contexts and wrote my doctoral dissertation on the fire-walking rituals of the Anastenaria in Greece.[6] For years, whenever I lectured on the topic, one of the first questions from the audience was 'Have you ever done it yourself?' This would prompt a long explanation about why this was not really an option for me in the particular settings I had studied. That is, until I began my fieldwork on the island of Mauritius in 2009.

On arrival, my partner (who is now my wife) and I rented an apartment in the coastal village of Pointe aux Piments. From our window we could see the sun set over a small Hindu temple made of concrete blocks and corrugated tin sheets, located by

the local beach. The Maha Kali Mata Mandir, as was its official name, was a *kalimai*, a sanctuary dedicated to the Mother
Goddess Kali. At its centre was a statue of the fierce deity, with
her four hands holding a trident, a bloody sword, a severed head
and a skull made into a bowl, collecting the blood of the ampu-
tated head. Over my first few months in Mauritius I would
spend most of my days around that temple. In the morning I
would sip a cup of tea at the small restaurant across the street
and observe the devotees as they went in to pray and make their
offerings. Throughout the day the temple was one of the best
spots to find people to interview, as it was the only place with
any significant activity in the area. And in the evenings I would
attend the various ceremonies there, where I had the opportunity to ask more specific questions about those practices.

Like other temples of the Mother Goddess, the Maha Kali
Mata Mandir organised an annual fire-walking ceremony called
Thimithi. This ritual has been performed in Tamil Nadu, the
southernmost state of India, for over two millennia. Today it is
practised by numerous Hindu communities around the world.
Legend connects it to the story of a young woman called Draupadi, who is often considered the incarnation of Kali. Born out
of a sacrificial fire, she was a princess of unparalleled charm
and beauty as well as being a fierce, powerful woman. Luck,
however, was not on her side. After a terrible misunderstand-
ing, she found herself married to all five of the Pandavas, sons
of King Pandu. When their cousins, the Kauravas, challenged
their claim to the throne, Draupadi got caught in the war of
succession, during which she suffered a series of hardships.
Her five sons were killed, she was abducted after the Pandavas
lost her in a game of dice and she endured numerous humili-
ations and attempts to defile her. After helping her husbands
prevail over the Kauravas, she underwent a trial by fire: to prove

her chastity and piety, she walked through flames and emerged unscathed. Thus was born the *Thimithi* ceremony, which is held to commemorate her story. Like Draupadi, participants in the *Thimithi* endure a number of hardships that culminate with their own trial by fire, and she is said to protect them from the flames by turning the burning embers into flowers.

As the day of the ceremony drew near, I spent most of my time observing the preparations and talking to devotees and temple officials. One morning, as I was interviewing a woman in the nearby grove, I noticed that some of the men were engaged in a lively discussion in front of the temple. Every so often they would look in my direction. Eventually, Prakash, the temple president, stood up and signalled me to come closer. I approached.

'Dimitris,' he said, in a formal way, 'I have been thinking. You have been living in our village for how long now?"

'A couple of months.'

'And you've been spending time with us, sharing our meals, attending our prayers.'

'Yes,' I said, not sure where this was going.

'You are one of us now,' Prakash declared.

As honoured as I was to hear that, I was sure that they had not called me there just to pay me a compliment.

'Well, I don't want to pretend to be a local,' I said. 'I am here to learn from you about your way of life and your customs.'

Prakash came to the point. 'So,' he said, 'you should also do the fire-walk.'

In Spain the ritual is a mark of San Pedran descent, proudly reserved for those who can claim blood ties to the local community. As such, no outsiders are allowed to take part. In Greece too the fire-walking rituals of the Anastenaria are passed down from one generation to the next, and so had traditionally been performed only by those who derived their ancestry from the region where the ritual originated, in present-day Bulgaria.[7] In recent decades some outsiders had been allowed to take part, but this was a gradual and delicate process that involved careful vetting by the elders. To become an Anastenari, one must experience a personal revelation, commonly in the form of a dream or vision that leads to a spiritual transformation and the establishment of a personal relationship with the saints. This was not my own experience. Besides, being an Anastenari was a lifelong commitment, and people might feel disappointed or betrayed if I did the fire-walk and later failed to return each year. In short, I was not expecting Prakash's invitation.

I stared at him for a second, trying to get a feel of the situation. There had been a light-hearted tone in his words, yet now he was nodding, indicating that he had meant what he said. Everyone's eyes turned to me.

I politely turned down the invitation. It was a great honour, I explained, but this was *their* tradition. I was not Mauritian or Hindu. I was just a foreign anthropologist, there to do research. It was therefore important for me to be able to observe and document the ritual, which I was going to witness for the first time in that village.

'OK,' Prakash said, looking amused. 'If God wants you to do it, then you will do it.'

'Trust me, Prakash, God does not want me to walk on fire,' I replied.

On the day of the *Thimithi* things got busy early. At dawn, the fire-walkers and their families started gathering in the nearby town of Triolet to perform prayers and purification rites. They were dressed in traditional garments: long saris for women and dhotis for men, most of them bright yellow. Many of them carried silver plates with flowers and food offerings for the goddess. A few hours later they formed a procession that crossed our village's main road for about 4 kilometres before reaching the temple by the shore. I walked along, observing, taking pictures and making notes on my voice recorder. The procession lasted several hours, during which devotees walked barefoot on the burning asphalt road, stopping at each cross-road to dance. Many appeared to fall into a trance, letting out agonising cries as they swayed and gyrated to the tune of drums and wind instruments. By the time we arrived at the temple, I already felt exhausted and dehydrated from the tropical sun. The shallow trench that had been dug in front of the temple was now full of burning coals, and the area around it was roped off, separating the fire-walkers from the crowd like a theatre stage from the audience. As everyone gathered in front of the fire pit, I could feel the tension.

I watched closely as people crossed the fire one by one. The first person to walk across the coals was the temple priest, followed by Prakash and other temple officials. Then came everyone else. I had been allowed to stand inside the roped-off enclosure to observe and photograph the event from close up. I was impressed by the sparks flying through the embers with each footstep and tried to capture them with my camera. At one point one of the organisers suggested that I should move closer to the fire, where I would be able to get better pictures. It was indeed a better spot. Kneeling down, I started shooting the action. Men, women and even children participated, and each walk was met by the crowd with the chant 'Om Shakti', an invocation of the Divine Mother.

I noticed a little girl – she must have been about nine or ten – standing in the line. She was very nervous, and kept looking at her parents, who were trying to encourage her. When it was her turn to face the fire, she froze on her feet, seemingly terrified.

At that point, however, backing out was not an option, for that would be an insult to Kali. A man grabbed her by the arm to get her moving. She resisted and started crying, kicking and screaming. Prakash came to the rescue. He waved the man to step aside and whispered something in the girl's ear. He then lifted her in his arms and carried her through the fire himself. Her parents seemed relieved, although it took her some time to stop crying. People didn't seem to worry much about this. Soon I saw more children, even infants, being carried over the fire. I was fascinated by people's facial expressions, which ranged from fear to determination and from pain to bliss. I tried to capture these emotions with my camera. I focused all my attention into the lens and became so absorbed that I never noticed the small conspiracy that was taking place around me.

A few moments later, I felt a tap on my shoulder. I took my eyes off the lens and looked up. It was Prakash, signalling me to get up. I obliged and looked at him, awaiting instructions. 'Turn around,' he said. When I did, I suddenly realised that I was standing in front of the fire pit and the entire village was watching me. Prakash smiled and said, 'Now you will know what the fire is like.' There was not much else to say or do at that point. To refuse would mean insulting my hosts and losing face in front of the entire community, and would probably also cause a disturbance in the ritual, as the remaining fire-walkers were already lined up behind me waiting for their turn. All I had time to do was say, 'Please hold my camera.'

Being caught by surprise had its benefits. Having looked at people's heart rates in the context of similar rituals, I knew that they tend to peak just before their walk. Yet, as my own fire-walk came unexpectedly, there was no stressful anticipation. I wonder what a heart-rate monitor would have revealed. Perhaps, like the Spanish fire-walkers, I might have reached extreme levels of arousal without being consciously aware of it. This might be why those few seconds felt like several minutes. Time slowed to a crawl. I became intensely focused. With my first step I sensed all the ferocity of the heat. I had measured the temperature of the coals in other fire-walks, and I knew that it could range between 400 and 800 °C (750–1500 °F). But I had no idea what it would feel like to actually walk on a surface that hot.

One of those steps felt particularly painful, and I immediately knew it was going to give me a blister, but I managed to show no signs of pain – or so people told me afterwards. Earlier, I had seen the flames spark under the feet of other walkers. I wondered whether this was happening under my own feet, but I avoided looking down. I kept facing the crowd, although I didn't really see anyone in particular. Just like the people of San Pedro had described, I felt hyper-aware, but at the same time it was all just a blur. And when it was all over, I felt a surge of exhilaration as the crowd cheered, along with a sense of pride, as if I had chosen to walk on the fire of my own free will.

Once the event was over, many people came to ask me questions. They wanted to know what I had experienced, what it felt like and what had made me do it – the kinds of questions I would usually ask people in my own interviews. I answered honestly, explaining that I hadn't really planned to do it – it was in fact some of the locals who had convinced me to go through with it. But the experience was thrilling, almost intoxicating. I felt the adrenaline rushing through my body and a kick of euphoria strong enough to last the rest of the day and beyond. Reflecting on my experience later, I was amazed at how this short burst of activity produced such strong, long-lasting emotions.

Although my experience was certainly not the same as

that of the locals, taking part in that fire-walk helped me get a glimpse of the intense emotions involved in such rituals. The roller coaster of fear, pride, excitement and joy that they provide to their practitioners is key to creating the unique experiences that my informants often described. Even as an outsider, I too got a small taste, however superficial, of those bonding effects. For me it signified acceptance in this community that I had come to study. And for the locals it signalled that I was willing to do as they did, even if that involved walking on fire. That day had brought me closer to them than ever before. In fact, many years later, I am still in touch with many of these people, and I always visit them when I am in Mauritius, even when carrying out research in other parts of the country. If it had that much of an impact on an outsider like me, what must it do for the permanent members of the community?

My fire-walking experience brought to mind another study I did in San Pedro, which examined fire-walkers' recollections of their performance.[8] In that study we found that, although everyone had vivid memories, the details of those memories were blurry. People remembered the central event – their own fire-walk – and how it made them feel. They described their excitement, enthusiasm and fear. 'It is such a powerful feeling,' a young man said. 'It is scary, but simultaneously awe-inspiring.' And another said, 'I was so excited that I felt like floating.' Beyond those emotions, however, there was little else they could remember. When I asked them about the details of the event – things like who was sitting next to them, who they talked to or where they went after their walk – they had no recollections of such things. No one remembered talking to me either. 'I think … you were not there last night, were you?' many of them said. In reality, I was facing the group the whole time, wearing a bright yellow shirt, and had approached each one of them to ask them questions.

This narrowing of perception resembles what the psychologist Mihaly Csikszentmihalyi called *flow*: a mental state in which we become so fully immersed in an action that our mind filters out all peripheral details, allowing us to become unconditionally absorbed into the experience.[9] Such 'optimal' experiences are often called *autotelic,* which means that people do not need any external motivation or justification to pursue them – the actions become a goal in themselves. Common to these experiences is the feeling of losing the sense of time, being focused entirely on the present moment to the extent that nothing else matters, and a sense of empowerment and effortlessness, as if being carried by a water current – which is where the term 'flow' comes from. This transcendental feeling of losing oneself lies at the core of some of the most meaningful human activities.

Csikszentmihalyi alluded to the possible links between flow and effervescence. But there is much more to effervescence than flow. Although flow can be experienced in collective settings, it is at its core an individual phenomenon. Fighter pilots, athletes, chess players, musicians and other artists often describe flow as a state of total involvement where the self becomes indistinguishable from the action. Many people may even experience similar states when practising a craft or hobby, during a sexual encounter or while exercising. Some of the most meaningful moments in our lives are activities that elicit flow. And there are indeed various solitary ritual experiences that can induce this feeling, including prayer, meditation and repetitive actions such as reciting mantras or creating mandalas. But what these and other transcendental experiences have in common is that they *restrict* the sense of self to the point of dissolution. The self becomes lost in the action, and this is experienced as bliss. Moreover, as is clear from many of these examples, flow states do not require emotional arousal.

Some collective rituals, in contrast, seem to create a different, more elevated experience. These rituals involve strong emotional and physiological arousal and, crucially, this arousal is shared between participants. The resulting emotional communion creates a dynamic system in which each individual's experience is affected and amplified by those of others, like a thousand streams of water merging to form a river that is faster and more powerful than any single stream could ever be. When this interactive kind of flow is present, the sense of self is *expanded* and the individual experiences a transcendental oneness with the group.

Durkheim conceived of collective effervescence as an emergent property of synchronous arousal, something far greater than the sum of its parts. And for him it was the whole that defined the parts rather than the other way round. While the solitary mystic seeks to find God within the self, collective rituals create the conditions for practitioners to find themselves in the group, so that they may experience transcendence as one. Through sharing their actions and emotions with other group members, participants feel an intense bond, to the point where the boundaries between the 'I' and the 'we' begin to blur. Just as my own informants put it when they told me that 'there are thousands of people there, but you feel like one'. It is a truly ecstatic sensation, which creates meaning and a collective sense of purpose, motivating individuals to relive the experience.[10]

Durkheim stressed the primordial significance of collective effervescence for early human societies. By periodically coming together to enact emotional rituals, the members of those societies were able to forge a strong group identity – a 'collective conscience', as he called it. By acting as one and feeling as one, those members were more likely to think as one. So powerful are these experiences that they feel sacred, which is why Durkheim considered that religion itself was born out of the unique feelings generated by such collective rituals.

In January 2016 a YouTube video of Aaliyah and Benjamin Armstrong's wedding reception in New Zealand went viral, getting over 20 million views within hours. The three-minute clip showed many of those in attendance performing a traditional Maori ceremonial dance known as the *haka*. This is a very physical group dance, involving vigorous synchronised movements such as pounding the chest and thighs and stamping the feet on the ground, accompanied by fierce posturing and loud rhythmic shouting. A successful *haka* performance is said to elicit *ihi*, which is a hair-raising feeling of exhilaration experienced by performers and observers alike.

The performance was organised by the groom's best man as a tribute to the couple's Polynesian heritage. In the video the groom's older brother can be seen leading a group of groomsmen and bridesmaids in a performance that moves the bride and groom to tears. Before long the couple and many of the guests join in the performance. At the end of the choreography the dancers are seen sweating and panting, exhausted from the physical effort and deeply emotional, affectionately hugging one another in a manifestation of the ritual's bonding effects.

Judging from this video, one might be surprised to hear that the *haka* has commonly been performed as a war dance, meant to fill those who perform it with aggression and intimidate the enemy before battle. Even in the absence of warfare, this dance is still performed by some military units in New Zealand. Perhaps more famously, it is also done by the members of the New Zealand national rugby team, the All Blacks, in front of their opponents before each game as a menacing display of power and defiance. When I visited New Zealand, I attended one such event, where a group of Maori danced in unison, beating their chests, stomping and letting out thunderous cries as they faced the audience, myself among them, with intimidating expressions on their faces. But this was no war dance. The *haka* is not used just to convey aggression towards opponents but also to show hospitality to friends. On a variety of occasions it can be performed to honour distinguished guests, mark important events or welcome visitors.

The dual nature of this Maori tradition is not unique. The *hosa* is a war dance performed by Shia tribes in southern Iraq. It involves synchronised movements and chants that are said to produce a state of exaltation that acts as a stimulant for warriors before facing their enemies. But the same ritual is also performed on happy occasions, such as marriages and important holidays. When Saddam Hussein visited the territory of those tribes, they performed a *hosa* in his honour. How can the same rituals move people to tears but also induce antipathy towards others?

Collective rituals are powerful social technologies that can excite, elevate and unite individuals into cohesive units, and even inspire them to create myth, religion and other meaningful pursuits. But, like all technologies, they can be used for better or for worse. It would be remiss to talk about those noble aspects of effervescence without also acknowledging its potential to foster division, discrimination and hatred. Emotional ceremonies are often painted in ideological colours and used to instil fanaticism and hostility towards outsiders. One has only to think of the effervescent character of Nazi parades, nationalist marches or the gatherings of religious fanatics and football hooligans, which can often lead down dark avenues.

I was in my late teens when I travelled to Athens with a friend to watch a football match. We arrived early and decided to explore the area. We had been walking around for a few hours when, completely out of the blue, I felt a blow to my head from behind. Before I realised what was happening, I found myself on the ground and a group of people were beginning to hit me. Punches and kicks were coming from all directions, and one of them was using a club. This was not a mere attempt to scare me; they were trying to do as much damage as possible. As I tried to protect my head, I worried that someone might pull out a knife – in situations like this, stabbings are quite common. No one said a word to me; they didn't have to. I immediately knew that the reason for the attack was that they didn't like the colour of my scarf. They were fans of a rival team – not even the one we were facing that night – who were patrolling the streets looking for blood.

My salvation came just as unexpectedly. Quite by chance, another group of fans, this time wearing the right kit, happened to be approaching. My friend ran to them and called to them for help. Outnumbered, my assailants ran away. The last thing I remember is watching them being chased down the street as my allies hurled rocks and beer bottles at them.

In many parts of the world, such scenes are all too common, as some sports fans become so attached to their team that they are willing to risk their lives or threaten the lives of others to defend its honour. Clashes between fans of opposing teams frequently take place inside and outside stadiums. Groups of fans are even known to travel long distances, often to another country, to engage in street fights with their enemies. In many instances they attack their adversaries with bare fists, as well as with flares, rocks, clubs and even firearms. In 2019 the leader of a fan association for the Serbian team Partizan was gunned down in downtown Belgrade in an act of modern tribal warfare. He had recently been released from prison after serving a sentence for the brutal murder of a fan of the French team Toulouse who had travelled to Belgrade to watch the game between the two teams. His execution appears to have been an act of revenge.

In many ways, sports fandom is not unlike religion, nationalism or other forms of ideology. In such contexts most people copy the preferences of their parents and peers, or simply support whatever team is popular in their area. But what begins as an arbitrary preference or mere adherence to tradition can turn into deep ideological commitment. The effervescent rituals performed in stadiums, temples and rallies act as a catalyst for this transformation.

Indeed, in a study conducted in the USA we found that, when sports fans watched games in the stadium, their emotional reactions were aligned, their hearts beating more synchronously than groups who watched those games together on television. Those in the stadium reported having more meaningful and transformative experiences that shaped their personal identity and expressed more loyalty to the community of fans. These bonding effects of participation were a product neither of individual arousal nor of the game itself. Rather, they were related to the degree to which this emotional arousal was physically shared in a group context.[11]

There are, of course, many other reasons for football's wild popularity. But the level of extreme loyalty that leads some fans to see their opponents as mortal enemies can only be forged through the collective rituals that take place in the terraces. There has never been a couch potato hooligan. When it gets out of hand, the power of ritual can be deadly.

Nevertheless, this conclusion may seem premature without examining the behavioural evidence. I began studying extreme rituals wanting to learn something about their social effects: their role in strengthening bonds between participants. Anthropological insights, psychological surveys, biological measurements and neuroscientific data all agree that these rituals create shared arousal that results in feelings of togetherness, and my own participation gave me a glimpse of their emotional impact. But, other than my own intuitions, I still had no concrete evidence that these effects really translated into increased social cohesion. Do such intense rituals actually have the power to change people's behaviour? And how can we find out?

6

SUPERGLUE

Deep in the Brazilian Amazon rainforest a group of young boys of the Sateré-Mawé tribe are nervously waiting for their coming-of-age ceremony. Elders prepare a pair of gloves made of palm fronds and bird feathers. The challenge the boys must face consists of wearing the gloves for a few minutes. But this is easier said than done. Some hours earlier a hundred bullet ants were collected from the forest and carried to the village inside a hollow bamboo trunk. These enormous ants have oversized pincer-like mandibles that can easily cut through skin. It is their other end, however, that makes them so menacing. Their venomous stingers can deliver a paralysing neurotoxin, which is said to cause the most painful sting of any insect. The entomologist Justin O. Schmidt, who subjected himself to all manner of insect attacks to create the Schmidt Sting Pain Index, described being stung by a bullet ant like 'walking over flaming charcoal with a 3-inch nail embedded in your heel'.[1] Others say that a single sting feels like a gunshot (hence the ant's name).

To handle the ferocious arthropods, a medicine man immerses them in a brew of crushed cashew tree leaves, which renders them temporarily unconscious. They are then woven into the gloves so that they cannot escape, their stingers facing inside. Once the ants have woken up, the medicine man blows smoke on them to agitate them. As soon as the initiates put their hands inside the gloves, the enraged insects begin to bite and sting.

The excruciating effects are felt at once. The venom causes swelling and paralysis. The boys sweat and shake uncontrollably. By the time the shaman passes on the gloves to the next initiate, each boy will have been stung hundreds of times. The elders lead them in a dance to help distract them. But as the time passes the effects only worsen. Initiates will develop fever, blistering, hallucinations and waves of burning pain. In Venezuela this ant is known as *hormiga veinticuatro* ('ant 24'), alluding to the twenty-four hours of suffering that follow its sting. The pain is so unbearable that there are stories of men who wanted to cut off their own hands to put an end to it. Yet this is just the beginning of their ordeal. To become a warrior, each boy will have to go through this ritual not once but twenty times.

The bullet ant initiation may seem extreme. But the Sateré-Mawé are not alone. The ethnographic record is rife with traumatic rituals that often involve so much stress and suffering that they have been called 'rites of terror'.[2] Anthropologists like to disagree on most things. It is all the more impressive, then, that the idea that these practices help maintain social order has rarely been disputed. Despite this consensus, however, attempts to validate this assertion have until recently been scarce. This has not been for lack of interest. As we have seen, collective rituals, especially extreme ones, are not easy to study. Unsurprisingly, then, early attempts to measure the effects of ritual intensity scientifically were confined to the laboratory.

In 1959 the social psychologists Elliot Aronson and Judson Mills invited sixty-three female students at Stanford University to join a discussion group on the psychology of sex.[3] To become members of this group they would first need to complete an 'embarrassment test'. Participants were told that the purpose of this test was to make sure they were comfortable with some of the sensitive topics that would be discussed in the sessions. In reality, it was meant to serve as a sort of initiation ritual.

The test consisted of performing a reading task in front of a group of other students. Some of the women were randomly assigned to a 'mild embarrassment' condition, in which they were required to read a list of words that were related to sex but would not make most people uncomfortable, such as 'virgin', 'prostitute' or 'petting'. Others were assigned to a 'severe' version of the test, in which the list contained vulgar words like 'fucking' or 'cock', and pornographic narratives with explicit descriptions of sexual activity. After completing the task, participants listened to a recording of the reading group's meeting, which had been designed to be dreadfully boring. A group of dull speakers engaged in a long, tedious discussion of the secondary mating characteristics of birds. The discussion was full of dry language and the speakers took long pauses, repeated themselves and made mistakes and contradictions. In the words of Aronson and Mills, this was 'one of the most worthless and uninteresting discussions imaginable'.

After the end of this discussion, participants were asked to rate the group and its members in terms of various attributes, such as how interesting they found the conversation and how bright and charming the group members appeared. The results showed that the mild initiation group provided ratings no different from those of a control group, who had joined the discussion without any entry test. But the severe initiation group viewed both the group and its members more favourably. Although all groups participated in the exact same activity, those who underwent the more intense initiation found it far more interesting and saw their peers as being more likeable.

In the context of American society in the late 1950s, when girls were brought up to be prudish and sex was a taboo topic, performing this task in front of an audience must have been truly embarrassing for those students. In fact, on seeing the list of words she was to read, one of the participants got up and left the room, withdrawing from the experiment. Still, this verbal task is no match for the kind of intense physical and emotional arousal involved in some real-life rituals, some of which include pain, bodily mutilation or psychological trauma.

A few years later, two psychologists at the University of California at Riverside decided to up the ante.[4] Harold Gerard and Grover Mathewson conducted a similar experiment, but one that involved a much more disturbing initiation. Instead of embarrassing words, they used electric shocks to induce pain on a group of unlucky volunteers. This was 1966, before most universities had established procedures for the ethical treatment of research subjects, so these kinds of experimental methods were not uncommon. The results of the experiment were consistent with those of Aronson and Mills. Participants who received shocks before joining the group expressed more positive feelings towards the group and its members. Moreover, those who received the more severe shocks gave even higher ratings than those who had been exposed to the milder ones.

These classical experiments provided relevant insights for the study of costly rituals. But even though the experimenters referred to their manipulations as 'initiations', the situations had little resemblance to real-life ceremonies. And although completing the tasks was related to membership of the reading groups, these groups were a far cry from the meaningful social interactions that people encounter in their everyday lives. More importantly, positive attitudes towards one's group are only important to the extent that they motivate actual behaviours. Although those studies were instrumental in pointing researchers in the right direction, evidence from real-life rituals was still scarce.

C

Scientific research consists of a series of comparisons. We compare what happens before and after an intervention; we compare a group that receives one kind of treatment with a group that receives another, or one that receives no treatment; we compare what happens at different times or among different populations; and so on. The artificial environment of the laboratory offers the opportunity to engineer and manipulate these differences, because the experimenter has control over what participants are exposed (and not exposed) to and what they are allowed (and not allowed) to do.

When we move out of the lab and into the real world, we give up most of this control. We may no longer be able to randomly assign individuals into various groups, or to manipulate the kinds of conditions they are exposed to. This means that we need to approach research design in a different way. Rather than creating these conditions ourselves, we must try to find instances where they occur naturally. For my purposes this meant finding a context in which members of the same cultural group performed rituals that substantially varied in their level of intensity from the mundane to the extreme.

I made a list of various potential field sites and began gathering information about them. Each of those places presented unique challenges and opportunities, so picking the most suitable site for my project was no easy decision. Anthropological research can take place anywhere where there are human communities, no matter how large or small, from the rainforests of the Amazon to the International Space Station. And although flying to space was not an option, there were many possibilities right here on earth. I started narrowing down my options based on the various factors that were crucial to my project – the naturally occurring conditions that would make my field experiment possible. After eliminating most other locations I finally came across one place that seemed to meet all my criteria: a small tropical island 500 miles off the east coast of Madagascar.

Just over half the size of the smallest US state of Rhode Island and lying in middle of the vast Indian Ocean, Mauritius is easy to miss on the world map. Some know it as the home of the dodo, the large flightless bird that became extinct as soon as human activity began on the island. Many have never even heard of it. Regardless, this tiny speck on the map is an extraordinary place.

Mauritius was one of the world's last sovereign countries to be populated by humans. In its brief history it has seen successive waves of Dutch, French and British colonisers before gaining independence in 1968. Those previous administrations initially brought thousands of slaves from Madagascar, Mozambique and various other parts of Africa to work on sugar cane plantations. After slavery was abolished, this was followed by even greater numbers of indentured labourers who migrated from India, China and other parts of Asia. The descendants of all those ethnic groups make up a true rainbow nation, whose inhabitants speak multiple languages and practise numerous religious traditions. This diversity makes Mauritius an ideal place to study ritual. Within the range of a few miles one can find temples of all major religions and attend a wide variety of ceremonies.

Some of the most fascinating of these rituals were brought to Mauritius by Tamil Hindus in the nineteenth century. Tamils are an ethnic group native to southern India and northern Sri Lanka, with a recorded history going back thousands of years. In addition to their place of origin, several million more live in diasporic communities around the globe. These communities speak Tamil, one of the oldest living languages in the world, and maintain a range of ancient traditions, including some truly electrifying ritual practices such as fire-walking, sword-climbing and body piercing.

Perhaps the most spectacular of all those ceremonies is the Thaipusam Kavadi, a long and painful pilgrimage practised in honour of the Hindu god Murugan, son of Shiva and Parvati, a form of the Mother Goddess whose reincarnations include Kali. Celebrated on the full moon of the Tamil month of *Thai*, this ritual is the culmination of the Thaipusam, the most important event for the Tamil community.

Although its origins are lost in time, this festival is said to commemorate the occasion when Murugan received his mighty spear from his mother. The demon Soorapadman had managed to trick Shiva into giving him special powers. After singing his praises for a thousand years, the demon received a blessing from the god so that no one but Shiva's own son could vanquish him. Shiva was childless, however, which meant that Soorapadman was now in effect immortal. Thus emboldened, he went on to execute an evil plan. Aided by his brothers, he captured the earth and the heavens, kidnapping the gods and turning them into slaves. The gods turned to Shiva for help and arranged for him to meet and marry Parvati. Their union resulted in the birth of Murugan, who led a divine army to face the demons. The battle was fierce and lasted six days, but Murugan finally prevailed, using the spear his mother gave him to deliver the final blow. Soorapadman repented and pleaded with the god to let him live so that he could serve him. Murugan granted his wish, turning him into a peacock, which would forever become his vehicle. To celebrate his triumph, participants in the Thaipusam Kavadi pierce themselves with needles that symbolise his lance and carry offerings decorated with peacock feathers.

Performed by millions of Tamil Hindus from South Africa to Australia and from parts of Europe and North America to various islands of the Indian Ocean, the Pacific and the Caribbean, the Thaipusam Kavadi is one of the most ancient as well as one of the most widespread extreme rituals in the world. The festival spans several days and involves a host of activities. The most extraordinary among them is the *kavadi attam*, during which devotees have their bodies pierced with sharp objects and carry heavy shrines (the *kavadi*) on their shoulders in a long procession to the temple of Murugan. Participation in this ritual is often the result of a vow made to the deity. Devotees may ask Murugan for something specific in return, such as healing from illness, professional development or academic success for their children. Others make the vow in retrospect, to repay the god for blessings they have already received. But many undertake this commitment for social reasons.

When I asked them why they performed the *kavadi*, people commonly referred to custom and group membership as the reasons behind their participation. 'We are Tamils, and that's what Tamils do,' they would say. 'It's our tradition.' They explained that from childhood they had seen others do it, so they too wanted to do it one day. Others referred to their progenitors: 'Our fathers did it, and so did their fathers, and so we continue in their footsteps.'

The day of Thaipusam is a public holiday in Mauritius. On that day, no matter where on the island you might find yourself, you cannot fail to notice that something momentous is about to happen. More than a hundred temples from every corner of the island organise processions. The smallest of those processions may draw a few hundred pilgrims, but the larger ones pull in thousands. Each is a true spectacle to behold. Yet there is one that stands out. A temple known as the Kovil Montagne is built on a hilltop at the foot of the Corps de Garde mountain in the town of Quatre Bornes, overlooking much of the island from the Indian Ocean in the west to the central plateau in the east. This was the first temple to organise the Thaipusam festival in Mauritius over a century ago. Today it is a major pilgrimage site, drawing worshippers from all over the country and even overseas.

The festival begins at the temple with the ceremonial hoisting of a flag that signals the start of the preparations. It depicts Murugan's symbols: the spear (*vel*) and the peacock. Each day leading up to Thaipusam, the god's statue is bathed with milk and turmeric water, dressed and adorned in flowers. Devotees perform additional prayers at home. They purify themselves by abstaining from meat, alcohol and sex. Some sleep on the floor, while others avoid small everyday pleasures: watching television, listening to music, playing sports, eating sweets or having soft drinks. They spend several days building their *kavadi*s: portable altars constructed on a wooden or metallic frame and meticulously decorated with icons, flowers, coconut leaves and peacock feathers. They are carried on the shoulders during the procession, to be offered to the deity at the end of a journey that lasts many hours.

At the crack of dawn on the day of Thaipusam, people gather at the nearby river dressed in traditional bright fuchsia or saffron robes. The pilgrims, accompanied by friends and family, bring their *kavadi*s and arrange them in orderly rows along the riverbank, where they are proudly displayed for everyone to see. They begin the day by performing purification rites in the shallow waters of the river. They bathe using turmeric before changing into loincloths and smearing their body with sacred ashes. They pray to Murugan and to his mother, Parvati, asking to be granted strength and courage for what is to come. There is a Hindu belief that all rivers are sacred because they are symbolically related to the Ganges; bathing cleanses both body and soul.

Soon the tranquillity is broken by loud cries. Before they undertake their pilgrimage, devotees must endure painful body piercings. A needle through the tongue symbolises – and enforces – a vow of silence that must be kept until they reach the temple. Some of the women may instead use a scarf tied around their mouth that serves the same purpose. Most of the men, however, endure multiple piercings. These range from a handful of needles on the cheeks and forehead to several hundred spikes perforating the entire body, as well as hooks from which they hang bells or limes. The needles are made of silver and resemble Murugan's lance, with heads shaped like leaves. Even when crammed, they are arranged in an orderly fashion, forming beautiful symmetrical patterns on the back, chest, arms and legs.

I once asked a teenage boy who was coming down from the temple how many piercings he had. He must have been around fifteen years of age. He looked exhausted but kept smiling proudly. 'Five hundred,' he said in broken English. I looked at him, incredulous at what I had heard. I could see a big scar on each of his cheeks and several dozen puncture wounds on his chest and arms, but there were nowhere near as many as that. 'Do you mean fifty?' I asked. 'No,' the boy insisted, 'five hundred!' This must be a language issue, I thought, so I asked again, this time using my broken French. 'Cinquante? Cinq-zéro?' 'No,' he replied, articulating each word. 'Five. Hundred. Five-*zero*-zero,' and turned around to show me his back. It looked like a sieve, every inch perforated.

As the piercings are being made, loud cries begin to ripple through the crowd. Although those who undergo the physical trauma certainly seem to be in agony, it is the women who scream the loudest as they watch their sons, husbands or brothers being tormented. These empathic reactions are an important component of painful rituals. As we saw in our study of the Spanish fire-walk, social connectedness facilitates emotional contagion. When devotees go through painful acts, their loved ones vicariously share their suffering, and as they do so the entire community becomes more bonded.

To be sure, even for an outsider this is not an easy spectacle to watch. Over the years I have seen students and members of my research team feel sick, cry or collapse at the sight of these piercings. And although it becomes easier over time, I always feel my stomach churn when I look at someone being impaled by a spear through the cheeks. I often have to resort to looking through my camera: the lens provides a sense of distance.

Many practitioners go even further, having their cheeks pierced by large metal rods that can be as thick as a broomstick and several metres long. Because of their length and weight, these rods need to be held with both hands and their bearers must bite down on the metal to prevent them from ripping through their face. As if that was not enough, some devotees drag chariots by chains attached to hooks pierced through the skin of their backs. These are supersized versions of the *kavadi* that look like temples on wheels. They are lavishly decorated, featuring full-size statues or representing mythological scenes. They may have multiple storeys and can be so tall that overhead power cables must be lifted with a bamboo pole so that they can pass underneath. I once observed a man drag an eighteen-wheel series of interlinked chariots through the hooks on his skin, like a locomotive pulling a train. Someone else was pulling a model mountain forged out of metal sheets, with a statue of Murugan at the top surrounded by live trees planted on its slopes. According to legend, Murugan is the lord of mountainous regions, which is why his temples tend to be on mountainsides.

With all their piercings in place, devotees assemble to form the procession to Murugan's temple. They place their *kavadi*s on their shoulders like yokes, and they will not put them down until they reach their destination. The word *kavadi* means 'burden' in Tamil, which seems like an appropriate choice. These structures can measure up to 3 metres (10 feet) tall and can weigh over 50 kilos (110 pounds). Each of them contains an icon of Murugan, as well as food offerings and brass pots full of milk, which will be offered to the god upon their arrival at the temple. It is said that Murugan protects the milk from spoiling. The procession follows a 6-kilometre (4-mile) route, which pilgrims cover barefoot. Some impose an additional hardship on themselves, walking on shoes made of upright nails. The alternative is not much less gruelling either, as the asphalt is scalding hot, baked by the tropical midsummer sun. For someone like me, who is not used to walking barefoot, even a single step is agonising.

The procession moves slowly, the temple *kavadi* always at the front: to carry it is considered a great honour and blessing, and the duty is entrusted to a different person each year. It is accompanied by the carriers of a peacock, a statue of Murugan, a golden lance, a wooden mace and a *lingam*, a phallic symbol of Shiva. A group of musicians set the pace, playing the *nadhaswaram*, a long clarinet, and the *thavil*, a barrel-shaped drum. The crowd stops at each crossroad to perform rites used to ward off evil – here, as in many cultures, intersections are considered to be liminal spaces, frequented by spirits and other dark forces. Each time they stop, the music picks up the pace and the pilgrims start dancing, swinging their bodies to the tune without letting go of their burdens. As the music escalates in rhythm and volume, many appear to enter a state of trance, spinning around with their eyes rolled back into their heads. Some cry out, which sends a wave of emotional contagion sweeping through the crowd. One by one, people start to shake and swirl, seemingly oblivious to what is happening around them. When they appear to lose control, family members who walk alongside them may gently touch them to help them regain a sense of their surroundings. Soon the music slows and the march resumes, until the next crossroads.

At this pace the procession takes several hours before reaching its end point. But as the pilgrims arrive at their destination, weary and dehydrated, the most demanding part is yet to come. To reach the temple they will have to carry their heavy burden up to the top of the hill. This means climbing 242 steps made of black volcanic rock, which becomes scorching hot under a full day's sun. At this point many seem to be at the brink of collapse, but somehow everyone manages to push through. At least, almost everyone.

In several years of attending the Thaipusam, I have only come across one instance of someone failing to complete the pilgrimage. It was a man, probably in his mid-forties, who was carrying an enormous *kavadi* up the hill. As he began to climb, I noticed that he seemed weak and exhausted. Every few steps he would take a long break, holding the rail with one hand and using the other to sustain the *kavadi* on his shoulders. His family looked worried, and someone offered to hold his burden for him until he got his strength back. He shook his head and kept climbing, slowly and painfully. But soon he paused again. He hunched over and then went down on one knee to keep his *kavadi* balanced on his back. His companions were now begging him to let them assist him. But that was not an option. This was his burden, and he alone would have to shoulder it. They urged him to take his time, which he did.

He stayed in that position for several minutes. But when he tried to stand up again, he couldn't. He rested some more and gave it another try. Two men grabbed him under his armpits and helped him get up, but soon he knelt down again. He made several attempts to stand up, but he couldn't. He raised his head and looked at the temple in evident despair. He was so close – just a few steps away! He had managed to endure the piercings, get through the day-long procession and bear the weight of the *kavadi* under the blazing sun. He had even climbed most of the steps up the hill. He had given it his all and had nothing left to give. As he finally allowed his companions to take his burden off his back, the man burst into tears. He remained there, defeated and humiliated, as he watched his *kavadi* complete its journey to the temple without him.

A while later, I saw him as he was leaving the temple. I tried to talk to him, but he made his excuses and left.

The Thaipusam Kavadi provided the ideal conditions for me to set up my naturalistic experiment. Within the context of this festival, members of the same community practise a patch-work of rituals, in which they participate in different roles and to varying degrees. This meant that it should be possible to compare how these factors affect people's attitudes and behaviours within their natural context.

The collective prayers that are held every evening at the temple involve sitting down and chanting for hours. They are devoid of any intense physical or emotional tension, and are therefore in sharp contrast to the superlative levels of arousal that the *kavadi* requires. Based on the anthropological theories on the social role of these rituals, the question arises: does taking part in the high-intensity ritual make people more pro-social?

Then again, not everyone is exposed to the same amount of suffering. Some *kavadi*s are small and others are enormous; some devotees have a single piercing while others have hundreds; and while each of those needles and hooks is painful, having a rod impaled through the face is another story altogether. Hence my second question: were those who experienced more pain more pro-social than those who experienced less pain?

Finally, as pilgrims carry their burdens, family members walk alongside them throughout the procession without engaging in any of those painful activities. Would the pro-social effects of the ritual, if any, extend to them as well?

In the behavioural sciences one of the most common methods employed to measure pro-social behaviour is what is known as an 'economic game'. Economic games are experimental tasks that involve monetary transactions between participants (in this context often called 'players'), which are bound by specific rules imposed by the experimenters. Perhaps the simplest of these tasks is what is known as the Dictator Game: players are given a predetermined amount of money and are told that they can choose to keep as much of that endowment as they wish and donate the rest to another player. This allows researchers to examine how generous each individual is in comparison with the others.

The main advantage of economic games is that the stakes are real. Subjects give away actual money that they could otherwise put into their own pocket. This is crucial, because when researchers ask people to report on their own attitudes and behaviours, their answers do not always correspond with what they actually think and do, especially when it comes to reporting traits that are seen as positive or praiseworthy in a particular society.[5] Whether consciously or unconsciously, people everywhere tend to inflate such socially desirable attributes. Economic games deal with this problem by asking people to engage in costly interactions. Rather than looking at how much money people *say* they would give away, why not look at how much they *actually* give?

In recent decades we have learned a lot about human nature by using these kinds of games. For example, the long-prevailing wisdom in many branches of economic theory argued that people make decisions based on rational and narrowly selfish cost-benefit calculations, driven purely by their wish to maximise utility – a model known as *Homo economicus*. However, when researchers started using behavioural experiments to look at how people make decisions, they found that *Homo economicus* only exists as a theoretical construct. In real life, our instincts, emotions, unconscious biases and social expectations often sway our behaviour in numerous ways.

Despite their value, however, formalised economic experiments also have a major downside: they can feel perplexingly strange to participants, because they are decontextualised and do not resemble situations they would normally come across in real life. After all, when was the last time someone stopped you in the street, handed you £10 and asked you whether you wanted to split it with an anonymous stranger?

To avoid this pitfall in our study, we used a task that felt like an activity people often engage with in real life: charitable giving. We would invite people to take part in a study and pay them 200 rupees for participating – a substantial amount in that context. Then we would inform them of a charity, so that we could see how much of that money they would be willing to shell out. To make sure they had enough options, we would give them the money in coins of 20 rupees, effectively creating a zero-to-ten scale that could be used to measure generosity.

This plan allowed us to increase the realism of the study. But it also created some unforeseen challenges. To conduct this kind of experiment we would need to procure a few thousand coins. This proved to be more difficult than I had anticipated. The only obvious place to get such a large stack of coins was the bank. The problem was that, for some reason, none of the local banks seemed willing to hand out so many coins. As we were getting dangerously close to the festival and still did not have the number of coins we needed, we held a meeting. We agreed that unusual circumstances required unusual measures. As robbing a bank was not really an option, we decided to go to the only place that might have that amount of cash on hand: the casino.

There, too, our request was met with incredulity by the teller, who called the manager to report our suspicious behaviour. Politely, the manager informed us that the casino only provided change for customers. There would be no coins for us, although we were welcome to stay and gamble if we wished to. As we roamed around, we noticed that the slot machines occasionally rewarded players by spewing out 20-rupee coins. It also dawned on us that each machine had a button labelled 'payout', allowing players to withdraw whatever amount they had deposited. Would this payout also come in 20-rupee coins, rather than bills, tokens or a voucher? Nervously, I inserted a 1,000-rupee note into the machine. I made a joke about this being the time to perform some rituals, and everyone came up with their own. Someone kissed the slot machine, another crossed his fingers and I appealed to Lord Murugan. As I pressed the button, we all held our breath. The fifty metallic clinks that followed in rapid succession were like music to our ears. By the end of the evening, we were all set.

On the day of Thaipusam we arrived at the temple early. The temple committee allowed us to use a reception room at the foot of the hill, where we set up our equipment and waited. We knew that, once the crowd reached the premises, things would be chaotic and we would only have a window of a few hours to recruit participants before the last of the devotees left the temple.

After climbing the steps to the top of the hill, pilgrims formed a queue, putting their *kavadi*s down before entering the temple one by one to make their offerings to Murugan, receive blessings and have their piercings removed by the priests. As they stepped inside, many of them burst into tears, overcome with joy and relief. Having completed their ordeal, they would now begin to walk down the other side of the hill towards the exit.

This was where our research assistants were stationed to invite them to take part in the study. Those who agreed entered the room, where we presented them with a brief questionnaire designed to assess how painful their experience had been. When they had completed the survey, we thanked them for taking part and gave them their compensation. But as they were leaving the building, an actor hired by our research team asked them whether they wished to donate some of their earnings to a local charity. They were handed an envelope and directed towards a booth where they could place their donation in a charity box in complete privacy, so that their choice would remain anonymous. Each envelope was marked with its own hidden code, allowing us to link it to each participant's answers to the questionnaire without compromising anonymity.

To see how these donations compared with other occasions, we followed the same procedure in different contexts. A few days earlier, we had recruited people after they participated in collective prayers performed at the same temple as part of the same festival, and a few weeks later we collected data from a control group in another, non-religious location, outside the context of any ritual. All of our participants lived in the same town and had taken part in the Thaipusam festival. This meant that, as they were recruited randomly, any major differences in their behaviour should in theory be due to their participation in the specific events rather than any personality traits or demographic characteristics.

When we analysed the data, we found that those in the control group (who had not attended any ritual) gave on average 26 per cent of the money they had earned to charity.[6] This is a sizeable portion, considering that they could have kept the entire amount for themselves, but similar to the typical allocations made by those who play Dictator Games in the lab. In comparison, those who took part in the collective prayer (the low-intensity ritual) gave significantly more: about 40 per cent on average. Still, participants in the *kavadi* ritual donated almost twice as much as that, their average contribution reaching over 75 per cent of their earnings. So, after engaging in this painful ritual people gave three-quarters of their entire endowment to charity.

In fact, when we looked at the relationship between pain and donations, we found a significant positive correlation: the more pain devotees experienced during the ritual, the more money they gave to the charity. But the pro-social effects of this ritual were not limited to those who experienced the painful activities at first hand. Those who accompanied them in the procession also made comparable donations. Those observers stood by their kith and kin as they were getting pierced, walked alongside them as they were carrying their burden, supported them and cried for them. And in doing so, they vicariously experienced their sacrifice. Not only did they feel like the active performers did, but they also behaved like they did. On the day of the *kavadi* the entire community became more generous.

In our study we focused on aspects of this ritual that we could measure. But other manifestations of pro-sociality may be observed with the naked eye. On the day of Thaipusam the entire local community bands together. As the procession passes through the town, people open their doors not just to watch but also to help. They bring out hoses and pitchers, dowsing the feet of *kavadi* bearers to relieve them from the pain of walking barefoot on the blistering tarmac, and they wipe the sweat off their foreheads with towels. They also care for the thousands of people who accompany the procession, setting up tables and makeshift canopies where they offer them refreshments, fruit and a few moments of shade. At the temple, volunteers spend the day cleaning, running errands and cooking meals that will be offered freely to everyone at the end of the evening, using ingredients that have come from hundreds of donations. That night, each family also cooks the 'Sept Cari', an elaborate traditional meal comprising seven different vegetarian curries served on a banana leaf and accompanied by rice, a tapioca dessert and various snacks and drinks. The locals take great pride in inviting not only family and friends but also strangers to partake in these meals. The most affluent members of the community may feed hundreds of people that night. Each time I attended the *kavadi* I was invited to several of these feasts. The invitations were extended with such sincerity and persistence that I often ended up having more than one dinner that evening.

C

To outsiders, extreme rituals like the Thaipusam Kavadi may seem puzzling. It is, however, the very intensity of those ordeals that underlies their pro-social effects. The strong bonds forged in the face of shared suffering may be an evolutionary adaptation that helped early human communities pull together and overcome adversity when faced with existential threats such as war, predators or natural disasters. This is why some of the most extraordinary examples of human cooperation are to be found in the midst of such existential threats.

The anthropologist Brian McQuinn joined a group of rebels who were fighting against Muammar Gaddafi's dictatorial regime in Libya. During his fieldwork McQuinn came to understand that these men formed relationships with each other that were as strong as, or even stronger than, those with their close family. But when he collected data from the entire battalion, he found that front-line fighters, who were engaged in direct armed conflict with enemy forces, forged much stronger ties than logistical supporters such as mechanical and health workers, who had no exposure to combat. Those ties were so profound that these fighters were often willing to lay down their own lives to protect their comrades. Although they were not related by blood, these soldiers expressed feelings

---

of brotherhood towards each other and often reported being more bonded with their battalion than with their own family. When describing those emotions, they explained that there was something about the experience of going through combat that outsiders were not capable of understanding. Knowing that their comrades had shared that intimate experience with them was what made their relationship unique.

In the words of Vietnam War veteran Major Robert J. Reilly,

> the strongest motivation for enduring combat [...] is the bond formed among members of a squad or platoon. This cohesion is the single most important sustaining and motivating force for combat soldiers. Simply put, soldiers fight because of the other members of their small unit. [...] Most do not risk their life for lofty ideals [...] they do it for the members of their cohesive group.[7]

In a similar vein, Jesse G. Gray, a philosophy professor who served as a lieutenant during the Second World War, had this to say:

> Numberless soldiers have died, more or less willingly, not for country or honour or religious faith or for any other abstract good, but because they realised that by fleeing their post and rescuing themselves, they would expose their companions to greater danger [...] No -ism, not nationalism and not even patriotism, no emotion in which men can be indoctrinated and then manipulated, but only comradeship, the loyalty to the group is the essence of fighting morale. [...] The commander who can preserve and strengthen it knows that all other psychological or physical factors are little in comparison.[8]

In essence, extreme rituals appear to simulate these conditions to reap their pro-social benefits. Rather than wait for warfare or some other disaster to occur, many communities are able to galvanise their members by proactively providing them with powerful ritual experiences. And sure enough, the sentiments expressed by those who undergo those intense collective rituals often echo those of military combatants. As a young man who took part in such a ritual told me: 'The next day, you see another person in the street, and you know you've been through this ritual together, you've bonded, you now have a different relationship to this person. Even if someone was your enemy, when you're there, they become your comrades, your brothers.' This deep and unconditional identification with other group members results in a special kind of bonding.[9]

In most cases, membership of a social group requires some kind of trade-off between our personal identity (our sense of who we are as individuals) and our social identity (the things that we share with other group members). Our personal self is formed through our unique life experiences, those key moments in our lives that have shaped our personality. In contrast, collective identities are typically based on more abstract ideas, ideals and doctrines – for example, about one's nation or religion – and generalisations about other group members. As a result, there can be a hydraulic relationship between those two selves: activating one's collective identity requires downplaying one's personal self and vice versa. When I think of myself as a Greek, I am not thinking about my personal experiences or traits. Rather, I am evoking those prototypical characteristics, symbols and doctrines that are meant to represent Greekness in my mind: it might be the country's flag or its outline on the map, aspects of its history and culture or the various generalisations that I have come to form or have been taught over the years about the Greek psyche. Neither am I thinking of any particular relational ties I have with specific people – my parents, my sister, my friends. Those are more likely to be activated when I think of my personal self – they are important to me, but not to all Greeks.

This abstract form of social identification is the result of socialisation. By regularly participating in a group's practices and being exposed to its doctrines, norms, symbols and traditions, we come to perceive ourselves as organic members of society who share a host of generic similarities and interests with other members. This is the kind of solidarity that holds complex, often heterogeneous groups together by encouraging the acceptance of and allegiance to an abstract social order. The frequent, low-arousal rituals of the kind Whitehouse called doctrinal are sufficient in reinforcing this type of solidarity. The regular services of religious groups, the daily hoisting of the flag in the army and a company's weekly happy hour all work to emphasise the collective self while downplaying the individual self.

Imagistic rituals are different. By putting participants through extraordinary experiences that are shared between group members, they activate the personal and collective self at the same time. To a group of individuals who have gone through those experiences together, it is the same formative memories which mark their narrative self that also represent the group in their mind. What makes a group of initiates feel like a unit is not so much the doctrines they have been taught: first and foremost, it is their shared experiences of initiation. Rather than suppressing their sense of individuality, imagistic rituals make it more salient but at the same time indistinguishable from their social self.

Psychologists have called this sense of unity with the group *identity fusion*, a term that reflects people's feeling that their personal identity becomes fused with their collective identity.[10] Researchers have devised a number of methods to measure it. For example, a verbal measure can be administered in the form of a survey, where respondents can indicate their level of agreement with statements such as: 'I am one with my group', 'I am strong because of my group' and 'My group is me'. Another method involves a visual aid in the form of a pictorial illustration of two circles, one representing oneself and the other representing one's group. Respondents are asked to describe how they see themselves in relation to their group by arranging the two circles as far apart or as close together as they like. Those who feel entirely fused with their group might even overlap the two circles completely, making no distinction between themselves and their peers.

When people become highly fused with a group, they come to align themselves not merely with the collective in an abstract way but with its individual members, with whom they form personal ties, whether real or imagined, as if they were their own kin. Rather than members of impersonal groups, they become brothers and sisters in arms. Studies show that highly fused individuals perceive threats to their group as personal affronts to themselves. When a fellow group member is threatened, they show emotional reactions similar to those they exhibit when their family members are threatened.[11] Compared with non-fused individuals, they are more willing to help their comrades and fight for group values, even if this means making costly sacrifices, and they express more willingness to fight and die for their group.[12] Imagistic rituals can result in this kind of superglue.

The anthropologist David Zeitlyn studied the initiation rituals of the Mambila people in Cameroon. Each year, a group of young boys are brought into an enclosure in the forest called a *jere*, which only men are allowed to enter. They perform a ceremony that involves taking a secret oath and being smeared with mud. As they are being ushered through this rite, they are unable to see a man who is hiding in the darkness, dressed as a ferocious spirit and wearing an outsize mask. Suddenly he leaps behind them and attacks them. Terrified, the children try to flee, whereupon the adults capture them and throw them back towards the monstrous spirit.

> Children failing to pass the mask and escape the *jere* formed an hysterical knot trying to pluck up courage to run the gauntlet. The children were clearly thoroughly terrified despite the fact that the older boys must have had similar experiences on several previous occasions. [...] The adult men stood about laughing, or helping the Mask at the door by catching boys who tried to slip past while it was man-handling another boy. One boy was so scared that he forced his way through the fence. Others were caught trying to do the same.[13]

A few decades after he conducted his fieldwork Zeitlyn returned to Cameroon with a team of collaborators to examine the effects of these initiation rituals in shaping collective bonds.[14] They surveyed almost 400 Mambila males, roughly half of whom had performed the initiation ritual in their youth, while the other half had not. They found that those who had undergone the ordeal felt more fused with their community and reported being more willing to fight and make sacrifices to defend their group. Although decades had passed since their initiation, the experience had left indelible marks on their group identity.

◯

The implications of the ritual superglue are as far-reaching as they are obvious: imagistic ceremonies can help forge highly cohesive groups, for better and for worse. In contexts that emphasise inclusivity they can become important vehicles for unity. This, for instance, is what we found when we surveyed people who took part in the Thaipusam Kavadi in Mauritius. This ritual is celebrated as a national holiday, and often attended by members of other religious communities, who coexist in relatively peaceful ways. In that setting, we found that participation increased people's sense of national unity: after performing the painful ritual, participants' sense of national pride increased – they saw themselves as more Mauritian. But at the same time they also saw the other local groups as more Mauritian. Interestingly, these judgements varied according to the degree to which those groups participated in the Thaipusam Kavadi. Unsurprisingly, they saw their own group, Hindus, as being the most Mauritian, followed by Christians, who often participate in the celebrations, and lastly by Muslims, who do so more rarely.

By contrast, in communities that face out-group threats (whether real or imagined), these rituals can foster hostility and the endorsement of violence. For example, a study conducted in Brazil found that football fans who were more fused with their team were more likely to engage in physical violence against fans of rival teams.[15] And in a study conducted among prisoners in Spain, researchers found that those who were more fused with their religious group were more likely to commit acts of terrorism.[16]

We have examined some of the psychological mechanisms that contribute to the bonding effects of participation in extreme rituals. But our findings from Spain and Mauritius suggest an additional aspect of these rituals, which is crucial to their societal outcomes: rather than being confined to a small group of individuals who experience the traumatic ordeals at first hand, under the right conditions they can also extend to the entire community. To further investigate how this happens, we will now turn from what happens *within* individual minds to what happens *between* them, by exploring how these rituals' symbolic character makes them powerful communicative devices.

7

SACRIFICE

In 1860 Charles Darwin wrote in a letter to his colleague Asa Gray: 'The sight of a feather in a peacock's tail, whenever I gaze at it, makes me sick!'[1] The reason for Darwin's bad mood was that the peacock's extravagant tail posed a difficult puzzle. According to his theory of evolution, those individuals who are better adapted to their environment will be more likely to survive and reproduce. As a result, successful individuals will pass along the traits that contributed to their success, and over generations those useful traits will become more common at the expense of less useful ones. This is the process known as *natural selection*.

Most traits, even extreme ones, have obvious utility. A cheetah's long tail is used to balance and steer while turning at high speeds; a hummingbird's elongated beak allows it to extract nectar from tubular flowers; and a porcupine's long quills help it fend off predators. But how could the peacock's outrageously long tail make the bird more fit? Measuring up to 2 metres (just over 6 feet) and aptly known as a 'train', it adds drag during flight and weighs down its bearer, making him less agile as well as more conspicuous to predators. How can such a burden be allowed to persist in the evolutionary process?

Darwin thought hard about this conundrum, and he was eventually able to come up with the solution, which he called *sexual selection.*[2] To find the answer, he had to take into account those members of the peafowl species that do not carry large tails: the peahens. If the females of a species develop a preference for a particular trait in males (let's say, lions with bigger manes or birds with brighter plumage), then they will be more receptive to the sexual advances of males that possess that trait. As a consequence, those males who have more exaggerated versions of the trait will have higher mating success. Since males endowed with these ornaments will be more desirable mates, the females who prefer mating with them will be more likely to have sexier sons, thus increasing their own chances of spreading their genes. What is more, those females will pass on their preference for long tails to their daughters, thus perpetuating the cycle. Obviously, the inverse can also happen if males develop preferences for extravagant female traits. In this way the ornament and the preference become coupled in a feedback loop that can result in the runaway selection of these attractive traits even if they have no direct utility to begin with.[3]

The Israeli biologist Amotz Zahavi noted that these traits, whether physical or behavioural, play an important communicative role.[4] One of the many examples of such traits that Zahavi investigated is a peculiar habit observed among certain species of antelope. When African gazelles spot a predator, they often engage in what is known as *pronking* or *stotting:* they repeatedly jump as high as they can, springing vertically into the air with all four feet raised. At first glance, this behaviour seems really puzzling. If the gazelle spots a lion, then its best course of action might be either to lie low in the tall grass of the savannah hoping to go unnoticed or to turn around and run for its life. Performing gymnastics in plain sight of a hungry predator seems like the worst possible idea. For even if the hunter had previously not noticed the gazelle, it has undoubtedly seen it now.

To an observer, stotting may appear to be strange, if not suicidal. In fact, some ethologists considered stotting to be just that: a voluntary sacrifice of the individual gazelle, which seeks to attract the attention of the predator to provide other members of its herd with a chance to escape. After all, the gazelle seems to be taunting the lion, almost daring it to attack. How else could this strange behaviour be explained if not as suicide by provocation?

There is, however, an important caveat to the altruistic suicide hypothesis. As the most altruistic gazelles will be the ones who end up being eaten by lions while those that flee or lie low get a chance to spread their genes, this behaviour will not fare well in the long term. Therefore, even if some gazelles did commit altruistic suicide, evolutionary pressures would eventually select against this. Besides, if the purpose of stotting is to give other group members a chance of escaping, then an individual should only stot when there are more gazelles around. As it turns out, they are in fact *more* likely to stot in front of a predator when they are alone. What then can explain this eccentric behaviour?

When Zahavi studied predator–prey interactions in gazelles and many other species, he realised that there was a very different solution to this puzzle. After carefully observing and quantifying thousands of encounters between hunters and hunted, he discovered that these flamboyant displays did not make gazelles more likely to be attacked by lions. On the contrary, stotting animals were actually *less* frequently assaulted by predators. Similarly, he observed that larks often sing while being chased by falcons. In the midst of a high-speed chase that requires all the lung power the little bird can muster, such a waste of energy would seem to be disadvantageous. Nonetheless, falcons tend to give up on larks that sing during the chase.

Looking at this evidence, Zahavi proposed that such displays, which might otherwise seem irrational, function as signals that convey important information to the predator about the individual's qualities that might otherwise be hard to observe. By handicapping itself, the animal is in fact advertising its fitness rather than its vulnerability, for it is only the strongest animals that can afford to squander such valuable resources. Zahavi called this the *handicap principle*, which can explain the evolution of physical or behavioural traits that advertise an individual's fitness by assuming seemingly unnecessary costs.

If you challenge someone to a fist fight by declaring that you agree to have one hand tied behind your back, you are sending a strong signal of confidence in your superior physical strength. This is a *costly* signal, because a bluff that is called may result in serious injury. Therefore, weaker individuals who falsely advertise their fighting skills have more to lose than stronger ones, who might indeed be up to the task. For this reason your opponent will probably think twice before accepting the challenge. After all, if you are willing to enter the fight with such a severe handicap, you must be really fit – or perhaps really crazy, which might be an equally effective deterrent.

An analogous principle can be found in some sports. In certain horse races, for instance, the fastest horses are handicapped by having to carry heavier weights, which give them a disadvantage compared with slower horses, which carry lighter weights. Someone who is not at all familiar with the quality of the contenders would be able to identify the best racehorses solely based on the size of their handicap. The handicap thus becomes a reliable signal of an underlying quality that would otherwise be hard to observe.

In nature, these kinds of signals are bound to evolve when they provide benefits to both receivers and transmitters. As long as it sees them coming, a healthy adult gazelle can normally outrun or outmanoeuvre any of the big cats, so a predator is better off focusing its energy on younger, older or injured gazelles. For the predators, the great majority of strikes do not end in success, and in the unforgiving heat of the African savannah each encounter results in great expenditure of energy, leaving both predator and prey exhausted. Big cats often need hours to recover their strength before initiating a new hunt, so haphazardly pursuing unattainable targets carries the risk of starvation. By engaging in this kind of communication, it is therefore not only the prey but also the predator that is spared a lot of unnecessary trouble.

What is more, other receivers may also benefit from the transmission of these signals. For example, members of the same species may use these cues to gauge the fitness of potential mates, the strength of potential competitors or, in social species, the value of potential allies.

Humans, too, can and do benefit from the use of costly signals, and nowhere is this more evident than in the domain of ritual. The performance of public ceremonies often involves substantial costs. The most common costs paid by ritual practitioners come in the form of time and energy investments. These can be conceived both in terms of what one is doing (for instance, a pilgrimage can be time-consuming and exhausting) and in terms of forgone opportunities (that is, what one *could* be doing instead). Time is finite, and participation in regular ritual activities adds up. If you attend church every Sunday morning, over a lifetime you could end up spending a full year of your life in the temple. All that time could be spent in any number of other ways, including working, pursuing relationships or providing parental care to your offspring.

In addition, most rituals involve monetary costs, which may include travelling, purchasing special clothing and other supplies, making material offerings or organising lavish feasts. And some rituals even involve physical risks. Ritual practices such as fire-walking, snake-handling or bodily mutilation pose significant dangers to their practitioners, including physical harm, infection and, in extreme cases, even death. It is precisely thanks to these costs that rituals are able to function as reliable signals.

A famous demonstration of the idea that rituals may draw some of their utility from their costs can be found in the potlatch ceremonies practised by various native tribes of the Pacific Northwest.[5] A potlatch is an opulent feast held by wealthy and powerful members of a community on important occasions. This can be the birth or naming of a child, a wedding or funeral, or the passing of chiefly privileges to one's eldest son. During these feasts the hosts present those in attendance with expensive gifts – the word *potlatch* itself means 'to give' in the Chinook language.

Historically, it was not uncommon for these potlatches to escalate into a full-blown competition among chiefs, who tried to outperform one another in their ability to give away valuable goods or even to destroy them by throwing them into a bonfire. Such valuables included expensive canoes, furs, woven blankets and 'coppers' – large ornamental plates made of expensive imported copper that were owned by the upper classes. In extreme cases entire villages were set ablaze and slaves were sacrificed. Those who were able to squander more resources than their rivals during the potlatch managed to increase their status and elevate their position in the local hierarchy, while those who could not keep up were often driven into bankruptcy and humiliation.[6]

In 1885 the Canadian government enacted a ban on potlatch ceremonies because they saw them as wasteful behaviour that went against Christian views on the virtue of frugality, and out of fear that the redistribution and destruction of wealth would undermine capitalist values. For precisely the same reasons, the potlatch was hailed by twentieth-century Marxist groups as an example of a non-market economy. In the 1950s *Potlatch* became the name of a leading French avant-garde publication. This publication could not be bought: it could only be gifted from one person to the next.

Ironically, however, the potlatch exemplifies one of the hallmarks of the modern capitalist consumerist society: the ability of the upper classes to use their wealth in order to manifest and reaffirm their power and social status through the public squandering of resources. This can involve purchasing luxury items such as designer cars or expensive paintings, paying for extravagant services such as flying in private jets or making donations in exchange for naming rights. This strategy is what the sociologist Thorstein Veblen described as 'conspicuous consumption'.[7] In engaging in spending behaviours that seem to be without any utility, conspicuous consumers are effectively using their financial capital to buy social capital. The reason they are able to do this is precisely that the items they are purchasing lack the added utility that could reasonably be justified by their cost: a $4,000 handbag by Louis Vuitton is no more practical than a generic $20 handbag, and driving a million-dollar sports car in the city will not get you to work any faster than a more spacious (and quieter) $20,000 runaround.

What consumers are really paying for with the purchase of such luxury items is prestige, because in order for financial capital to be converted into social capital it must first become publicly visible. Similarly, the only way to judge the relative wealth of a chief is through observing his ability to spend it in public. Only a very wealthy chief can afford to destroy valuable coppers, so destroying coppers functions as a reliable signal of his underlying financial power.

Thanks to this ability to communicate information about important but otherwise hard-to-observe qualities of their practitioners, costly rituals can help solve a number of problems related to social living. One of the most important problems any sexually reproducing organism must face is choosing a mate. The reason this is a problem is that some of the most desirable traits in a sexual partner are not always easy to observe. These include physical attributes such as health, fertility and physical prowess, material and social capital, and personality traits such as loyalty, generosity and adherence to social values. Throughout human history a variety of rituals have helped to solve this problem by providing clues about who might genuinely possess such desirable traits.

For instance, many traditional ceremonies function as choreographed courtship displays and are directly linked to mating. These ceremonies often involve dancing or performing demanding and even dangerous feats, which is an excellent way to showcase fitness-related qualities such as symmetry, coordination, strength and stamina. Among Wodaabe pastoralists in West Africa the *gerewol* dance operates as a mating competition. Over several nights young men adorned with bright face paint, colourful clothing and flashy jewellery dance for hours as the entire community watches. Observers comment on their appearance, technique and stamina. At the end of the evening, young girls pick out the best performers and invite them to spend the night with them.

Ritual

Likewise, the famous *adumu* rite of the Maasai people (often called the 'jumping dance') is part of a coming-of-age ceremony (*eunoto*) for young warriors. During this dance, the young men take turns repeatedly jumping as high as they can while maintaining an upright posture – a physically exhausting task. The entire community gathers to observe the competition, which provides the dancers with an opportunity to display their strength and endurance in front of their potential brides.[8] In similar fashion, the Umhlanga coming-of-age ceremonies for Zulu and Swazi girls involve the performance of the 'high kick', a traditional dance move among several African tribes that requires thrusting one's leg up as high as possible, often until the foot is well above the head.[9] This manoeuvre, which requires extraordinary flexibility, is a reliable signal of health, fitness and fertility.

In addition to showcasing physical prowess and skill, rituals offer opportunities for displaying beauty, taste and wealth. In parts of Europe and the USA upper-class girls of marriageable age are formally introduced into (make their *debut* in) high society as women in a ceremony known as a debutante ball. Although the character of these rituals may have changed in recent years, traditionally debutante balls served the same purpose as the leks where flamingos gather to dance and find a mate.

One of the most famous of these events, known as the International Debutante Ball, is held every two years at the Waldorf Astoria hotel in New York. It is attended by the offspring of celebrities and socialites such as politicians, billionaires and royalty. Preparations can take over a year, during which time the girls choose their dress and take dancing and etiquette lessons. Before the event they attend the Bachelors' Brunch, where they meet wealthy members of Manhattan's most exclusive bachelors' clubs. The ball takes place in the Grand Ballroom, which is decorated in gold and pink for the occasion. Dressed like brides, the girls walk into the room escorted by a male companion (typically chosen at the Bachelors' Brunch) and are paraded ('presented') one by one in front of the guests. They then proceed to dance and chat with several of the male attendees. During the night they will be judged on their looks, dancing skills and manners. As the event is by invitation only and the cost of attending is similar to what some people earn in a year, potential suitors can be certain that the boys and girls in attendance come from wealthy, well-connected families.

While debutante balls are typically only for the elites, similar traditions are widespread in many cultures. In the Americas, the *quinceañera* is a celebration of a girl's fifteenth birthday. This coming-of-age ritual combines Catholic and indigenous elements and originally served to present the girl to the local society as eligible for marriage. Initiation came with certain privileges only reserved for adult women, such as wearing make-up, jewellery and high heels, shaving the legs and plucking the eyebrows, and being allowed to date. In the USA and Canada many girls go through a similar ritual one year later, during their 'sweet sixteen' birthday celebration. In most respects these ceremonies resemble wedding rehearsals. The girls are dressed like brides, arrive in expensive cars escorted by male guardians and spend the evening dancing, greeting guests and receiving gifts.

The debutante balls of the aristocracy and the *quinceañeras* and 'sweet sixteen' parties of the masses are designed to serve the same basic functions. For the hosts, the benefit is the chance to shine in front of a large pool of potential mates, whom they can try to impress with their beauty, elegance and fitness. This is why wealthy families often try to increase their audience by booking larger venues, paying for newspaper announcements and hiring professionals to curate and post online videos of their daughters' *quinceañeras*. But these rituals also benefit the guests by conveying important information about the qualities of the host. For the entire evening the girls are the centre of attention. They dance for hours in front of the crowd, which scrutinises their every move.

Dancing is so ubiquitous in courtship rituals not only because it creates bonding but also because it allows observers to make judgements about the biological fitness of the dancer. Good dancers are perceived as more attractive, and studies show that the moves that are considered to be the sexiest are different for males and females.

A group of psychologists in England made video recordings of women dancing and used 3D motion-capture technology to create digital avatars so that facial features and other individual characteristics would not be observable. They then showed those animations to 200 people and asked them to rate the quality of each dancer.[10] The results showed that the key moves making a good female dancer were hip swing (a distinctive feminine trait associated with fertility) and the asymmetrical movement of thighs and arms, which may provide an indication of health and motor coordination. In contrast, the sexiest male dance moves were associated with traits that show strength and dominance, such as upper-body movement and expansive postures.[11]

There is, of course, a great deal of cultural variation in aesthetic preferences in general, and dance moves in particular. But there is also evidence of cross-cultural consensus on which moves are sexiest, as indicated by studies that compared Americans with Koreans and Germans with Brazilians.[12]

Aesthetic preferences aside, when it comes to choosing a long-term mate, some of the most important traits are also among the most difficult to observe.[13] These are character traits such as sexual fidelity, family values and other socially desirable attributes. Here, too, costly rituals may offer useful information on the mating value of potential life partners, because performing these rituals is an indication of acceptance of the community's distinctive norms and values: willingness to bear the costs of the ritual signals that the individual is determined to be a good member of the group and uphold its moral codes. Indeed, a study performed in New Zealand found that ritual participation was statistically related to increased fertility rates, suggesting that those who practise more rituals may be perceived as more suitable long-term mates.[14]

Of course, whether the cost of a ritual can increase the perception of mating quality is an empirical question. My colleagues and I conducted an experiment in Mauritius to find out. We created dating profiles for a number of local young men and showed them to a group of young unmarried women. We asked these women to evaluate each profile based on how likely they would be to agree to a date with that man, as well as how suitable they thought he might be as a husband. What they didn't know was that we had carefully manipulated the profiles to create three different conditions. While the men's head shots and all other details about them remained constant, we varied the background images in their profiles to convey specific information about their ritual habits.

In one condition those images included generic themes such as landscapes or abstract artwork. In a second condition the images gave the impression that the man in question regularly attended public rituals: for example, a photo of a temple or a *tilak* – a touch of ash or vermilion paste on the forehead that Hindus are given in the context of various ceremonies. Finally, in the third condition, the images specifically suggested that this man had performed the costly ritual of Thaipusam Kavadi, which involves a great deal of pain and suffering: for example, a photograph of the procession or one of the portable shrines participants in this ceremony carry.

Using these variations, we wanted to see how ritual participation would affect these men's mating value. In addition to the unmarried women, we also showed the profiles to a group of parents and asked them to make similar judgements on behalf of their daughters. That is, we asked them how approving they would be of their daughter going out on a date with each man, and how suitable they found him in terms of the potential to be a good husband.

When people assessed the men's mating value, we found that ritual participation played a key role in their judgements. For the women as well as for their parents, those who practised more rituals were seen as better partners, especially when it came to marriage. But while for the potential brides the type of ritual did not seem to make much of a difference, their parents showed a clear preference for those who performed the more costly ritual. No matter the age, education or religiosity of those making the judgement, they saw ritual practitioners as higher-quality material. Not only was ritual the most important predictor of mating quality, but the more effort invested in those rituals the better, as those who participated in the painful ritual were judged even more favourably.

The reason the parents' evaluations are important is the historical role of the family in mate selection. Among Mauritian Hindus, in particular, the family plays a very important role in mate choice, either by suggesting, vetting, vetoing or outright dictating who their offspring are going to marry. Of course, in Mauritius, as in much of the world, this is rapidly changing as young people are increasingly empowered to pick their own mates. Nevertheless, in most societies throughout human history marriages have served as a means of building strategic alliances between families, who have exercised great influence over their offspring's reproductive choices, exerting a powerful selective pressure that favoured the practice of culturally sanctioned rituals.

Thanks to this ability to communicate socially important information, rituals can help solve social dilemmas that extend beyond the confines of the family. For its very survival, any human group depends on sustained cooperation between its members. In small-scale societies, cooperation is usually not as much of a problem: as most individuals are genetically related to one another, interactions are more personal and everyone's interests are more or less aligned. What is good for the group is typically also good for the individual. But as human communities start to grow in size and complexity, collective action becomes ever more challenging because it is increasingly susceptible to the problem of free-riders.

Consider an extended family inhabiting a single plot of land. For several generations the members of this family have been living around a large central yard, dwelling with their parents until marriage and then building their own home directly above or next door to them. As a result, all fifty of the current residents of the plot are related by either blood or marriage ties, sharing the land with progenitors, siblings, cousins, aunts and uncles and in-laws. This has been the most common pattern in much of human history, and to this day remains one of the most typical living arrangements in the world.

Imagine that one night two burglars break into one of the households and try to rob it. The homeowner's cousin sees them climbing through the window. He calls his brothers, who surround the house and confront the intruders, engaging them in a physical fight and reclaiming the family's property. By helping their cousin, the men are also promoting their own interests, as they may count on him to do the same should the inverse situation occur in the future. Besides, the better off their relatives, the stronger their own safety net should they find themselves in need of financial help. And by defending their cousin, they are also protecting their nieces and nephews, who carry some of their own genes. It's a win-win.

Now imagine that one of the cousins enlists in the army. One day an enemy state declares war against his country, and before long he receives marching orders to the battlefield. When he has to face the enemy as part of his battalion, he has two options: he can try to be a hero, placing himself in the front line and risking life and limb to defend his comrades, or he can lie low, hiding in the crowd and watching his back while hoping that others will be brave enough to win the battle for the group. Which course of action should he choose?

In the latter scenario, cooperation is clearly the best outcome for the group. If all the soldiers coordinate their efforts and display bravery, they will win the battle. If everyone defects by being cowardly, they will all die. But if the group is large enough, victory can be achieved even if several of its members defect. So long as a sufficient fraction of soldiers pull their weight, the collective goal can still be accomplished. The problem is that, from the perspective of any single individual member of the group, the best course of action is to defect and hope that others will cooperate. This way, they can reap the benefits of the collective effort without assuming any personal risks.

This type of coordination problem is all too common in human groups. Taxes benefit everyone. But for any given citizen the most advantageous course of action would be to avoid paying their contributions while enjoying the protection of the state and the benefits of public welfare and infrastructure funded by other taxpayers. Cooperators end up paying more than their fair share, while defectors get a free ride.

In other situations, cooperation may consist in exercising restraint. When resources accessible to all group members are finite, this often results in what is known as a 'common pool problem'. Let's say, for example, that a group of fishermen rely on a lake for their livelihood, and let's assume that there are enough fish in the lake for everyone to get by. In fact, even if a few individuals took more than their fair share, the fish population would still be able to replenish itself. But if too many people start overfishing, the fishery will eventually be depleted and everyone will starve. This kind of problem is often described as the 'tragedy of the commons', because it constitutes a situation that from the perspective of any group is truly tragic: while everyone in the group gains from cooperation, the most beneficial course of action for any individual is to defect. Therefore, if everyone, or even most, act according to their own interests, everyone loses. Given that the stakes could not be higher, cooperation dilemmas pose a momentous question: how can groups of unrelated individuals avoid exploitation by free-riders?

In 2018 Joel Martinez was sentenced to forty years in prison by a federal court in Boston for stabbing fifteen-year-old Irvin de Paz to death. The evidence was indisputable: the prosecutors had obtained secretly recorded video footage of Martinez bragging about his crime. But the murder was nothing personal. Martinez had never met his victim before. Taking the boy's life was simply a requirement in order to become a member of

Mara Salvatrucha, a notorious criminal gang also known as MS-13.

The initiation is a two-step ordeal: first, candidates must carry out an execution: a rival gang member, a police officer or anyone who has fallen out of favour with the gang leaders. If they succeed, the next step is what is called a 'jump in': gang members form a circle around the initiate and give him a brutal beating for thirteen seconds. Unluckily for him, Martinez's 'jump in' was also caught on camera. The footage shows the gang leader slowly counting up to thirteen as various other members punch him to the ground and kick him around. Once they have finished, the boss helps him stand up, hugs him and declares with a big smile: 'Welcome to the Mara, you bastard.'

The initiation rituals of MS-13 are not unique. Criminal organisations around the world have similar horrific ordeals. Being showered with firecrackers or smeared with faeces, enduring sexual abuse, drinking their own blood or committing murder and other atrocities are just some of the physical and psychological traumas that initiates must go through to be accepted as members.

The logic behind these initiations provides an efficient solution to a pressing cooperation dilemma: in order for a group to survive, it must rely on the loyalty of its members. But how can the group decide who can be trusted? Of course, all aspiring members will readily pledge their commitment. But words are cheap. When push comes to shove, a single act of defection (for instance, someone snitching to the police) may bring the entire group down. The solution to this problem is to make group members pay a hefty price for their membership *in advance*.

Some behaviours, such as the stotting of the gazelle or the jumping dance of the Maasai, convey reliable information thanks to their direct relationship with a trait that is hard, if not impossible, to fake (in this case, physical fitness). An old or injured gazelle cannot jump as high as a healthy one, and neither can a sick or frail human dancer. Jumping becomes a direct index of prowess that cannot be easily forged, hyped or imitated by low-quality signallers. But traits such as commitment and loyalty are not directly observable – they can only be inferred through indirect evidence. Some rituals manage to solve this problem not by providing direct evidence of those traits but by making those indirect signals so costly that no one would be willing to pay such a high price unless they were truly committed group members. Actions speak louder than words, and the higher the stakes of defection, the louder these actions must be to ensure the honesty of the signal.

In the 1970s legal scholar Dean M. Kelley wondered why liberal churches in the USA were in decline while conservative churches seemed to be thriving.[15] In the open marketplace of ideas provided by an environment of religious freedom and plurality, believers have plenty of options to choose from. Under such conditions, one might expect that worshippers would be inclined to abandon churches that charge a high price for salvation and turn towards those which offer it at a bargain price. Why was this not happening?

Kelley proposed a counter-intuitive answer: conservative churches were thriving not *despite* being strict – they were striving *because* they were strict. By severely limiting their members' lifestyle through imposing stringent restrictions on what they eat and drink, how they dress, what activities they practise and who they interact with, these churches actually presented a *more* attractive option, he argued. The stricter they were, the more serious and valuable they appeared in the eyes of their congregants.

When the economist Laurence Iannaccone carefully

examined data from various religious denominations, he found that they supported Kelley's theory.[16] His analysis showed that churches that imposed stricter requirements on their members had higher attendances, received more donations from devotees and had stronger social ties and lower risk of desertion. This, he argued, was because the high price of belonging acts as a deterrent to free-riders, those who might enjoy the benefits of membership without contributing substantial effort or resources. By weeding out those low-quality members, strict churches increase their value and are able to attract and retain more committed congregations.

This is why groups that require high levels of loyalty tend to have costly initiation rites. Across the world, military organisations incorporate high-intensity rituals in their training regimes, and the more elite the unit the more challenging those ordeals are. To become a member of the US Navy SEALs (one of the world's fiercest special operations forces), candidates must go through one of the most notorious military initiations, tellingly named Hell Week. The process involves various extreme physical and psychological hardships that are designed to weed out all but the most toughened and committed cadets. The programme is so merciless that in recent years more SEALs have died in training than in combat.

Indeed, anthropologists have noticed a pattern: societies that rely more on social solidarity to achieve their goals tend to have more dramatic initiation ceremonies.[17] A historical analysis found that the cost of initiation rites across human cultures is related to the severity of the coordination problems that they face.[18] Using ethnographic records, the researchers analysed male initiation rites practised across a representative sample of sixty societies from around the world. Looking at patterns of violent conflict among those societies, they found that the prevalence of warfare was associated with more costly rituals. Moreover, among societies that faced mostly internal conflict, initiation rites were less fierce and their effects tended to be temporary. Such rites involved, for instance, putting on body paint or experiencing sensory deprivation. In contrast, among groups who engaged in external warfare and therefore faced greater existential threats, initiations tended to be much costlier and to leave visible reminders on the initiates' bodies. Those rites included genital mutilation, scarification, body piercing and painful tattoos. In addition to the cost of performance itself, such acts furnish their practitioners with permanent identity markers.

Just as the peacock's tail allows the peahen to judge his fitness based on the cost invested in growing his extravagant plumage, so costly rituals allow group members to assess an individual's commitment based on the costs invested in extraordinary actions. In so doing, these rituals become safeguarding mechanisms for deterring free-riders and facilitating cooperation between those who share the same commitments by providing benefits to both the senders and the receivers of the signal.

For the senders, the primary benefit comes in the form of increased status. Performance of a group's rituals equals the symbolic acceptance of that community's values. As a result, individuals who are willing to pay significant costs to participate in those rituals are seen by other group members as more likely to uphold their own ideals, and therefore more trustworthy. Similar to the potlatch ceremonies, where chiefs convert financial capital into social capital, some extreme rituals allow participants to use somatic capital (their own bodies) to increase their social status.

This logic of signalling is not lost on ritual participants. In a series of experiments the anthropologist Aldo Cimino asked people to imagine themselves as members of various groups and set them the task of designing initiation rituals for those groups.[19] For each group, subjects were presented with a description and pictures of individuals performing group-related tasks. Half of these groups required a high level of cooperation in order to perform their goals: one engaged in Arctic expeditions where they had to climb dangerous ice caps and find shelter from the extreme weather and wild animals; another provided humanitarian aid in war-torn countries, where they sometimes came under fire and had to work together to survive. The other half of the groups required low levels of cooperation. They consisted of members who shared the same interests, such as naturalists and music lovers, who got together to organise exhibitions or compete among themselves. Cimino found that people intuitively associated more cooperative groups with costlier rituals: when they had to design initiations for the highly cooperative groups, participants were twice as likely to prefer more stressful rituals and to support putting pressure on other group members to go through those rituals.

After going through his own initiation, a newly minted member of a street gang in Brooklyn, New York, reflected on his experience: 'That's something I'm going to remember, you feel me? I'll always remember that shit. For years and years.' His face bruised and swollen from the beating, and with blood still dripping from his eye, he expressed affection for his tormentors, who had gone through the same ordeal themselves:

I love my brothers, man, they did what they had to do … They understood; they've been there; they had to get through it, you know what I'm saying? Those are the guys I want to stand toe to toe with, that I wanna be in battle with; they went through what I went through today. That shit was real.[20]

These social gains are why low-status individuals are often willing to go the extra mile to signal their commitment to the group by investing more heavily in the practice of costly rituals. By way of example, in a study of a piercing ritual in Mauritius, we found that people of different socio-economic backgrounds behaved very differently in the context of the same ceremony. Those who were of high status used their financial capital to build bigger and better-decorated portable shrines to offer to Lord Murugan during this ceremony. In contrast, those of low socio-economic status participated in the ritual in more painful ways, by putting more needles through their body during the ceremony. As they lacked financial capital, they paid for the status that this ritual affords in the only currency they had: their own blood, sweat and tears.[21]

Some rituals require great sacrifices of their practitioners. But do these sacrifices actually pay off? During her fieldwork in southern India, the anthropologist Eleanor Power asked the residents of two rural communities to offer judgements about the character of their fellow villagers. She also recorded how frequently they participated in public worship. She found that those who invested more time and effort in the performance of public rituals were perceived by other members of their community not only as being more devout but also as having a variety of pro-social attributes. For example, they described them as more hard-working, generous and wise.[22]

To see whether ritual participants were able to cash in on

these reputational benefits, Power later analysed the social networks of those villages by recording various types of social support relationships between individuals. This analysis allowed her to see who people turned to when they needed emotional or financial help, advice and guidance, or favours and errands. She found that those who invested more heavily in public ritual performance, either by participating in frequent but low-intensity rituals throughout the year or by practising painful rituals once a year, had more social ties within their villages and were better able to utilise those ties when they were in need of support.[23]

But are the receivers of these signals justified in trusting that ritual practitioners are more committed group members? A number of empirical studies suggest that such increased trust towards those who undertake high ritual costs is not misguided. In Israel, male members of religious communes (*kibbutzim*) who spent more time attending collective rituals were found to be more cooperative when they played economic games with other members of the community.[24] Among the members of an Afro-Brazilian religion known as Candomblé, those who participated in more public rituals were shown to be more generous.[25] And, as we saw in Mauritius, those who endured more pain during a public ritual gave more money to charity. In further studies we found that those effects lasted beyond the duration of a single ceremony: those who participated more frequently in painful rituals throughout their lifetime also behaved more altruistically in economic games.[26]

Across all these different contexts it seems that those who perform costly rituals are indeed more cooperative group members. By allowing the community to assess its members' loyalty to the group, costly rituals can therefore increase cooperation and strengthen the social glue. Indeed, in her social network analysis in India, Eleanor Power found that those who went through rituals together formed stronger connections among themselves, and the more intense those rituals the more cohesive the group was as a whole.[27]

Costly rituals help communities grow stronger, and this can have major implications for their long-term survival and prosperity. This was demonstrated by a historical analysis of nineteenth-century communal societies in the USA.[28] Scouring the literature on eighty-three such societies, the researchers measured the cost of membership in those communes by compiling a list of all the norms their members had to abide by. Specifically, they looked at two types of costly requirements: things members were required to do that were not directly helpful to them, such as spending time memorising religious texts or buying and wearing specific clothes; and things members were prohibited from doing that would have been beneficial to them, such as having sexual relationships or communicating with the outside world. They then looked at how long each of those communes managed to survive before its eventual demise. They found that there was a positive correlation between the number of costly requirements a commune imposed on its members and the total lifespan of that group. The higher the price of membership, the longer the group survived.

In addition to communicating important information about their practitioners, costly rituals signal equally crucial information about the community itself and what it stands for. We humans are cultural learners. Rather than figuring out the world from scratch, we rely on our fellow humans to help us learn most of what we know. Therefore, following the example of others can often be highly beneficial to us. But indiscriminately imitating others might make us none the wiser. Instead, we have evolved learning biases that help us decide which individuals are good role models and when it might be useful to imitate their behaviour.[29]

For example, children and adults in all societies are more likely to imitate the behaviours of prestigious and successful individuals, and especially of those who are members of the various groups to which they themselves belong.[30] After all, they already know that those individuals must possess some knowledge and skills that have led to their success and status within that society. This prestige bias runs so deep in us that it can often be exploited – for instance, by marketers who use celebrities in commercials even when those celebrities have no expertise whatsoever related to the products being advertised.

In the course of evolution, every action brings a reaction. Thus, because our cultural learning biases may sometimes be hijacked, leaving us susceptible to manipulation by others, there has been a selective pressure for learners to look for tangible evidence that the behaviour of their role models is sincere. This is where CREDs come in.

CRED stands for 'Credibility Enhancing Display', a term introduced by the Harvard evolutionary anthropologist Joseph Henrich to explain how certain costly behaviours may function to raise the credibility of the beliefs or ideals they relate to.[31] Before deciding to commit to a collective cause, we look for evidence that the cause is worthy by examining how committed to it other community members appear to be. If people claim to believe in Santa Claus but do not engage in any regular worship to honour him, even small children will eventually realise that Santa is not a supernatural being of any high standing. But if those who claim to believe in Lord Murugan walk the walk by putting skewers through their cheeks for him, this conveys not merely that those individuals are truly committed but also that Murugan is a god worthy of commitment. Actions speak louder than words.[32]

In this process, costly rituals serve as honest displays of commitment that benefit the individuals, the group and the group's culture, creating a positive feedback loop. Committed individuals are able to increase their status and become better connected, and groups with more committed members become more cohesive. This may provide groups that have costly ritual requirements with a significant evolutionary advantage, allowing them to outdo groups that do not. Meanwhile, as the beliefs associated with those costly ritual practices appear more credible, they will be more likely to be endorsed and transmitted among the group's members but also to be copied by other groups. And because those beliefs are symbolically expressed by the enactment of the costly ritual practices, new believers will now be even more likely to endorse those practices.

There is a self-reinforcing power to costly rituals, which is manifested not only in their social functions but also in their psychological properties. These rituals signal important information about their practitioners, and this signalling is not only directed outwards, towards other community members. It can also be directed inwards, towards the self. Rather than merely *demonstrating* commitment, costly rituals are also effective in *building* commitment – and thereby creating meaning.

In 1951 a young psychology professor named Leon Festinger arrived at the University of Minnesota to take up a position at the Laboratory for Research in Social Relations. At the age of thirty-two, he already had a reputation as an accomplished laboratory experimentalist. Unlike many of his predecessors, however, Festinger also stressed the importance of studying social phenomena outside the narrow confines of the lab by examining behaviour in real-life contexts. He was an avid reader of anthropological theories, and towards the end of his career he closed down his psychology lab and turned his focus to prehistoric archaeology. In Minnesota he met other like-minded scholars such as his former student Stanley Schachter and another young professor by the name of Henry Riecken, who had recently arrived from Harvard. The trio shared an interest in how people come to attribute meaning and importance to various experiences and how they reconcile contradictory beliefs, emotions and behaviours.

The opportunity to delve deeper into this topic came when Festinger read a newspaper article about a UFO cult in Chicago. They were called the Seekers, and they were preparing for the end of days. The cult leader, a woman by the name of Dorothy Martin, claimed that she was receiving telepathic messages sent by the Guardians, a race of extraterrestrial beings that hailed from a planet called Clarion. The aliens had reached out to Martin to warn her: a massive earthquake, followed by an enormous tidal wave, was going to wipe out the USA and most of the Americas on 21 December 1954. The rest of the world would be destroyed soon thereafter. But for those who believed in the prophecy there was still hope: the aliens had promised to send a flying saucer to pick up Martin and her followers and transport them safely to Clarion.

Martin's following was small but fervent. Convinced that the end was nigh, many of them had left their families, quit their jobs and given away their possessions. Together, they attended regular meetings and ceremonies, and braced themselves for the apocalypse. When Festinger saw the newspaper article, he had an idea: what if the world didn't end in December? What would the Seekers say and do then? He picked up the phone and called Martin, expressing his interest in joining the cult and embarking on a new life on the planet Clarion. A few days later Festinger, Schachter and Riecken, along with some of their graduate students, joined the group in a mission to conduct undercover ethnographic research.

During the days leading up to the expected doomsday, multiple alien arrivals were predicted. Before each rendezvous, the group was instructed to remove anything metallic from their persons, as per the aliens' request. Belts, wristwatches, eyeglasses and bras were discarded, and buttons and zips ripped off. People gathered in Martin's garden and waited for hours in the snow, scanning the sky for flying saucers. They never came. But despite the initial disappointment, each time the prophecy failed their beliefs only seemed to grow stronger. When doomsday came and went, the group eventually came to the conclusion that the catastrophe had been averted thanks to their efforts. Their prayers had spread so much light that the Guardians had decided to spare the earth from destruction.

Rather than abandoning their beliefs, the Seekers' response to the failed prophecy was to double down. Previously, the group had met in secrecy, but now they started organising public ceremonies to summon the flying saucers. And while they had previously avoided the press and were highly selective about their membership, now they sought interviews and engaged in an aggressive proselytising campaign. As a result, their numbers started growing – at least for a while. Responding to complaints from the local community, the police threatened legal action. Alarmed by this development, the core members of the group fled the city. Martin moved to Peru, from where she continued to communicate her revelations to her followers by post. After spending a few years in a monastery in the Andes, she returned to the USA under the name of Sister Thedra and started a new cult in Arizona.

Festinger's time among the Seekers led to the publication of one of the most influential books in the history of social psychology, titled *When Prophecy Fails*.[33] It argues that human beings strive for internal consistency. When our beliefs and our actions clash with each other, we experience a kind of psychological discomfort that Festinger called *cognitive dissonance*. To reduce this unpleasant state, we are motivated to reconcile the contradiction between what we believe and how we behave. But here lies the novelty of Festinger's theory: while it seems obvious that we should act according to what we believe, the opposite also happens: our actions themselves have the power to alter our beliefs and attitudes.

In the case of the Seekers, the group members had already invested too much in their beliefs. They had given up their jobs, abandoned their families and turned their entire lives upside down. The realisation that all this had been for nothing would have been hard to bear. To reduce this dissonance, they updated the prophecy in retrospect and tried to enlist more social support in the belief by proselytising others. If more and more people embraced their belief system, then it had to be true after all.

Festinger's work sparked a wave of empirical and theoretical work on how people come to interpret their own actions.[34] The study on the severity of initiation that we saw in Chapter 6 was one of the many tests of Festinger's insight (Elliot Aronson, the lead author of that study, was Festinger's student). That experiment found that subjects who were randomly assigned to undergo a costly initiation to join a group came to attribute more value to that group. Researchers call this phenomenon 'effort justification'. According to this perspective, some things are valued not despite but *because* of the effort they require.

Across various contexts we find that more costly things are also more valuable: you get what you pay for. An athlete who trains hard every day will probably perform better than someone who only trains once a week. A four-year degree will probably provide better skills than a two-year degree. Good things take effort. In fact, some of the most meaningful things in our lives are also among the toughest: winning a championship, defending our country or raising children.[35] It therefore stands to reason that when something requires a lot of effort, it must also carry great significance. This rule of thumb is a useful heuristic, a mental tool that allows our brain to make inferences about the relative value of things. In fact, it is such a basic way of assessing the behaviours of other people that we inadvertently apply it to our own actions. This, in a nutshell, is the claim made by self-perception theory, which both expands and simplifies Festinger's insights.[36]

From this perspective, then, ritual actions serve as evidence of commitment not only to those who witness their performance but also to performers themselves. As a group's ritual practices are symbolically associated to that group's beliefs and values, enacting the practices helps the group's members internalise those beliefs and values. Thus, as expressed by the anthropologist Roy Rappaport, to participate in a ceremony is necessarily to conform to it:

> To say that performers participate in or become parts of the orders they are realising is to say that transmitter-receivers become fused with the messages they are transmitting and receiving. In conforming to the orders that their performances bring into being, and that come alive in their

performance, performers become indistinguishable from those orders. [...] Therefore, by performing a liturgical order the participants accept, and indicate to themselves and to others that they accept, whatever is encoded in the canon of that order.[37]

Another anthropologist, Edward Evans-Pritchard, summarised it more succinctly by saying, 'If one must act as though one believed, one ends in believing [...] as one acts.'[38] Rituals do not merely reveal group affiliation – they actively create it.

One implication of this is that even private ritual practices, such as praying in solitude at home or hoisting a flag in one's garden when no one is watching, can strengthen practitioners' devotion to the ideas and the groups associated with those practices. Of course, Rappaport cautioned, participation in a society's rituals does not guarantee the observance of its norms. 'We all know that a man may participate in a liturgy in which commandments against adultery and thievery are pronounced, then pilfer from the poor box on his way out of church, or depart from communion to tryst with his neighbour's wife.' After all, cultural rituals are not meant to control behaviour directly, but rather to present an exemplary framework of behaviours that are deemed socially acceptable.

Participation in a ritual in which a prohibition against adultery is enunciated by, among others, himself may not prevent a man from committing adultery, but it does establish for him the prohibition of adultery as a rule that he himself has both enlivened and accepted. Whether or not he abides by that rule, he has obligated himself to do so. If he does not, he has violated an obligation that he himself has avowed.[39]

Another implication of the self-signalling perspective is that the impact of ritual participation is dose-dependent: the more energy practitioners invest in a group's rituals, the more they are bound to endorse its values. At the same time, by virtue of being shrouded in ritual, those ideas feel more valuable and sacred. As we have seen in Chapter 4, ritual actions are perceived as special. But as those actions are causally opaque, they beg interpretation. In fact, the heavier the cost of participation, the greater the need for sense-making. Thus the cost of ritual actions not only affects participants' view of themselves and their groups but also makes those actions more meaningful in themselves. This link between ritual cost and meaning has received empirical support. In ethnographic studies and surveys, I have found that across several communities costlier rituals are considered to be more meaningful and important in people's lives.[40]

Seen through this lens, then, traditions that may at first glance seem wasteful become powerful social technologies that allow practitioners to internalise group values, build trust and form cooperative units. Thanks to these multi-level effects, they can also achieve what might be their most surprising function of all. As we shall see in the next chapter, through the effort, struggle and even suffering that they require, these rituals may often help improve the lives of their practitioners.

8

WELL-BEING

In a small rural village in mainland Greece, a group of people gather inside a large, ascetic-looking room. Other than some long wooden benches on either side and a small shrine holding a few icons covered in red cloths, the place is mostly empty. But as people begin to gather, it will soon be packed far beyond what seems like its normal capacity. Most of the visitors appear to be familiar with the space and greet each affectionately, albeit solemnly. Yet the mood is not festive. They seem uneasy, almost troubled. As a musician starts playing the lyra (a pear-shaped string instrument played with a bow), everyone stops talking and their faces turn sombre.

Slowly, people begin to swing to the tune, breathing heavily and letting out long sighs of discomfort. They are visibly distraught, although there is no apparent cause. An old woman repeatedly throws her arms in the air and screams loudly, as if trying to fight some invisible nemesis. When people try to comfort her, she pushes them away with sharp hand movements, shouting, 'No, no, no!' As two large goatskin drums join the lyra, she stands up and begins to move towards the shrine, taking small steps to the rhythm of the music. She picks up a smoking censer, which she carries around the room. As she makes her way through the crowd, people lean towards her to breathe in the smoke. An old man picks up one of the icons and joins her in dancing around the room. One by one, others follow them into a hypnotic improvised dance, carrying the heavy icons around the room.

The smell of incense now fills the stuffy, overcrowded, over-heated chamber, which feels suffocating. The sound of the large drums reverberates so loudly that you can feel their beat in your gut. Before long the dancers are swirling frantically in the crowded hall, sweating, panting, screaming and crying. So strong are these emotional displays that many of the observers in the room are also moved to tears. As for the dancers, they keep going for well over an hour, occasionally collapsing on the floor from exhaustion, only to resume dancing when they have regained their senses. Eventually the music slows and the activity comes to a halt. But not for long. After a brief break the whole process is repeated, again and again, for the better part of three days.

This was the scene I encountered in 2005, the first time I visited the village of Agia Eleni, which would later become the site of my doctoral fieldwork. It is one of a handful of small communities of Orthodox Christians called the Anastenaria, known for their particular devotion to Saints Constantine and Helen. The ecstatic rituals they perform for those saints have played a key role in holding those communities together, even as they faced exile and persecution throughout the centuries. The Anastenaria themselves consider this collective dance to be central to their personal and group identity, but they do not see it as a jolly occasion. On the contrary, they experience it as stressful, even agonising. When asked to describe what it is like, they often use words like 'strain', 'struggle' and 'suffering'. The very name of these communities comes from the Greek verb *anastenāzo*, which means 'to sigh', owing to their loud groaning as they dance. Nevertheless, they also describe their experience as a process of profound fulfilment, which can result in spiritual and even physical healing.

Take, for example, Stella, the elderly woman who led the dance that night. When I asked her why she took part in that ritual, she said: 'Because I got sick. I was suffering. If it hadn't been for the Anastenaria, they would have locked me up [in a psychiatric clinic].' When she was younger, Stella struggled with mental illness. She experienced anxiety and could no longer find any joy in life. She felt tired and did not want to do the household chores. Eventually, she stopped socialising and did not even want to leave the house. She was just idly watching her youth go to waste. 'I was sitting in a chair, staring at the window for two years,' she told me.

Concerned about her situation, her family took her to the city to see a doctor, who confirmed that she was suffering from depression ('melancholia', as they called it in those days). But at a time when biomedical interventions for mood disorders were just in their infancy, the doctor could not do much to help her. Desperate to find a solution, they called the village elders, and after deliberation they came to the conclusion that she should join the Anastenaria. She did, and it changed her life. She no longer felt depressed.

Stella's case is far from unique. Numerous cultures all over the world perform healing rituals. At first glance, such claims may sound dubious, to say the least. If anything, some of those rituals often seem to involve substantial health risks rather than any tangible benefits. But, as we have seen before, the fact that ritual does not have a direct impact on the physical world does not mean that it has no impact at all. It is not just the numerous personal experiences that ethnographers have amassed. A substantial body of research shows that ritual can impact health and well-being in subtle but important ways, and that these impacts can be studied, understood and measured.

India is the home of some of the world's most ancient ritual traditions. It is thus not surprising that a lot of field studies on ritual come from India too. In one such study an international group of researchers examined the effects of participation in Diwali, the Hindu festival of lights.[1] Originally held as a harvest festival, Diwali celebrates the victory of light over darkness with a five-day observance that includes a series of collective prayers and shared meals and culminates with a firework display. In this context the team recruited people who celebrated Diwali in two different metropolitan areas in the northern part of India. They visited them before, during and after the festival, each time carrying out a battery of interviews and surveys to assess their social, mental and emotional well-being. They found that, as the festival unfolded, people were in a better mood, experienced more positive emotions and felt more connected to their community. In fact, these effects started to kick in even before the festival began. The more time people spent engaged in the preparations the better they felt, suggesting that the anticipation of the activities may already have beneficial effects.

A similar study was led by anthropologist Jeffrey Snodgrass in the nearby state of Madhya Pradesh, although in a very different setting.[2] Snodgrass conducted two years of fieldwork among some of the Sahariya tribes, who have inhabited the Kuno tropical forest for centuries. When Kuno was designated as a state wildlife sanctuary, all twenty-four of the Sahariya villages in the area were forced to resettle and each family was given a plot of land to cultivate a few miles outside the forest. This brought radical changes in their way of life, as they had to adjust to a new form of subsistence as settled farmers. To make matters worse, they became geographically and socially isolated, which made them more vulnerable to raids by bandits and bullying by politically powerful herders. All this had a dramatic impact on their health. The Sahariya suffered acute stress following their relocation and continued to experience chronic stress for the rest of their lives. DNA analyses found that displaced individuals had shortened telomeres (the tips at the ends of chromosomes that protect us from ageing and disease).[3] Such premature shortening is an indicator of psychosocial stress and is associated with poor health and reduced life expectancy.

The Sahariya embrace a mix of indigenous and Hindu beliefs and observe many of the major Hindu rituals. Snodgrass and his team wanted to see whether participation in those rituals would help them cope with distress. To do this, they investigated the health effects of two religious festivals. The first was Holi, also known as the festival of colours, which takes place in March to celebrate the end of winter and the arrival of spring. Celebrations start the night before, when Hindus build bonfires and burn effigies of the evil demon Holika. On the day of Holi, people take to the streets to drench each other with water and smear everyone with brightly coloured powders. They tease and play pranks on one another, even on those of higher status, as on that day it is acceptable to break social rules that are strictly observed the rest of the year.

The second event was Navratri, another spring festival, which takes place a few weeks after Holi and is held in honour of various female deities such as Durga, Lakshmi or Saraswati, according to local preferences. It involves various preparations that culminate in two days of processions, praying, dancing and singing, often accompanied by trance and possession states, and followed by communal meals. In the context of those two festivals the researchers collected daily saliva samples, which allowed them to measure levels of the hormone cortisol, which increases rapidly when we are stressed. To complement these measures, they also used surveys that assessed symptoms of anxiety and depression.

In the course of their ethnographic observations the anthropologists noted that social tensions were not uncommon during those festivals. As large swaths of people interacted freely in the streets and at home, there were often frustrations, misunderstandings and even physical fights. But despite those tensions, when the researchers analysed their data and compared them with baseline measurements collected before each ritual, they found that participation had positive effects on participants' mental and physiological health. Symptoms of depression and anxiety were dramatically reduced, and their subjective mental and emotional well-being had improved significantly. These subjective improvements were also mirrored in the hormonal data, as cortisol levels dropped after the performance of each ritual.

Despite the occasional tensions that may arise at any social gathering, festivals like Diwali, Holi and Navratri are joyous occasions, similar to celebrations like Carnival or Mardi Gras. After all, whatever other purposes they may serve, collective rituals have always been a source of public entertainment, providing people with opportunities to put their daily preoccupations aside, make merry and have some fun. It is therefore unsurprising that participation in those events would have positive outcomes.

The relationship between collective rituals and well-being, however, is not restricted to such euphoric events. In many contexts, rituals that may appear stressful, painful or downright dangerous are often culturally prescribed remedies for a variety of maladies. For example, the Zār ceremony practised in various parts of Africa and the Middle East, which involves dancing for hours to the brink of collapse, is believed to help practitioners overcome depression, anxiety and various conditions that are attributed to spirit possession; in Mexico, worshippers of Santa Muerte crawl in the dirt on their hands and knees for long distances to implore the deity to cure them of infertility and other problems; in North America, native tribes practise the Sun Dance, a healing ceremony that involves piercing or ripping the flesh; and all around the world, people undertake pilgrimages that push the limits of human endurance as a way of seeking solutions to their problems.

Some might argue that for their practitioners these rituals are not as stressful as they may seem to an outsider. Is it possible that these individuals do not mind the pain or have a higher tolerance for it? In fact, people have often asked me whether there is a masochistic side to these extreme rituals. Could it be that the individuals who are attracted to such practices have a penchant for pain and actually experience it as pleasurable? I do not think this is what is happening, and the anthropological evidence also suggests otherwise.

People who participate in these rituals typically describe their experience as one of anguish rather than pleasure. Even in cases when ritual performers are expected to display bravery and suppress any signs of discomfort, one only has to look at their faces. Indeed this is what my colleagues and I did in a study of facial expressions in the context of a fire-walking ritual. Using high-definition cameras to record this ritual, we extracted over 2,000 still images of people's faces as they were walking on burning embers. We then showed those photos to independent judges in a laboratory and asked them to evaluate the emotional expressions reflected in those faces. Even as participants in this ritual try to appear unaffected by the stress and pain of walking on burning embers, all the judges were able to recognise their growing agony as their ordeal progressed.[4]

These findings are also consistent with analyses of biometric data. Every time I looked into people's physiological states during the performance of such extreme rituals, I was amazed at just how intense their bodies' reactions were. In some of those rituals, as we have seen, participants' heart rates spiked at levels that I thought would be impossible in healthy adults. Another measure of arousal, electrodermal activity, revealed that during the Thaipusam Kavadi ritual stress levels were orders of magnitude higher than any other stressful event people experienced in their everyday life.[5] And even participants in a piercing ritual performed in the context of a BDSM conference (where one might suspect that participants would find the pain pleasurable) showed tangible signs of suffering. Researchers who collected saliva samples during this event found a 250 per cent increase in levels of the stress hormone cortisol.[6]

In addition to the pain and stress they cause, many of these traditions carry the risk of injury, scarring or infection. They often take place in the context of massive gatherings, leading to overcrowding and poor sanitary conditions that challenge the immune system and expose practitioners to the risk of communicable diseases. Because of these risks, the World Health Organization has raised concerns about the well-being of pilgrims, and in 2012 the top medical journal *The Lancet* dedicated a special issue to policy recommendations with regard to such mass gatherings.[7] In light of such serious concerns, it is remarkable that in so many contexts these risky practices are often said to have positive health benefits. Can this possibly be true?

◯

In 2012 a group of scientists reported a study, once again conducted in India, designed to investigate the health effects of participation in a mass religious gathering.[8] And by 'mass gathering' they meant really massive. The Kumbh Mela is one of the most important Hindu pilgrimages, whose origins are lost in time. It takes place at the banks of four major rivers, where pilgrims gather to pray and wash away their sins by bathing in the sacred waters. The celebrations are held on a twelve-year cycle, with smaller versions taking place every sixth year. Even those smaller pilgrimages can attract well over 20 million people. But the biggest event, the Maha Kumbh Mela, which takes place on the banks of the Ganges near Allahabad, is the largest gathering of human beings on the planet, with an estimated attendance that in recent years reaches up to 150 million.

The celebrations last a month, and many pilgrims spend this entire period camping in harsh conditions. They live in makeshift tents or sleep on the ground, exposed to the subtropical sun during the day and near-freezing temperatures at night, at the mercy of the elements. They bathe and drink from the Ganges, which is one of the most polluted rivers on earth, into whose waters chemical waste, garbage and untreated human sewage are dumped by the numerous cities that lie along its course. In addition, pilgrims are exposed to extreme overcrowding, high levels of noise, shortage of basic goods and services, and physical exhaustion.

One might expect that such conditions would have devastating effects on people's health. The researchers decided to study these effects by comparing 416 pilgrims who attended the Kumbh Mela to a control group of people who did not. One month before the pilgrimage, participants were asked to report symptoms of physical or psychological illness and to evaluate their overall well-being. These measures were repeated one month after the end of the pilgrimage to provide a measure of change. Remarkably, the data analysis showed that those who took part in the pilgrimage experienced fewer psychological and physical health symptoms and had an increase in subjective well-being.

Of course, while the Khumb Mela is a very demanding ritual, its participants are still likely to enjoy their time camping at the riverbank. But what about all those other rituals, which directly impose pain and suffering on their practitioners? Intrigued by the Kumbh Mela findings, I contacted one of the authors of that study, a social psychologist by the name of Sammyh Khan. I asked him whether he thought that their findings might also extend to the more extreme rituals that I was studying. I also offered some unsolicited critique of the methods they had used in their research. As a good scientist, Sammyh welcomed my criticism and we engaged in a long series of online conversations on the potential outcomes of extreme rituals and how to study them. Seeing that we shared the same research interests, we decided to meet in person to discuss a potential collaboration. I invited him to give a talk at my institution, and we worked on a grant proposal to fund a joint project. We eventually managed to get the funding, which allowed us to buy equipment and put together a team to investigate the health effects of the Thaipusam Kavadi ritual in Mauritius.

The Thaipusam Kavadi was an ideal setting for this study, because it involves serious physical hardships that push the limits of the ritual well-being hypothesis. The numerous body piercings cause wounds that remain open and are continuously irritated throughout the day, presenting a considerable risk of skin or bloodstream infection. The skewers inserted through the cheeks cause large holes and pose a serious threat of skin tearing and nerve damage. Additional risks include bleeding, granulomas, the formation of keloid scars, and disfigurement. The ritual is performed under the scorching tropical sun that bakes the asphalt streets. The pilgrims, who walk barefoot, often suffer burns and blisters on their feet. It is common to see people faint from heat exhaustion on that day, and over the years many members of my research team have suffered heatstroke and sunburn, despite seeking protection from the tropical sun whenever possible – something devotees are not able to do. While the intense nature of this ritual provided a good case study for our project, it also imposed great challenges.

Our goal was to measure the effects of this intense experience on participants' physical and psychological well-being. To do this, we needed to quantify the intensity of ritual participation. One way of achieving this would be to look at the external causes of suffering by somehow assessing the amount of pain each individual was exposed to during the ritual. Another way would be to look at the consequences of that exposure by measuring the bodily manifestations of suffering. We decided to do both. The most painful activities involved in the Thaipusam Kavadi are the metallic piercings on the pilgrims' bodies. Some devotees may have a single needle through their tongue, while others have hundreds throughout their body. By counting the number of piercings each participant endured, we were able to obtain an estimate of the pain they were exposed to.

It is only expected that this pain, combined with all the other hardships devotees face throughout the procession, will lead to high levels of stress. But how high? To find out, we measured people's electrodermal activity by recording their skin conductance. When we are stressed, the sympathetic branch of the autonomic nervous system is aroused, triggering our eccrine glands to release sweat. This is why our palms sweat when we are nervous or scared. This sweat makes our skin more conductive to electricity, so by placing two tiny electrodes just a few centimetres apart we can track the flow of an imperceptible current to measure this autonomic response. This reaction is automatic and beyond any conscious control, which is why skin conductance is one of the main elements of a polygraph test, also known as a 'lie detector'. Although the idea that this test can actually detect lying falls in the realm of pseudoscience, it does do a good job at measuring stress.

Our second challenge was to quantify the health outcomes of participation in this ritual. Health is a broad and complex concept and has no single measure. Thankfully, Sammyh's background was in health psychology and he had plenty of experience collecting this type of data. Using a series of survey instruments designed to assess subjective health and wellbeing, we gathered information from a group of participants in the Thaipusam Kavadi and from a control group: people from the same area and the same cultural background who did not participate in the painful ritual that year. In addition to these survey instruments, we also obtained physiological data. Overall, we monitored the two groups for a two-month period extending before, during and after the ritual.

Apart from these technical issues, the most important challenge we needed to overcome was how to conduct this study without disturbing the ritual. For the members of the local community this festival is the most important time of the year, taking place at their most sacred temple in honour of their most important god. The last thing any of them would want on that day would be to have a group of nosy researchers getting in the way of their pilgrimage. Thankfully, recent technological advances allowed us to conduct our measurements remotely, without interfering with the ritual. We used a portable health monitor, a tiny device the size of a wristwatch that participants wore on their arm. This device recorded physical activity, stress levels, body temperature and sleep quality. And as its battery could last an entire week, we did not need to disturb participants on the day of the ritual. We collected our measurements over a two-month period, which included one month before and one month after the festival itself. Over this period we visited our participants once a week to download the data from the devices and obtain additional measurements of heart rate, blood pressure and body mass index.

The data revealed just how demanding this ritual was. Our participants withstood, on average, sixty-three body piercings on that day, with some putting over 400 needles in their body. This also left observable traces in their physiology: their electrodermal activity was far higher than on any other day, suggesting the pilgrims were indeed in agony. Some, however, went further than most: people who suffered from chronic illness tended to engage in more intense forms of the ritual, and so did those who suffered from social marginalisation, that is, individuals of low socio-economic status. Those who were in greater need were willing to pay a higher price. And high it was: people who reported suffering from some health condition withstood ten times more piercings than those who didn't.

Remarkably, this torment did not have any long-lasting negative impact. Just a few days later, every aspect of their physical health was back to normal. And in fact, their mental health was substantially improved. Compared with those who did not attend the ritual, participants experienced an increase in psychological well-being and quality of life, and those improvements were in proportion to the degree of suffering they experienced during the ceremony. In other words, the more pain and stress they faced during the ritual, the greater the improvement they experienced afterwards. As a more concrete example, the half of the group with the most needles in their bodies saw a 30 per cent increase in psychological health compared with the half that endured fewer piercings.

At first glance, such results may seem paradoxical, because the activities involved are distressing and pose direct threats to practitioners' health. Nevertheless, given everything we now know about ritual, these outcomes are not altogether surprising. The reason some of those ceremonies have survived for millennia is that they exert powerful effects at the physical, psychological and social levels – effects that may be found individually in other domains but are combined in unique ways in the context of ritual.

As we have seen, rituals play important psychological functions. Thanks to their highly structured and reliably predictable nature, they serve as an anchor in the storm that is our world. By providing a sense of order and control over the frequently disorderly and uncontrollable situations we face in our daily lives, they help us cope with anxiety. Moreover, engaging in regular ritual activities requires effort and commitment, which helps performers practise discipline and strengthen self-control. As an illustration of this, a series of studies found that performing rituals before meals helped people make better food choices and control caloric intake, and left them feeling more empowered to pursue a healthier lifestyle.[9]

By sanctifying rituals and prescribing their regular performance, religious traditions provide external encouragement that amplifies this self-regulatory potential. Cultural systems set clear goals and motivate people to strive to achieve them. These goals may not be pleasurable in themselves: most people do not enjoy being deprived of food or having needles stuck into their bodies. Conquering such objectives requires exercising willpower, which, like a muscle, becomes stronger with use.[10] The sense of accomplishment that comes with completing these challenging tasks boosts self-confidence, helping to motivate practitioners to tackle other kinds of challenges. This may help explain some of the health-promoting habits associated with religion, such as lower substance abuse and safer sexual behaviours.[11]

While these effects operate largely unconsciously, cultural rituals also create more explicit expectations. We have seen that people intuitively perceive rituals as having causal power. Recall the studies of little children from Chapter 2, where preschoolers believed birthday parties cause people to age, and the experiment with adults from Chapter 3, which found that pre-shot rituals made basketball players appear more likely to score. Cultural rituals amplify this intuition by making it obvious and using it to create positive expectations and provide hope.

When patients are given a sugar pill by a physician who tells them that it is an active drug, they often experience improvements in their condition. This is known as the *placebo* effect. It works by inducing a positive outlook that can lead to a drop in stress hormones, alleviating pressures on the immune system and aiding in the healing process. Thus, while they cannot fix a broken bone or shrink a tumour, placebos may go some way towards alleviating pain, migraines, insomnia, anxiety and depression. Long before the idea was even discussed by psychologists, all human cultures used healing rituals to stimulate the immune system. In the context of these ceremonies, intuitive expectations about the efficacy of ritual actions may be combined with beliefs about the role of supernatural agents or forces, as well as faith in cultural wisdom: if so many others have put their trust in this ritual, we guess that they must be on to something.

The social framing of healing rituals can be helpful in additional ways. More often than not, those who seek a cure in these rituals suffer from mental illness or psychosomatic disorders. This is not surprising. Most people are more likely to visit a medical doctor for a broken bone than they are to visit a psychiatrist for anxiety or depression. This is because in many parts of the world such conditions may be associated with shame or loss of status, which deters patients from seeking help. But when they visit a religious healer, the maladies that plague them may be attributed to spirits, witches or other external forces. This allows patients to reinterpret their condition in ways that may be more socially acceptable as well as more palatable to themselves. In fact, in many cases, what was previously thought of as an illness may now be seen as a blessing. Among the Anastenaria, those who seek healing are thought to be suffering because they have been chosen by the saints. Their symptoms are not manifestations of illness – they are a toilsome but rewarding and honourable path to accepting the saints' calling.

Perhaps the most important contribution of ritual is in providing a sense of connection. Participants in collective rituals are members of enduring communities of individuals who share similar backgrounds, values and experiences. Ritual observances help them strengthen those ties, and become symbolic markers of membership, proof of their commitment to the group, increasing their status and strengthening and expanding their social networks within the community.

Having wider social ties means having more friends you can turn to in times of need, more people who are willing to listen to your problems and more resources and expertise to draw from. As a result, those who have stronger support networks are better able to cope with stress, lead healthier lives and have healthier relationships.[12] In contrast, people with poor social support are more vulnerable to loneliness, depression and social marginalisation.[13] They are at greater risk of cardiovascular disease, substance abuse and suicide, and are likely to die younger. This is why social support is identified as a key component of psychological health and well-being.

The above effects operate in a top-down fashion, relying on the ability of the mind and society to influence the body. But rituals can have additional, bottom-up effects: they exert their influence by directly tinkering with participants' brain chemistry. Take, for example, the reward system, which regulates levels of neurotransmitters such as dopamine and serotonin to produce heightened sensation, elevated mood and an overall sense of well-being. This system evolved to motivate actions that are crucial to our survival, such as feeding and mating. This is why a surge in dopamine produces feelings of bliss and a sense of deep meaningfulness that is often experienced as an altered state of consciousness. Addictive substances such as recreational drugs or alcohol are very effective in triggering this circuitry. Since ancient times, various ritual traditions have used hallucinogenic drugs to induce powerful feelings by directly interfering with dopamine and serotonin activity in the brain. So effective can these substances be in producing spiritual experiences that they have been called *entheogens*, a Greek word that means 'generating the divine within'.

Drugs, however, are not the only entheogens. Those same experiences can be achieved by manipulating the body and the mind. By controlling corporeal movement and posture, breathing or sensory stimulation, some rituals essentially function as natural entheogens. For instance, studies show that certain forms of deep meditation can have significant effects on brain chemistry. Practising *yoga nidra* has been found to increase dopamine levels in the ventral striatum,[14] while *vipassana* meditation, mindfulness meditation and transcendental meditation all modulated serotonin levels.[15] Curiously, transcendence can be experienced through activities that seem to fall on opposite extremes of arousal: both quiescence, the state of hyper-relaxation induced by deep meditation, and the hyper-arousal of shamanic trance can bring about similar feelings of absorption and result in states of dissociation.

Engaging in high-intensity rituals that involve emotional arousal, physical pain and exhaustion, repetitive music and dancing, fasting and/or sensory overload causes an electrochemical storm in the brain, triggering the reward system to release a cocktail of feel-good molecules. Serotonin helps regulate mood by inhibiting negative feelings: it acts like a tranquilliser, suppressing pain, improving sleep, reducing aggression and violence, and making you more sociable. Dopamine, on the other hand, is more directly associated with pleasure. It creates pleasurable sensations, excitement and motivation to actively pursue those sensations. When serotonin and dopamine levels are in imbalance, you may experience loneliness, anxiety, depression or a host of other mental disorders. This is why most antidepressants focus on restoring serotonin and dopamine levels in the brain.

When arousal is sustained for long periods, it can also stimulate the production of endogenous euphoriants, our brain's own recreational drugs. These substances play important roles in regulating motivation by elevating mood, reducing discomfort and anxiety, and alleviating pain. Pain is a very important sensation because it helps us avoid dangerous situations. As a general rule of thumb, if something hurts, you should probably not do it (with some notable exceptions, such as going to the dentist). But when we experience prolonged pain, stress or physical exhaustion, this signals to our brain that a struggle for survival is taking place. Childbirth, warfare, fighting, fleeing and other life-and-death situations often involve pushing ourselves to our limits. Under such circumstances pain can become a serious distraction or impediment. The function of the endogenous opioid system is to allow our body to keep going when the going gets tough. Just like the painkillers prescribed by our doctor, evolution has designed its own painkillers to allow us to push through without being debilitated by pain.

Consider the experience of long-distance runners. When racing mile after mile, they sometimes reach a state that is known as the 'runner's high': a euphoric feeling of excitement and reduced discomfort, often accompanied by a dreamy sensation of floating and losing the sense of time. Runners often describe this state as similar to flying, being high or having an out-of-body experience. It is at once hypnotic and empowering, making them energised and simultaneously relaxed and worry-free. These remarkable effects are the workings of specific brain circuits such as the endogenous opioid system and the endocannabinoid system.

In a study that my colleagues and I conducted, we found that people experienced similar effects after engaging in various physically demanding ceremonial acts such as body piercing, dancing and walking on upright knives or burning coals. Sure enough, those who undertook these exhausting and painful activities showed evidence of distress in their physiology: their heart rates reached levels similar to those we had recorded in Spain, well over 200 beats per minute. But this suffering actually left them feeling better: the more effort they exerted, they less tired and more euphoric they felt afterwards.[16]

Like their synthetic counterparts, endogenous euphoriants are implicated in treating chronic pain and depression, boosting immune function and improving subjective well-being. This is why people who exercise regularly have better moods and are less likely to suffer from depression and anxiety disorders. Pharmacological treatments for these disorders work by regulating some of those same neurotransmitters triggered by highly arousing experiences such as extreme rituals. As a matter of fact, medical research shows that intense physical exercise can be as effective as antidepressant medication in treating Major Depressive Disorder. The problem, of course, is that people suffering from mood disorders usually lack the motivation to be physically active, which results in a vicious cycle. Cultural rituals may help circumvent this problem by exerting external pressure to participate.

This has led the sociologist James McClenon to propose that shamanic rituals involving absorption, dissociation and altered states of consciousness shaped the biological basis for religion and spirituality. These rituals, he argues, would have been the primary means of healing in early human societies. Thanks to their therapeutic benefits, they exerted selective pressures that favoured genotypes associated with hypnotisability. With the increased prevalence of these genotypes, religious sentiments, myths and ideas became possible and were used to justify the use of those rituals.[17] McClenon's idea is speculative, but it is an intriguing one. If it holds any truth, it would imply that the benefits of shamanic ritual techniques have selected for individuals who were susceptible to them. And this, in turn, would mean that we are descended from people whose genetics predisposed them to seek certain kinds of ritual experience. We literally evolved to perform rituals.

Extreme rituals manage to utilise suffering to reap health and social benefits. On the face of it, there is also risk in suffering: for instance, there would seem to be the danger that practitioners might keep ramping up the intensity, compromising their immune system or sustaining serious injury. Strangely enough, those cases are unusual. Just as most marathon runners do not run until they drop of a heart attack, ritual participants seem to know the limits of their endurance and (with a few exceptions) only push their bodies up to those limits.

Another potentially dangerous side effect of healing rituals might come from over-reliance in their power. Despite its documented benefits, ritual is obviously no panacea, nor can it be a substitute for biomedical interventions. Thankfully, most ritual practitioners are well aware of this. When a group of farmers perform a fertility ritual, they do not stop tending their plants. They still make the technical and physical effort required to ensure a good crop. Similarly, people who perform healing rituals do not typically stop seeing their doctor. For the most part, the relationship between ritual practices and biomedical ones tends to be complementary rather than antagonistic. It seems that, even when people believe that their rituals have some kind of direct effect on the world, they still have an understanding that this is a different kind of effect from the physical causality of the natural world.

A far greater danger lies in trusting pseudo-scientific practices such as homeopathy. Like rituals, these practices may have some beneficial placebo effects, but, unlike rituals, people turn to them with the belief that they involve some process of scientific causation. As a result, they may treat them as equal alternatives to medicine, which can have dire repercussions for their health.

On some occasions, though, people can become convinced

that ritual actions are subject to the same inescapable effects of physical causation. When that happens, things can go terribly wrong. One example of this kind of conviction is manifested in a bizarre phenomenon known as 'voodoo death'. It occurs when someone believes that an evil spell has been cast on them, and as a result they become so terrified that they begin to experience severe psychosomatic symptoms that lead to sickness and, in extreme cases, mortality. This type of negative placebo effect is called a 'nocebo': a patient who is told that a particular drug has negative side effects is often likely to experience those side effects. It is therefore no surprise that most descriptions of this rare phenomenon come from physicians.

One such was Walter Cannon, a professor at the Harvard Medical School who became fascinated by the topic during the early twentieth century and collected reports from various cultures around the world.[18] In certain Australian aboriginal cultures, for instance, there is a belief that pointing a bone at someone can result in their death. This bone must be from a specific animal – an emu, a kangaroo or even a human – and must be prepared in a special ceremony, sometimes involving threading it with human hair, and administered by the tribe's specialist ritual killers. Indeed, there are several ethnographic narratives about victims of bone pointing who fell ill and eventually died. The phenomenon is thus also known as 'bone-pointing syndrome'. Cannon interpreted these cases as 'death from fear'. When victims truly believe that the ritual will result in their death, they are overcome with fear and as a result become apathetic, refuse to eat and simply wait to die. Death can thus become a self-fulfilling prophecy.

An important factor in this process is one's social environment. When someone is said to have been inflicted by sorcery, the belief is not only in that person's mind but also in everyone else's mind. The entire community begins to treat them as doomed or dead. They may stop talking to them, avoid, ignore or pity them, or even start performing funerary rites for them. It is not therefore only the inner world but also the entire social world of the victims that collapses around them, speeding up the fulfilment of the prophecy. It is a kind of forced suicide – or, as some have called it, 'psychic homicide'.

Maxwell Maltz, a famed cosmetic surgeon, talked about one of his patients, a Mr Russell, who visited him at his office in New York in the 1950s. Mr Russell was born in a Caribbean island where beliefs in the power of voodoo were widespread. When he told his girlfriend that he had spent all his savings on cosmetic surgery on his lower lip, she became enraged and announced that she had placed a voodoo curse on him. At first, the man did not pay much attention to her threats. But the next day he discovered a small lump on the inside of his lip and became convinced that it was an 'African bug', which, according to legend, would slowly consume his spirit. By the time he went back to his doctor some weeks later, he was a shell of a man. 'The Mr Russell who had first called upon me had been a very impressive individual, slightly too-large lip and all,' Maltz recounted.

> He stood about six feet four, a large man with the physique of an athlete and the bearing and manner that bespoke an inner dignity and gave him a magnetic personality. [...] The Mr Russell who now sat across the desk from me had aged at least 20 years. His hands shook with the tremor of age. His eyes and cheeks were sunken. He had lost perhaps 30 pounds. The changes in his appearance were all characteristic of the process that medical science, for want of a better name, calls aging.[19]

Maltz, who had seen this type of phenomenon before, did not dismiss his story. Instead, he removed the lump (which in reality was nothing but a superficial scar from his surgery) and showed it to him. The patient, now convinced that the curse was lifted, made a speedy and complete recovery.

Cannon describes how local witch doctors treated voodoo death in a similar way: they would make a small incision on the patient and then produce a small piece of bone, tooth or claw and show it to the patient, who would now believe that the mighty spell had been undone. The cause of their illness had thus been determined and eliminated. And as the cause was the psychosomatic stress produced by the belief in the efficacy of voodoo, this would actually heal them.

One might be tempted to dismiss Cannon's and Maltz's stories as mere anecdotes, embellished with hyperbole and racist overtones to fit the writing style of their time. However, the annals of medicine are peppered with similar cases, and experimental research confirms that expectations can have major effects on health, both positive and negative.[20] Long before sugar pills were used as placebos and nocebos, rituals served exactly the same role.

Phenomena like voodoo death are rare. Most cultures discourage the use of ritual for harming others or settling personal rivalries. These activities are commonly demarcated as belonging to the realm of witchcraft. In societies where beliefs about the efficacy of such techniques are widespread, one can typically also find strong norms and laws that ban their practice. Take, for example, the penal code of the Central African Republic, which stipulates that sorcery is punishable by five to ten years in prison, fines and forced labour. In fact, things can get even worse. In Saudi Arabia, witchcraft can carry the death penalty.

On the whole, generations of trial and error have forged ritual traditions that operate on multiple levels to produce advantageous effects for those who practise them. These distinct but cumulative effects, related to the physical experience of performance, the individual's expectations regarding the efficacy of the practice, and the social consequences of participation, can combine to have a powerful positive impact on the performer's health. As a result, numerous studies have found that religious individuals have better physical and mental health, greater life satisfaction and better overall quality of life. Notably, these benefits seem to have little to do with the religious beliefs of those individuals, and much to do with their participation in the ritual lives of their communities.[21]

Obviously, ritual is no replacement for biomedical interventions. But in many cases, especially in contexts where such interventions are not readily available to everyone, it may fulfil important complementary functions by helping people cope with stress and illness and find courage and motivation. This is especially so when it comes to mental illnesses, which may be accompanied by social stigma. Some of the rituals we have seen have been practised by generation after generation for thousands of years. Although this does not automatically mean that they should be taken at face value, it does suggest that we should take them seriously. That is, we should not be too quick to dismiss the possibility that they have something important to offer to the millions who engage in them. For we now have evidence that many of these practices, even some that may seem frightful or appalling to us, have the capacity to bring comfort, support, resilience and healing.

Above all, rituals, even seemingly extreme ones, provide

people with deeply meaningful experiences. In his book *The Sweet Spot* the psychologist Paul Bloom argues that, despite many claims to the contrary, humans are not natural hedonists. Of course, comfort and pleasure are important to us, but there is much more to a good life. This is why Abraham Maslow placed such things as safety and security in the middle rather than at the top of his hierarchy of needs. To live a rewarding life, we are also motivated to pursue activities that involve effort, difficulty and struggle. Bloom distinguishes between two kinds of chosen suffering. The first kind involves things like hot baths, spicy foods, intense exercise or sadomasochism. To the people who engage in those activities, the sensations involved are experienced as pleasure. The second kind of chosen suffering is very different. It is the kind involved in climbing mountains, raising children and performing extreme rituals. Presumably, mountaineers do not find injuries and blizzards pleasurable, and parents do not enjoy the sleep deprivation. Similarly, fire-walkers do not seek foot burns, and participants in the Thaipusam Kavadi do not take delight in having their skin pierced by needles and skewers. 'Such activities are effortful and often unpleasant. But they are part of a life well lived.'[22]

9

HARNESSING THE POWER OF RITUAL

As I was writing this book, the world was facing the greatest existential threat of the new century to date. In December 2019 a new type of virus named SARS-CoV-2 was discovered in China. This pathogen, which became more simply known as the 'coronavirus', was thought to have originated in some mammalian species, perhaps a bat or pangolin, and then transmitted to humans who came into close contact with these animals, possibly in a wildlife market in the Chinese city of Wuhan. Once the first human was infected, person-to-person transmission took off rapidly, causing COVID-19, a life-threatening case of severe acute respiratory syndrome. By January 2020 over 1,000 people had tested positive, and the virus had been detected in various countries outside of China. Three months later, over a million had been infected, and three months after that cases reached 10 million, then 100 million. The spread was exponential. The World Health Organization declared the outbreak a global pandemic. There was virtually nowhere in the world that was virus-free.

The coronavirus pandemic sent shockwaves around the world, forcing governments to implement unprecedented measures. A range of 'social distancing' rules came into effect, dramatically limiting physical interaction in public places. Schools and businesses were shut down. International travel was banned, events cancelled and citizens told to stay home. Entire countries went into lockdown, and those who left their home without approval were given hefty fines or even arrested. In some places, curfew violations even resulted in public beatings by the police. The effects of the catastrophe were quickly felt at a global scale as incomes shrank, jobs were lost and entire economies collapsed, creating the biggest spike in unemployment the world had seen in a century. As citizens looked to their political leaders for guidance, many failed to rise to the occasion, wavering in their responses to the crisis and issuing contradictory directives. Faced with uncharted territory, medical experts kept revising their predictions. And the media bombarded the public with grim imagery and figures as the death toll kept rising. Even the world's most powerful nations seemed unable to prevent the disaster. For a long time there was no light at the end of the tunnel. Until a vaccine emerged, no one could predict when things would go back to normal, or even what this 'new normal' might look like.

By changing people's lives in unparalleled ways, the pandemic underscored certain core aspects of human nature. The new social distancing rules made everyone realise the importance of human connection and physical interaction. Self-isolation reminded us that we crave contact with nature. At the same time the crisis also demonstrated the human need for ritual and highlighted its transformative power.

Responding to the COVID-19 pandemic, universities around the world mobilised to curtail the spread of the virus by suspending all campus activities. Teaching was moved online, dormitories closed, research put on hold. Overnight, millions of students saw their lives change in ways no one could have imagined just weeks earlier. My university was no exception. The day after the administration announced the lockdown, I met with my students for what was going to be our last in-class meeting of the academic year. Everyone was nervous. There was not much teaching that day, as I spent most of the class discussing the way forward and trying to offer some reassurance. The situation was dire, but we were going to get through it.

After I outlined the process of transitioning to the new online format, I asked my students whether they had any questions. Many of them raised their hands. But the first question was not about my class. 'Will there be a graduation ceremony?' a student asked. Everyone seemed anxious to hear the answer. I explained that, although graduation had not officially been cancelled at the time, I suspected that it would be – and sure enough, it was. Judging from their faces, that was the most disappointing news they received that day.

Having read this far into this book, you will probably not find my students' concern all that surprising. We care deeply about rituals because they help us find meaning and cope with many of life's challenges. Because of their highly structured nature, they provide a sense of predictability and control over the uncertainties of everyday life. By bringing people together to enact collective ceremonies, they provide a sense of connection and unity. And by marking key moments in our lives, they give us a sense of accomplishment and growth. In a world full of ever-changing variables, ritual provides a much-needed constant. The coronavirus outbreak turned all that upside down by presenting a rather unique predicament. At times of extreme anxiety, people intuitively turn to ritual to find a sense of regularity and normality. But the shelter-in-place orders meant that some of the most common coping strategies had suddenly become unavailable. And while the need for social cohesion was greater than ever, restrictions of movement and social distancing rules were making it ever harder for people to connect.

Under these extraordinary circumstances, individuals around the world responded by seeking rituals wherever they were available. Google searches for prayer surged to an all-time record. For every 80,000 new cases of COVID-19, the number of searches for prayer doubled.[1] People also started creating new rituals tailored to the new reality, as well as finding new ways to celebrate age-old ceremonies. The American comedian Jimmy Kimmel and his wife, Molly, encouraged those in quarantine to start holding 'formal Fridays', weekly ceremonial dinners to be attended in formal attire even if the attendees were at home on their own. 'The idea is to get dressed up as if you are going somewhere, even though you are going nowhere,' he explained. These kinds of rituals helped people maintain a sense of structure and normality and reclaim the feeling of control. Or, in Kimmel's own words, 'We do this for no reason other than to pretend we are humans rather than parrots living in a cage. So if you have a tux, take it out and put it on.'

While at-home rituals are relatively easy to implement, holding collective ceremonies at a time of social isolation posed a much greater challenge. Nonetheless, people everywhere forged ahead, finding creative ways to maintain a broader sense of human connection. For instance, the residents of a neighbourhood in the Italian town of Bella decided that maintaining social distancing did not mean that you could not be social. Using long bamboo sticks, they furnished cane poles equipped with cup holders complete with wine glasses. From the safety of their balconies, they were thus able to reach across the narrow streets and clink their glasses to toast their neighbours.

City dwellers around the world also took to their balconies

to pay tribute to healthcare workers, who were widely hailed as the heroes of the crisis. At the same time every day, they simultaneously opened their windows to cheer, clap or bang pots and pans together in a standing ovation to those who worked in the front line. As entire cities began to reverberate with the sounds of acclamation, this ritual soon became a symbol of connection and resilience, providing a sense of unity and reassurance. Everyone was in this together, and together they would overcome.

Similar rituals of appreciation and unity spontaneously emerged around the globe. In various US neighbourhoods, elementary school teachers started driving in car parades to cheer up their students. In turn, students and parents organised processions that drove past teachers' homes, expressing their appreciation by honking, planting placards and scribbling messages in chalk on pavements. On the Spanish island of Mallorca, police officers paid homage to the local citizens by singing and dancing in the streets. And in San Bernardino, California, a group of high-school students synchronised their voices remotely to form a virtual choir.

As the COVID-19 crisis dragged on, everyday activities such as commuting to work, going shopping or attending school were no longer part of the daily routine for many. People often felt the sense of time drifting away and their days becoming less meaningful. What is worse, some of the more special moments that define our sense of self and provide a feeling of personal progress and accomplishment were being cancelled. But no matter what the circumstances, those rituals were simply too important to give up.

Like most other things, many rituals were moved online. Virtual proms used teleconferencing platforms to allow high-school students to get together without leaving their rooms in order to celebrate a special night, interact and even dance.

Media outlets such as MTV and *Teen Vogue* organised nation-wide proms attended by thousands of students, featuring live music performances and speeches by guest celebrities. Meanwhile, birthday parties were among the first ceremonies to go mobile. Drive-by celebrations consisted in friends and relatives rolling up in cars decorated with balloons, streamers and banners, and honking, shouting birthday wishes and dropping birthday presents through their car windows. This would sometimes be formalised into a procession, with cars lining up to form a birthday parade. Soon, *quinceañeras*, bar mitzvahs and other rites of passage were added to the list of drive-by celebrations. Neighbours, and even complete strangers, would often get in on the action, adding to the commotion. Some families posted the event in local newspapers, inviting anyone who might be in the neighbourhood to drive by and honk their wishes.

Schools and colleges organised online or drive-through graduations, and some even found ways of creating some truly unique experiences. The Indian Institute of Technology in Bombay created personalised avatars for each of their students and invited them to a virtual ceremony where they were handed their diplomas by the Nobel Prize winner Duncan Haldane, who also attended in digital form. In New Hampshire, Kennett High School held its graduation ceremony on top of Cranmore Mountain. Each student and their family rode a ski lift to the summit, where they received their diploma and posed for pictures. Even when some schools cancelled their graduation ceremonies altogether, students and parents often took matters into their own hands. When a father in Louisiana saw his daughter crying because her college graduation had been called off, he decided to take action. He built a stage in his front yard, complete with a podium, sound installation and seating area. He ordered regalia and even brought two keynote speakers, the girl's aunt and the family pastor.

In Manhattan, Reilly Jennings and Amanda Wheeler were on their way to the New York City Marriage Bureau to get married when they heard the bad news: because of the outbreak, the Office of the City Clerk was suspending all ceremonies effective immediately and until further notice. The couple were devastated. But despite their initial disappointment, they decided that they were not going to let anything ruin the happiest day of their lives. They contacted a friend who was an ordained minister, and two hours later they tied the knot under his fourth-floor window. A handful of guests stood on the pavement while others watched through a car sunroof as the celebrant read a passage from Gabriel García Márquez's *Love in the Time of Cholera*. A few moments later he pronounced the couple married, to the sound of cars honking and neighbours applauding from their windows.

While some rituals celebrate new beginnings, others serve to provide closure. Like so many other things, the coronavirus pandemic also changed the way people handled grief. Throughout history, humans have performed intimate and elaborate mortuary rites to honour their dead. Muslims wash the body thoroughly before burying it. Hindus congregate at the Ganges and other rivers to burn the mortal remains on funeral pyres. Christians hold wakes or 'viewings', where friends and family gather to pay their respects to the deceased. Jews watch over the dead body at home over a seven-day mourning period. In all cultures, people groom, dress, kiss and caress the dead bodies of their loved ones. From the dawn of our kind, these deeply human acts have helped people come to terms with the reality of death, express their grief, seek solace and find the strength to move on. During the pandemic, however, government restrictions and the fear of contagion deprived millions of people of their traditional ways of grieving, leaving them feeling powerless and compounding their pain.

In many countries, hospitals and elderly care facilities were closed to visitors. For many of those who were in hospice care, the biggest fear was the possibility of dying alone. For their families, it was the thought of losing them without a proper send-off. But no matter what the circumstances, end-of-life rituals were simply too important to omit. Many people ignored the prohibitions and risked contracting the disease and receiving fines or even a jail sentence in order to perform funerary rites. Others were forced to adapt age-long customs to the new situation. Mourners held virtual funerals; pastors administered last rites over the phone; and cemeteries organised live-streamed events where families could watch mask-wearing staff perform memorial services over the graves of their loved ones.

The new kinds of ceremonies that emerged during the coronavirus pandemic reveal an important truth about rituals: while they typically resist change, they serve functions that are much too important for humans to live without, and as such they can be quick to adapt when new circumstances demand it. This has happened before, and it will happen again. An example of such novel circumstances can be seen in the various ceremonies held by anatomy departments in universities around the world.

So many of the advances of modern medicine, in specialities ranging from surgery and organ transplantation to radiology, dentistry and all areas of internal medicine, would not have been possible without the knowledge gained from dead bodies. The dissection of human cadavers has greatly increased our knowledge of the internal workings of the human organism. It has allowed medical students to get invaluable practice and medical researchers to experiment on new techniques, and helped accelerate the discovery of new treatments and procedures, making them safer and more efficient and saving numerous lives in the process. In order to treat the living, physicians need to practise on the dead. Despite the tremendous importance of this research, however, and although death is the only certainty in life, the availability of cadavers for scientific research has always been limited.

In the past, anatomists often resorted to dubious practices to acquire cadavers for dissection. Often they were stolen from graveyards, obtained from hospitals and death rows without the consent of family members, or bought on the black market, no questions asked. Such was the demand for bodies that 'anatomy murder', killing someone for the sole purpose of selling their body to medical researchers, has historically been a relatively common occurrence. Obviously, such practices are no longer acceptable. Contemporary medical science relies on voluntary body donations for its training and research needs. Nonetheless, bodies are still in short supply.

One of the biggest impediments to the anatomical gift is the worry that the deceased will not have a respectful ending or that their relatives will be left lacking a sense of closure. In the absence of mortuary rituals, neither the dead nor the living can move on. This is why most medical schools and anatomy laboratories around the world hold memorial services in honour of body donors.[2] The Department of Anatomy of the University of Otago in New Zealand holds a 'clearing of the way' ceremony at the beginning of each academic year. This traditional Maori ritual is used to purify the dissection room and recognise the dead body as sacred (*tapu*). At the end of the year, a thanksgiving service is held for the donors' families and friends. In Thailand, each semester in the dissection laboratory begins with a dedication ceremony attended by Buddhist monks. The donors' names are read aloud, and they are awarded the title of 'Great Teacher'. At the end of the course, a ceremonial procession is organised in which students carry their 'teachers' to the site of their final cremation.[3] In China, medical apprentices bow to the dead bodies when they enter the anatomy lab and decorate the refrigerators in the morgue with flowers on Tomb-Sweeping Day, when Chinese people visit the graves of their ancestors. One Chinese university in Dalian has built a memorial hall to commemorate the lives and achievements of body and organ donors. And in the USA, the Mayo Clinic holds a 'Convocation of Thanks' ceremony at the end of each academic year, where anatomy faculty and students share their gratitude through speeches, poetry, music and artwork. These events are attended by the donors' families, who are invited to honour their loved ones individually by reading obituaries. In addition to these memorials, anatomy labs also cover the costs of a burial or cremation of the donor's remains, according to local customs and the wishes of the donors.

The memorial rituals held by anatomy departments provide an invaluable service to the donors' families, to medical schools and to society at large. For the students, professors and researchers, these memorials offer an opportunity to express gratitude to the donors and their families. In addition, they help them decrease the anxiety and discomfort associated with handling the dead by providing reassurance that they are allowed to carry out dissections without guilt or feeling that they are committing sacrilege. Moreover, in contrast to the antiquated view that medical professionals should be detached from their patients, these ceremonies encourage them to humanise the dead and see them as people, who deserve to be treated with respect, dignity and appreciation. For the donors' families, memorial rituals offer the chance of a final farewell and help them come to terms with their loss.

Not to be underestimated, these rituals help raise awareness of the importance of body donation in scientific research and education, and illustrate to the public that donated bodies are treated with respect and dignity. Potential donors will be more likely to make such a deeply personal commitment when they know that they will be given proper tribute and that their beloved ones will have the chance to honour them and find closure. By celebrating death, body donor memorialisation rituals help save lives.

Loss and grief are often experienced in situations other than death. But while death has been surrounded by ritual since time immemorial, this has not always been the case for other kinds of loss. One of the most obvious examples is divorce. While all cultures have elaborate marriage rituals, divorce ceremonies are rare. Exceptions include the United Church of Christ and the United Methodist Church, which have special divorce liturgies and prayers. Some religions, such as Judaism and Islam, have specific proceedings for issuing a religious divorce, but these are more legalistic than ceremonial in nature and rather resemble a court hearing. At the other end of the spectrum, the Catholic Church does not even recognise divorce as an option, although under certain circumstances an annulment is possible. For most people, therefore, getting divorced is a purely legal procedure. While starting a marriage is thoroughly ceremonial, ending it is merely a matter of paperwork. As a matter of fact, in most cultures divorce is probably the only major life transition without a dedicated rite of passage.

This lack of a specific ritual to mark such a consequential life event is largely due to historical reasons. In the not so distant past, divorce was relatively rare. Conservative cultural norms, religious and legal restrictions, and the subjugation of women have for centuries made voluntary separation all but impossible in most parts of the world. Even where special provisions existed, high costs, bureaucratic obstacles and social pressure placed divorce out of reach to all but a few. But the twentieth century saw a global explosion in separation rates. In some developed countries now, more than half of all new marriages end in divorce. And as social attitudes change in less wealthy regions, with more women entering the workplace to become financially independent, divorce rates keep going up there as well. As a result, millions of people each year go through one of the most emotional, significant and stressful life changes – yet it is only acknowledged through the signing of a legal document. This can leave the former couple with a sense of emptiness, unable to process their new status as single individuals or single parents, often feeling oddly unable to move on with their lives.

Acknowledging the need to facilitate this major life transition, religious as well as secular institutions are creating novel divorce ceremonies. Such rituals, for example, have been in high demand in Japan. The Mantokuji Buddhist temple in the prefecture of Gunma used to be a convent that provided refuge to women who wished to escape their abusive husbands. Today the temple offers women a divorce ritual that consists in writing their grievances on a piece of paper and flushing it down the temple toilet. Japanese entrepreneurs also offer divorce ceremonies where couples, often accompanied by friends and relatives, destroy their wedding rings with a hammer while undoing their vows.

Similar ceremonies are becoming popular around the world. In the USA they are often organised by 'divorce coaches' or 'divorce planners'. They range from very simple to highly elaborate, and they can be deeply personal and solemn or widely attended and festive. A bad relationship may be marked with the destruction of shared photographs and memories. A good one may be acknowledged by offering thanks. In all cases, their goals are the same: to facilitate transition. They provide the couple with an opportunity to grieve for the end of their marriage and come to terms with their changed status. Moreover, they communicate this new status to their social circle, helping everyone to process and acknowledge their new, independent social roles. In addition to marking the end of their relationship, such ceremonies inaugurate the beginning of their new lives.

Other modern attempts to harness the power of ritual extend to groups far larger than couples. At the end of each summer hordes of individuals from around the world congregate in Nevada to take part in an extraordinary human gathering known as Burning Man. A makeshift city the size of the Italian town of Pisa is erected in the middle of the desert, only to be dismantled a few days later, leaving no trace behind. During that week Burners participate in an extravaganza of cultural and artistic experiences, wearing wild costumes, riding surreal vehicles, enjoying spectacular light displays and attending all manner of fantastical interactive art installations. Sensory pageantry is everywhere and in abundance. The event culminates in the ceremonial burning of the two gigantic structures that loom at the centre of the ephemeral city. A towering wooden effigy known as 'The Man', visible from every part of the playa (the flat desert basin), is set ablaze on the penultimate night. The final and perhaps most spectacular part of Burning Man takes place on the last night, when everyone gathers to watch the burning of the temple.

When the sculptor David Best was invited to build an installation at Burning Man, he started collecting scrap wood from a toy factory without any concrete idea of what to make of it. A few days before the event, Michael Hefflin, one of the crew members working on the project, died in a tragic motorcycle accident. The team thought that Michael would have wanted them to complete the project they started, so they decided to go to the desert and build 'something'. As they started erecting a large wooden structure, visitors to the installation who heard about their loss spontaneously started putting the names of people they had lost in it, and later gathered to watch it burn at the end of the event. It was only then that Best realised he had built a temple.

The following year Best was invited to build another temple, and he christened it the Temple of Tears. This time, thousands of people came to watch it burn, adding the names of loved ones who had perished. Even when the following year's structure was called the Temple of Joy, people continued to use it as a memorial, a space in which they could grieve and put the past behind them.

Every year since then, the temple has been covered with thousands of notes, photographs and memorabilia. Many bring the ashes or favourite objects of a loved one, or even a hated one: an abusive spouse or parent, or a bad relationship that they wish to leave behind. Most of them leave heartfelt messages.

'John, I wasn't done with you,' someone wrote. Another note read: 'Mum and Dad, I am trying so hard to stop my resentment.' Someone else seemed to think of an impending divorce: 'Soon we will be living separate lives. I hope you find what you search for and what makes you happy.' There are those who mourn the loss of a pet, while others look to overcome their own fears, failures or regrets. 'I am sorry, baby, we were not ready for you,' said one of the messages. Another one read: 'I will be a better friend than I was a partner.' Such simple symbolic acts seem to have a surprisingly powerful effect on those seeking to overcome their grief, rid themselves of painful memories and celebrate new beginnings. As the temple is reduced to ashes, thousands of onlookers watch silently, many of them in tears. The solemn character of the temple burn comes in sharp contrast with the previous night's burning of the Man, a joyful event accompanied by fireworks, music and wild partying.

Burning Man defies a strict definition. Burners are quick to stress that it is not a festival – it is much more than that. If pressed to define it, they may describe it as a community, a movement, a social experiment or a pilgrimage. Whatever you might want to call it, it is a cultural phenomenon that has known astounding success. Within thirty years of its inception in 1986, attendance increased from a few dozen individuals to over 80,000 in Nevada and hundreds of thousands in satellite events around the world. This success is due to Burning Man's ability to create meaningful experiences for its members.

In surveys conducted every year, Burning Man attendees overwhelmingly report experiencing strong feelings of connection and community during the event and very high levels of satisfaction overall.[4] Consistently, over three-quarters of participants say that their experience has to some degree been transformative, even when they did not attend the event specifically seeking or expecting such a transformation. Among them, more than 90 per cent report that these transformative experiences lasted beyond their stay in Black Rock City and over 80 per cent state that they had a permanent effect in their lives.

It is not surprising, then, that Burning Man has unusually high levels of loyalty. The great majority of participants say that they identify as Burners and that they plan to return to the event – and most of them do. In 2019, over three-quarters of attendees had participated in previous burns, many of them returning year after year.

The deeply spiritual experiences Burners report, as well as their high levels of loyalty and community, resemble those of some religious groups. Indeed, many have drawn this parallel explicitly. Yet Burning Man lacks any official dogma or central authority, and the demographics suggest that participants are about as secular as they come: just over 5 per cent of Burners identify as religious, although almost half say that they are spiritual. All the same, the similarities with religion are no accident.

To create meaningful experiences for their members, the organisers of Burning Man took a page from the playbook of religious movements. Co-founder Larry Harvey studied classic works in the anthropology, psychology and sociology of religion to understand the transformative power of ritual. 'Beyond the dogmas, creeds, and metaphysical ideas of religion', he wrote, 'there is immediate experience. It is from this primal world that living faith arises. [...] The human urge to make events, objects, actions, and personalities sacred is protean.'[5] Harvey called on Burners to disregard any notions of belief and instead immerse themselves in this immediate experience of the rituals that lie at the heart of Burning Man. These rites address fundamental human needs, he explained. 'The desire to belong to a place, to belong to a time, to belong to one another, and to belong to something that is greater than ourselves, even in the midst of impermanence.'

For Burners, the ritual experience begins as soon as they walk through the gate, where people hug and greet each other with the phrase 'Welcome home!' They refer to Black Rock City as their home and the outside as 'the default world'. That home is treated as sacred, demarcated by the straight lines of a pentagon and protected from the polluting influence of the outside world. Upon their departure, Burners must remove all Matter Out of Place (MOOP). This is a concept borrowed from the anthropologist Mary Douglas, who used it to describe how cultural notions of purity and pollution are used to designate the things society holds sacred. According to Douglas, purification rituals create symbolic boundaries that separate the domain of the sacred from that of the profane. Anything that transgresses those boundaries is seen as a source of pollution and danger, not because it is inherently unclean but because cultural norms dictate that it does not belong there. In a shopping mall, wearing shoes is considered clean while walking barefoot is unclean; in many religious temples, the opposite is true. When the transgression is unavoidable or necessary, a purification ceremony ensures that it is not harmful. For instance, a priest must perform cleansing rites before entering the altar. At the end of Burning Man, Burners conduct 'line sweeps' in order to find and remove all MOOP. Precise rules dictate the number, arrangement, distance and movement of MOOPers. Even the tiniest particles must be removed, including hair, wood splinters or glitter, and everything is meticulously documented and inspected. There is even a blog dedicated to the art of MOOPing. Various other rituals help further demarcate the boundaries between Burning

Man and the outside world. As in other rites of passage, people even leave their default name behind and adopt a 'playa name', which is bestowed on them by another Burner.

Another thing that must be left behind are monetary transactions. Burners practise 'radical self-reliance', which means that they are responsible for their own subsistence and must bring all the supplies they need to survive with them on their journey to the desert. Once through the gate, the only place where money can be used is the main café. Other than that, buying and selling are strictly forbidden. Those who are found using money may be asked to leave. Bartering is not allowed either. Instead, gifting is one of Burning Man's core principles. People freely hand out gifts, each according to their skills, interests and means. Those gifts can be anything, whether material or immaterial – from food, alcohol and drugs to haircuts, massages, yoga classes and, of course, art. Everyone is encouraged to give these gifts unconditionally, without any calculation or presumption of reciprocation or exchange. In addition to material possessions and services, Burners donate their time and labour, as everything in Black Rock City is made by volunteers.

The gift economy of Burning Man is modelled on traditional ceremonial customs. Consider the example of the Massim people of Papua New Guinea, who maintained a complex system of ritual exchange that consisted in giving and receiving shell necklaces and armbands. Although those objects did not have any particular value or practical utility in themselves, the islanders would go to great lengths to exchange them, travelling great distances and taking substantial risks by crossing the treacherous waters of the Pacific Ocean in their unwieldy canoes. This resulted in a circular gifting pattern known as the 'Kula ring'. In essence, one may say that these practices bring no net benefit, as goods are simply recycled. But as the French sociologist Marcel Mauss observed in his classic essay *The Gift*, they can in fact have important social utility. Mauss noted that systems of ritualised exchange create a set of social obligations. Unlike economic exchanges that might produce equivalent outcomes, each act of donation creates feelings of gratitude and community, increasing both personal satisfaction and social solidarity. There is, in fact, no such thing as a free gift. Each act of giving comes with the expectation of repayment in one form or another. But on the whole, these gifts create a cycle of mutual responsibilities, establishing a network of reciprocal relationships that encompass the entire community.

Abandoning monetary transactions is one of the many sacrifices that Burners are required to make. There are no shops or restaurants, no showers and no mobile phone reception. The desert sun can be scorching hot, but the desert nights are freezing. Windstorms are a regular occurrence, and the ultra-fine playa dust covers everything and gets everywhere, including the lungs. It is so alkaline that it causes chemical burns to the feet, a condition known as 'playa foot'. As we saw in Chapter 7, these costly sacrifices may serve to ensure commitment. By filtering out those who are unwilling to give up their everyday comforts, they select for individuals who fully embrace the values of the community, while making it easy to spot free-riders. Celebrities and affluent individuals who try to maintain some level of luxury while on the playa are frowned upon. The numerous opportunities to witness these sacrifices in the hostile desert environment raise trust and facilitate cooperation between Burners. And to those who have never taken part, these sacrifices act as credibility-enhancing displays that mark group membership as valuable and desirable.

It may be tempting to associate Burning Man with hedonistic enjoyment. Music, alcohol, sex, drugs and all kinds of partying are certainly part of the deal. But those things can be found much more easily in other contexts. You don't have to travel to the wilderness to get drunk, get high or have sex. The exceptional success of Burning Man is due not only to these pleasures but also, and perhaps mostly, to the effort and hardship that make for a meaningful experience. In point of fact, in the early years of the movement, participation was easy and enjoyable. The Burn was held at Baker Beach in San Francisco and was free to attend. Even so, growth was slow and the crowd was not invested in it. After the event moved to the distant and inhospitable environment of the desert and an ever steeper participation fee was added, attendance accelerated at an exponential rate, until it had to be capped by federal authorities. A fence was added to keep outsiders out, guarded by a perimeter patrol equipped with night-vision and radar systems to detect intruders. Soon, Burning Man spawned numerous regional events and branched out to dozens of countries.

The success of Burning Man highlights the power of ritual to create meaningful experiences and build fellowship. And yet these experiences take place over the space of only a few days, after which people go back to the default world. Getting thousands of individuals to get along, cooperate and be merry over the span of a week is no small feat. But building cohesive groups that need to work together day in day out is a whole other story. If ritual is an effective design principle for building a utopian society, can it also boost cooperation among more permanent groups?

○

When I moved from Greece to Denmark, I was often struck by the many cultural differences between the two countries – an experience known as 'culture shock'. Providing a full account of Danish peculiarities from the perspective of a non-Dane from the Mediterranean could yield enough material to write another book. But one of the domains that especially stuck out was the workplace. Denmark has one of the highest productivity rates in the world, with a thriving industry, skilled workforce and efficient bureaucracy. With that in mind, and in line with the Danes' reputation for conformism and rule-following, one might expect Danish companies to look like well-oiled assembly lines, where workers tirelessly and mindlessly execute orders coming from higher up in robotic fashion. Nothing could be further from the truth.

The Danes work less than almost any other nation in the world, while at the same time taking more holidays. According to Organisation for Economic Co-operation and Development (OECD) data, in 2019 Danish workers on average clocked in a meagre 26.5 hours of work per week, compared with 37.4 for Greeks, who topped the European list. That is an annual total of 346 hours fewer than the OECD average, 399 hours fewer than Americans and a whopping 757 hours fewer than Mexicans, the hardest-working of all nations.[6] Unsurprisingly, then, when I got my first job in Denmark, things felt much more relaxed than what I was used to. In fact, to many foreigners like myself, the Danish workplace often felt a bit too relaxed, as even those short working hours did not seem very intensive. A significant part of each working day was spent in seemingly unproductive activities like drinking coffee, eating lunch, having cake or consuming beer. Regular meetings were convened even when there was nothing on the agenda. Retreats were organised, where much of the time was spent singing, drinking and playing games. And a variety of parties and celebrations were regularly sponsored by employers.

At first, all this seemed bizarre, often amusing and at times even annoying. To an outsider, it might appear that the Danes have a poor work ethic, or at least a bad sense of urgency. But the numbers tell a very different story. In addition to being one of the most productive and innovative workforces in the world, Danish workers are also among the happiest, reporting one of the highest satisfaction rates globally. And while at first glance the numerous rituals of the Danish workplace may have seemed odd or wasteful, as soon as I embraced them it became clear to me that they contributed something vital to the efficient, productive and enjoyable work environment. This power of ritual to transform the workplace is why some of the most successful companies around the world are ritualised by design.

Most workplaces in Denmark observe several daily breaks – typically a morning coffee break, a lunch break and an afternoon coffee break. These breaks are not simply about taking time from work. They are social events that help to forge connections among colleagues. Even those who were not hungry or had brought their own food would come out of their office and join everyone in the dining room or the canteen. Skipping the common meal because you were working on a project would not score you any points with your boss. Danish companies, large and small, encourage these events and support them generously. Most of them have fully equipped kitchens, expensive coffee machines and spacious dining rooms where staff can share their meals. My wife's employer even brought in a chef to cook lunch every day at the company she worked for.

Rather than considering such expenditures a waste of resources, these organisations realise that the social benefits of sharing meals among colleagues more than make up for the costs. Eating together is an intimate act, usually reserved for close relatives and friends. Sharing food therefore symbolises community and helps strengthen bonds among colleagues. Research shows that people enjoy eating with others more than eating alone, and that food tastes better when consumed in the company of others. From infancy, eating food together is perceived as a cue for social connection. Those who share food are seen as more friendly and intimate. Moreover, those who eat together trust each other more and collaborate more efficiently. A study conducted at Cornell University found that people who ate from shared plates became more cooperative and less competitive towards one another than those who ate from separate plates.[7]

This is presumably why many of Silicon Valley's tech giants offer their employees free meals or employ full-time chefs and baristas on the premises. At the Airbnb offices in San Francisco, chefs provide home-made snacks and beverages. Facebook offers its employees a whole gamut of free restaurants, cafeterias and even ice cream shops. Pinterest hosts a happy hour for all company employees every Friday. Kickstarter has a rooftop garden where employees can pick fresh fruit and vegetables. And Google has installed food stations known as 'microkitchens', strategically placed between departments to encourage interaction between different teams. Ironically, these companies even clash with local authorities over their insistence on spending more rather than less money on their workers. In 2018, succumbing to pressure from local restaurant lobbyists, San Francisco decided to ban employers from providing workers with free meals on their premises. After a year of controversy and negative reaction, the ban was scrapped.

Workplace rituals aren't just for leisure time. In Denmark, many of our work meetings were also highly ritualised. They occurred always at the same time and place, involved the same food and drinks and followed the same structure. It didn't matter whether there were any pressing work-related issues to discuss; most of the real work happened in the smaller teams that managed individual projects anyway. The group meetings of course helped those teams get valuable feedback, but mostly they provided people with a chance to connect with other group members, catch up with what everyone was doing and celebrate the latest accomplishments. Such outcomes were always presented as collective, so that everyone could share in the pride over a success, while feelings of failure could be diffused so as not to feel entirely personal.

In addition to these regular meetings and break-time activities, there were also several purely celebratory events. Some were meant to honour individual milestones, such as childbirth, promotion or retirement. Publicly acknowledging such non-competitive personal accomplishments boosted employees' morale and motivation and provided a sense of community and inclusion. Various other celebrations were held regularly. At the end of each week students and faculty attended a Friday Bar, complete with music, dancing and drinking. And the first item on the order of business every Monday morning was coffee and cake. Those cyclical rituals designated the working week and marked the time outside it as off-limits, helping employees disconnect from their work over the weekend. Indeed, personal time is treated as sacred in Denmark, a country that prides itself on its work–life balance.

Towards the end of the year each group organised a Christmas party, an event that was taken very seriously and involved extensive preparations. RSVPs were sent out weeks or months in advance, and spouses and partners were also invited. Senior management not only participated but invested significant time overseeing the arrangements, officiating at the celebrations and upholding traditions. Those included ceremonial speeches, lights and candles, games and multiple rounds of toasting, each accompanied by three *hurrahs* chanted in chorus. The high levels of sensory and emotional arousal involved in these ceremonies added to the perceived prestige and value of the organisation and provided a sense of a broader community of colleagues, connected through common customs and symbols. The various speeches and anecdotes shared on those nights helped reinforce the ethos and values of the community. And at the end of the day the celebrations were just good fun, creating fondness and a sense of nostalgia for these gatherings.

These collective activities effectively harness the power of ritual to solidify interpersonal relationships and boost team cohesion. Indeed, research shows that deliberately integrating rituals into their organisational structure allows companies to build a more organic, democratic and collaborative culture.[8] What is more, work group rituals make work-related tasks feel more meaningful, which makes for a happier as well as more productive workforce.[9]

In Chapter 4 we saw some of the basic ingredients of the ritual social glue. Many of those ingredients can be incorporated in organisational design in straightforward ways. Shared meals and regular meetings can be imbued with symbolism and group markers and enhanced by frequent repetition. But some other key ingredients of the ritual recipe may not be as easily accessible to all kinds of groups. Aspects such as synchronous movement, sensory pageantry and shared emotional arousal are key in turning the social glue into superglue. Inevitably, though, those ingredients will be more accessible to a sports team or military unit than an office environment. To make use of those ingredients, many companies deliberately put their employees through activities that resemble the experiences of athletes or soldiers. These corporate team-building rituals range from collective singing and dancing to panic rooms, paintball, extreme sports and even scary activities such as walking on broken glass.

For a long time, the traditional workplace has been a transactional and impersonal space. You get in, put in your hours and go home. Thus, upon joining an organisation that has embraced these ritual design principles, its liturgy of ceremonies may seem overwhelming, especially to newcomers who are used to a more sterile type of workplace. But through frequent repetition the oddities of each ritual quickly become familiar hallmarks of the organisation's culture. They help forge a unique group identity and mark the individual's place within it, creating meaningful experiences and providing a sense of agency and purpose. After all, it is precisely when a group's rituals cease to seem exotic, strange or comical and begin to feel familiar, comforting, even sacred, that a person knows they are truly part of that culture.

C

The ceremonies that emerge as a response to new challenges, as well as those enacted at Burning Man or practised in many workplace cultures, highlight an important truth about human nature. Rituals fulfil primal human needs that are central to our personal and social existence. That is what led religious studies scholar Catherine Bell to define ritual as a culturally strategic way of acting in the world.[10] Rather than being a mere matter of habit or routine, she argued, rituals offer solutions to various problems inherent in the human condition, which can be self-administered by individuals or prescribed by one's culture. Owing to these properties, and thanks to their ability to define abstract social relationships and coordinate thought and action, they have historically been in the service of ideological systems such as religious movements and organised states.[11] So successful have these institutions been in harnessing the power of ritual that we have come to equate it with them. But, while religions and states have tried to claim a monopoly on it, ritual both pre-dates and extends beyond them.

In the modern era, the grip of religious and state institutions on ritual is diminishing.[12] Around the globe, industrialised societies are becoming ever more secular as religious ideology gradually loses its centrality as one of society's organising principles. Fewer people participate in the liturgical life of organised religions, and those who attend do so less frequently. Moreover, human societies overall are becoming more democratic: despite regional fluctuations, there are overall far more democracies in the world in the twenty-first century than at any point in human history. As a consequence, the state-mandated rituals that are necessary for totalitarian institutions to assert their dominance are also becoming less common. Despite these trends, by our very nature we crave ritual, and thus the void created by the retreat of religious and state ceremonies is inevitably filled as other domains of life become more and more ritualised. This, however, does not always turn out as expected.

New rituals are born each day, but very few of them persist for any significant length of time. The ceremonies that we see around us are the survivors: those that have made it through a long and ruthless process of cultural selection. Social engineering attempts to draw on ritual's power are thus likely to fail unless they establish meaningful similarities to those traditions. Alas, an additional challenge is that rituals are only meaningful when practised in the right contexts. Many of the circumstances of our modern existence are vastly different from those our ancestors faced even a mere few decades ago. Life rhythms are faster and the social groups we identify and interact with are larger, more widespread and more heterogeneous than ever before. Simply copying ancient practices therefore does not guarantee replicating their results. It is one thing to go through an arduous coming-of-age ceremony that has been enacted by your ancestors for ages, accompanied by your peers and guided by the elders of your community; it is another altogether to be humiliated by a group of second-years in a fraternity initiation. Confessing your sins to a priest may be cathartic, but being asked personal questions by your boss in a corporate team-building session may feel embarrassing. And while screaming at the top of your lungs in a stadium may help you bond with fellow fans, being invited to do so by a motivational speaker in a suit may seem comical.

This raises an alarming possibility: the overall sense of the declining importance of traditional ritual practices in the industrial West has coincided with a long period of relative stability, in which we have been fairly isolated from many of the terrors of existential uncertainty. There is, however, no reason to think that many of the comforts we enjoy today may not come under threat in the near future. If anything, the COVID pandemic has illustrated how fragile our modern existence can be. It is not unthinkable that these could be just the opening rumblings of an age of upheavals, driven by unsustainable growth, the overexploitation of the earth's resources, the climate crisis and political failures. Should this be true, in the darkening times to come we may find that we have ever greater recourse to the powers of ritual, to give us peace of mind, foster solidarity and provide a sense of meaning and continuity. Will the new rituals of our age, which are often hastily invented rather than forged through lengthy trial and error, be up to the task? And will future generations be able to harness their power as intuitively and efficiently as our ancestors have done for millennia?

I started my journey with ritual as a sceptic. To me, the human obsession with ceremony seemed puzzling. I was not alone in that view. For a long time, ritual had rarely been the subject of scientific scrutiny, because scientists either rejected its utility out of hand or considered its inner workings to be a mystery. Now, for the first time, an interdisciplinary science of ritual allows us to appreciate that behaviours that seem wasteful may be both meaningful and beneficial. Studying those benefits for two decades has been an eye-opening experience, which has changed not just how I see rituals but also how I see my fellow humans. Ceremony is a primordial part of human nature, one that helps us connect, find meaning and discover who we are: we are the ritual species.

NOTES

1. The Ritual Paradox

1. Handwerk, 2003.
2. https://www.pgsindia.org/SinglePage.php?PageID=15
3. Homans, 1941.

2. The Ritual Species

1. Perrot et al., 2016.
2. Madden, 2008.
3. Bekoff, 2009.
4. Reggente et al., 2016; Watson, 2016.
5. Poole, 1996.
6. Meredith, 2004.
7. Goodall, 2005.
8. Kühl et al., 2016.
9. Rossano, 2006; 2010.
10. van Leeuwen et al., 2012; Dal Pesco and Fischer, 2018.
11. Meggitt, 1966.
12. de Waal, Frans, 1996, p. 151.
13. Deacon, 1997; Knight, 1994.
14. Dissanayake, 1988.
15. Jaubert et al., 2016.
16. Durkheim, 1915, pp. 216–17.
17. Rappaport, 1999, p. 107.
18. Sahlins, 1968; 1972.

19. Bocquet-Appel, 2011.
20. Scott, 2017.
21. Larsen, 2006.
22. Dulaney and Fiske, 1994.
23. Boyer and Liénard, 2006.
24. Fiske and Haslam, 1997.
25. Zohar and Felz, 2001.
26. Evans et al., 2002.
27. Klavir and Leiser, 2002; Woolley and Rhoads, 2017.
28. Watson-Jones, Whitehouse and Legare, 2015; Legare et al., 2015.
29. Rakoczy, Warneken and Tomasello, 2008.
30. Horner and Whiten, 2004.
31. Lyons et al., 2011.
32. McGuigan, Makinson and Whiten, 2011.
33. Over and Carpenter, 2012.
34. Legare and Nielsen, 2015.
35. Fairlie, Hoffmann and Oreopoulos, 2014.
36. Watson-Jones, Whitehouse and Legare, 2015.
37. Over and Carpenter, 2009.
38. Young and Benyshek, 2010.
39. McCormick, 2010.
40. Archer, 1999.

3. Order

1. Wayne, 1985.
2. Evans-Pritchard, 1951.
3. Malinowski, 1948, pp. 122–3.
4. Malinowski, 1922, p. 136.
5. Malinowski, 1948, p. 116.
6. Ibid., p. 70.
7. Delfabbro and Winefeld, 2000.
8. Joukhador, Blaszczynski and Maccallum, 2004.
9. Henslin, 1967.

10. Frazer, 1890.

11. Nemeroff and Rozin, 1994.

12. Chang and Li, 2018.

13. Gmelch, 1978.

14. Zaugg, 1980; Schippers and Van Lange, 2006; Wright and Erdal, 2008; Todd and Brown, 2003; Brevers et al., 2011; Dömötör, Ruíz-Barquín and Szabo, 2016.

15. Flanagan, 2013.

16. Bleak and Frederick, 1998.

17. Nadal and Carlin, 2011.

18. Keinan, 1994.

19. Sosis, 2007.

20. Keinan, 2002.

21. Lang et al., 2019.

22. Lang et al., 2015.

23. Skinner, 1948.

24. Wagner and Morris, 1987.

25. Legare and Souza, 2013.

26. Legare and Souza, 2012.

27. Xygalatas, Maňo and Baranowski, 2021.

28. Yerkes and Dodson, 1908.

29. Brenner et al., 2015.

30. Sosis and Handwerker, 2011.

31. Anastasi and Newberg, 2008.

32. Brooks et al., 2016.

33. Norton and Gino, 2014.

34. Lang, Krátký and Xygalatas, 2020.

35. Udupa et al., 2007.

36. Whitson and Galinsky, 2008.

37. Hockey, 1997.

38. Damisch, Stoberock and Mussweiler, 2010.

39. Gayton et al., 1989.

40. Foster, Weigand and Baines, 2006.

4. Glue

1. Biesele, 1978, p. 169.
2. Boyer, 2005.
3. Boyer and Liénard, 2006.
4. Zacks and Tversky, 2001.
5. Nielbo and Sørensen, 2011.
6. Nielbo, Schjoedt and Sørensen, 2012.
7. Kapitány and Nielsen, 2015.
8. Herrmann et al., 2013.
9. Schachner and Carey, 2013.
10. Liberman, Kinzler and Woodward, 2018.
11. Nielsen, Kapitány and Elkins, 2015; Wilks, Kapitány and Nielsen, 2016; Clegg and Legare, 2016.
12. Nielsen, Tomaselli and Kapitány, 2018.
13. Rakoczy, Warneken and Tomasello, 2008.
14. Nielsen, 2018.
15. Tajfel, 1970.
16. Park, Schaller and Vugt, 2007.
17. Shaver et al., 2018.
18. McElreath, Boyd and Richerson, 2003.
19. Wiltermuth and Heath, 2009.
20. Hove and Risen, 2009; Reddish, Fischer and Bulbulia, 2013.
21. Lang et al., 2017.
22. Dunbar, 2012.
23. Bernieri, Reznick and Rosenthal, 1988.
24. Chartrand and Bargh, 1999.
25. Wen, Herrmann and Legare, 2016.
26. Wen et al., 2020.
27. Bellah, 2011.
28. Ibid.
29. Stein et al., 2021.
30. Atkinson and Whitehouse, 2011.
31. Whitehouse, 2004.

32. McCauley and Lawson, 2002.
33. Ibid.

5. Effervescence

1. Bulbulia et al., 2013.
2. Konvalinka et al., 2011.
3. Xygalatas et al., 2011.
4. Zak, 2012.
5. Xygalatas, 2014.
6. Xygalatas, 2007.
7. Xygalatas, 2012.
8. Xygalatas et al., 2013a.
9. Csikszentmihalyi, 1990.
10. Walker, 2010.
11. Baranowski-Pinto et al., 2022.

6. Superglue

1. Schmidt, 2016.
2. Whitehouse, 1996.
3. Aronson and Mills, 1959.
4. Gerard and Mathewson, 1966.
5. Xygalatas and Lang, 2016.
6. Xygalatas et al., 2013b.
7. Rielly, 2000.
8. Gray, 1959.
9. Whitehouse and Lanman, 2014.
10. Swann et al., 2009.
11. Swann et al., 2010.
12. Whitehouse, 2018.
13. Zeitlyn, 1990, p. 122.
14. Buhrmester, Zeitlyn and Whitehouse, 2020.
15. Newson et al., 2018.
16. Gómez et al., 2021.

7. Sacrifice
1. Darwin Correspondence Project.
2. Darwin, 1871.
3. Fisher, 1930.
4. Zahavi, 1975.
5. Jonaitis, 1991.
6. Sahlins, 1963; Mauss, 1990 [1922].
7. Veblen, 1899.
8. Amin, Willetts and Eames, 1987.
9. Nielbo et al., 2017.
10. McCarty et al., 2017.
11. Neave et al., 2010.
12. Montepare and Zebrowitz, 1993; Fink et al., 2014.
13. Slone, 2008.
14. Bulbulia et al., 2015.
15. Kelley, 1972.
16. Iannaccone, 1994.
17. Young, 1965.
18. Sosis, Kress and Boster, 2007.
19. Cimino, 2011.
20. Burns, 2017.
21. Xygalatas et al., 2021.
22. Power, 2017a.
23. Power, 2017b.
24. Ruffle and Sosis, 2007.
25. Soler, 2012.
26. Xygalatas et al., 2017.
27. Power, 2018.
28. Sosis and Bressler, 2003.
29. Henrich, 2015.
30. Henrich and Henrich, 2007.
31. Henrich, 2009.
32. Norenzayan, 2013.
33. Festinger, Riecken and Schachter, 1956.

34. Inzlicht, Shenhav and Olivola, 2018.
35. Bloom, 2021.
36. Bem, 1967.
37. Rappaport, 1999, p. 118.
38. Evans-Pritchard, 1937.
39. Rappaport, 1999.
40. Xygalatas and Mano, forthcoming.

8. Well-being
1. Singh et al., 2020.
2. Snodgrass, Most and Upadhyay, 2017.
3. Zahran et al., 2015.
4. Bulbulia et al., 2013.
5. Xygalatas et al., 2019.
6. Klement et al., 2017.
7. Memish et al., 2012.
8. Tewari et al., 2012.
9. Tian et al., 2018.
10. Wood, 2016.
11. McCullough and Willoughby, 2009.
12. Ozbay et al., 2007.
13. Liu, Gou and Zuo, 2014.
14. Kjaer et al., 2002.
15. Newberg and Waldman, 2010.
16. Fischer et al., 2014.
17. McClenon, 1997.
18. Cannon, 1942.
19. Maltz, 1960.
20. Lester, 2009.
21. McCullough et al., 2000.
22. Bloom, 2021, p. 4.

9. Harnessing the Power of Ritual
1. Bentzen, 2020.

2. Štrkalj and Pather, 2017.
3. Pawlina et al., 2011.
4. Shev et al., 2020.
5. Harvey, 2016.
6. OECD, 2020.
7. de Castro and de Castro, 1989; Boothby, Clark and Bargh, 2014; Liberman et al., 2016; Miller, Rozin and Fiske, 1998; Woolley and Fishbach, 2017; Woolley and Fishbach, 2018.
8. Ozenc and Hagan, 2017.
9. Kim et al., 2021.
10. Bell, 1992.
11. Deacon, 1997.
12. Inglehart, 2020.

BIBLIOGRAPHY

Amin, M., Willetts, D., and Eames, J. (1987). *The Last of the Maasai*. London: Bodley Head.

Anastasi, M. W., and Newberg, A. B. (2008). A preliminary study of the acute effects of religious ritual on anxiety. *Journal of Alternative and Complementary Medicine* 14(2), 163–165.

Archer, John (1999). *The Nature of Grief: The Evolution and Psychology of Reactions to Loss*. London: Routledge.

Aronson, E., and Mills, J. (1959). The effect of severity of initiation on liking for a group. *The Journal of Abnormal and Social Psychology* 59(2), 177–181.

Atkinson, Q., and Whitehouse, H. (2011). The cultural morphospace of ritual form. *Evolution and Human Behaviour* 32(1), 50–62.

Baranowski-Pinto, G., Profeta, V. L. S., Newson, M., Whitehouse, H., and Xygalatas, D. (2022). Being in a crowd bonds people via physiological synchrony. *Scientific Reports* 12: 613.

Bekoff, M. (2009). Animal emotions, wild justice and why they matter: Grieving magpies, a pissy baboon, and empathic elephants. *Emotion, Space and Society* 2(2), 82–85.

Bell, Catherine (1992). *Ritual Theory, Ritual Practice*. Oxford: Oxford University Press.

Bellah, Robert N. (2011). *Religion in Human Evolution: From the Paleolithic to the Axial Age*. Cambridge, MA: Harvard University Press.

Bem, D. J. (1967). Self-Perception: An alternative interpretation of cognitive dissonance phenomena. *Psychological Review* 74, 183–200.

Bentzen, J. S. (2020). *In Crisis, We Pray: Religiosity and the COVID-19 Pandemic*. London: Centre for Economic Policy Research.

Bernieri, F., Reznick, J., and Rosenthal, R. (1988). Synchrony, pseudosynchrony, and dissynchrony: Measuring the entrainment process in mother–infant interactions. *Journal of Personality and Social Psychology* 54(2), 243–253.

Biesele, M. (1978). Religion and folklore. In P. V. Tobias (ed.), *The Bushmen*. Cape Town: Human & Rousseau.

Bleak, J. L., and Frederick, C. M. (1998). Superstitious behavior in sport: levels of effectiveness and determinants of use in three collegiate sports. *Journal of Sport Behavior* 21(1), 1–15.

Bloom, Paul (2021). *The Sweet Spot*. New York: HarperCollins.

Bocquet-Appel, J.-P. (2011). The agricultural demographic transition during and after the agriculture inventions. *Current Anthropology* 52(S4), S497–S510.

Boothby, E. J., Clark, M. S., and Bargh, J. A. (2014). Shared experiences are amplified. *Psychological Science* 25(12), 2209–2216.

Boyer, Pascal (2005). A reductionistic model of distinct modes of religious transmission. In H. Whitehouse and R. N. McCauley (eds), *Mind and Religion: Psychological and Cognitive Foundations of Religiosity*. Walnut Creek, CA: AltaMira Press.

Boyer, P., and Liénard, P. (2006). Why ritualized behavior? Precaution systems and action parsing in developmental, pathological and cultural rituals. *Behavioral and Brain Sciences* 29, 595–650.

Brenner, S. L., Jones, J. P., Rutanen-Whaley, R. H., Parker, W., Flinn, M. V., and Muehlenbein, M. P. (2015). Evolutionary mismatch and chronic psychological stress. *Journal of Evolutionary Medicine* 3, 1–11.

Brevers, D., Dan, B., Noel, X., and Nils, F. (2011). Sport superstition: Mediation of psychological tension on non-professional sportsmen's superstitious rituals. *Journal of Sport Behavior* 34(1), 3–24.

Brooks, A. W., Schroeder, J., Risen, J. L., Gino, F., Galinsky, A. D., Norton, M. I., and Schweitzer, M. E. (2016). Don't stop believing: Rituals improve performance by decreasing anxiety. *Organizational Behavior and Human Decision Processes* 137, 71–85.

Buhrmester, M. D., Zeitlyn, D., and Whitehouse, H. (2020). Ritual, fusion, and conflict: The roots of agro-pastoral violence in rural Cameroon. *Group Processes & Intergroup Relations*, 1368430220959705.

Bulbulia, J., Xygalatas, D., Schjødt, U., Fondevila, S., Sibley, C., and Konvalinka, I. (2013). Images from a jointly-arousing collective ritual reveal emotional polarization. *Frontiers in Psychology* 4, 960.

Bulbulia, J., Shaver, J. H., Greaves, L., Sosis, R., and Sibley, C. (2015). Religion and parental cooperation: An empirical test of Slone's sexual signaling model. In J. Slone and J. Van Slyke (eds), *The Attraction of Religion*. London: Bloomsbury.

Burns, James (dir.) (2017). *Inside a Gang Initiation with the Silent Murder Crips*. Vice video.

Cannon, Walter B. (1942). Voodoo death. *American Anthropologist* 44(2), 169–181.

Chang, Z., and Li, J. (2018). The impact of in-house unnatural death on property values: Evidence from Hong Kong. *Regional Science and Urban Economics* 73, 112–126.

Chartrand, T., and Bargh, J. (1999). The chameleon effect: The perception–behaviour link and social interaction. *Journal of Personality and Social Psychology* 6(76), 893–910.

Cimino, A. (2011). The evolution of hazing: Motivational mechanisms and the abuse of newcomers. *Journal of Cognition and Culture* 11, 241–267.

Clegg, J. M., and Legare, C. H. (2016). Instrumental and conventional interpretations of behavior are associated with distinct outcomes in early childhood. *Child Development* 87, 527–542.

Csikszentmihalyi, Mihaly (1990). *Flow: The Psychology of Optimal Experience*. New York: Harper & Row.

Dal Pesco, F., and Fischer, J. (2018). Greetings in male Guinea baboons and the function of rituals in complex social groups. *Journal of Human Evolution* 125, 87–89.

Damisch, L., Stoberock, B., and Mussweiler, T. (2010). Keep your fingers crossed! How superstition improves performance. *Psychological Science* 21(7), 1014–1020.

Darwin, C. (1871). *The Descent of Man and Selection in Relation to Sex*. London: John Murray.

Darwin Correspondence Project, 'Letter no. 2743', http://www.darwinproject.ac.uk/DCP-LETT-2743 [accessed on 23 October 2021].

de Castro, J. M., and de Castro, E. S. (1989). Spontaneous meal patterns of humans: Influence of the presence of other people. *The American Journal of Clinical Nutrition* 50, 237–247.

de Waal, Frans (1996). *Good Natured: The Origins of Right and Wrong in Humans and Other Animals*. Cambridge, MA: Harvard University Press.

Deacon, Terrence (1997). *The Symbolic Species: The Co-Evolution of Language and the Brain*. New York: Norton & Co.

Delfabbro, P. H., and Winefeld, A. H. (2000). Predictors of irrational thinking in regular slot machine gamblers. *Journal of Psychology: Interdisciplinary and Applied* 134(2), 117–128.

Dissanayake, Ellen (1988). *What Is Art For?* Seattle, WA: University of Washington Press.

Dömötör, Z., Ruíz-Barquín, R., and Szabo, A. (2016). Superstitious behavior in sport: A literature review. *Scandinavian Journal of Psychology* 57(4), 368–382.

Dulaney, S., and Fiske, A. (1994). Cultural rituals and

obsessive–compulsive disorder: Is there a common psychological mechanism? *Ethos* 3, 243–283.

Dunbar, R. (2012). Bridging the bonding gap: The transition from primates to humans. *Philosophical Transactions of The Royal Society B (Biological Sciences)* 367(1597), 1837–1846.

Durkheim, Émile (1915). *The Elementary Forms of the Religious Life*. London: Allen & Unwin.

Evans, D. W., Milanak, M. E., Medeiros, B., and Ross, J. L. (2002). Magical beliefs and rituals in young children. *Child Psychiatry and Human Development* 33(1), 43–58.

Evans-Pritchard, E. E. (1937). *Witchcraft, Oracles, and Magic among the Azande*. Oxford: Clarendon Press.

Evans-Pritchard, Edward (1951). *Social Anthropology*. London: Cohen & West.

Fairlie, R. W., Hoffmann, F., and Oreopoulos, P. (2014). A community college instructor like me: Race and ethnicity interactions in the classroom. *American Economic Review* 104(8), 2567–2591.

Festinger, Leon, Riecken, Henry W., and Schachter, Stanley (1956). *When Prophecy Fails: A Social and Psychological Study of a Modern Group that Predicted the Destruction of the World*. Minneapolis, MN: University of Minnesota Press.

Fink B., Weege B., Neave N., Ried B., and do Lago, O. C. (2014). Female perceptions of male body movement. In V. Weekes-Shackelford and T. K. Shackelford (eds), *Evolutionary Perspectives on Human Sexual Psychology and Behavior*. Berlin: Springer.

Fischer, R., et al. (2014). The fire-walker's high: affect and physiological responses in an extreme collective ritual. *PLOS ONE* 9, e88355.

Fisher, R. A. (1930). *The Genetical Theory of Natural Selection*. Oxford: Clarendon Press.

Fiske, A., and Haslam, N. (1997). Is obsessive–compulsive disorder a pathology of the human disposition to perform socially meaningful rituals? Evidence of similar content. *The Journal of Nervous and Mental Disease* 185, 211–222.

Flanagan, E. (2013). Superstitious Ritual in Sport and the Competitive Anxiety Response in Elite and Non–Elite Athletes. Unpublished dissertation, DBS eSource, Dublin Business School.

Foster, D. J., Weigand, D. A., and Baines, D. (2006). The effect of removing superstitious behavior and introducing a pre-performance routine on basketball free-throw performance. *Journal of Applied Sport Psychology* 18, 167–171.

Frazer, J. G. (1890). *The Golden Bough: A Study in Comparative Religion*. London: Macmillan.

Gayton, W. F., Cielinski, K. L., Francis-Keniston, W. J., and Hearns, J. F. (1989). Effects of preshot routine on free-throw shooting. *Perceptual and Motor Skills* 68, 317–318.

Gerard, H. B., and Mathewson, G. C. (1966). The effect of severity of initiation on liking for a group: A replication. *Journal of Experimental Social Psychology* 2(3), 278–287.

Gmelch, G. (1978). Baseball magic. *Human Nature* 1(8), 32–39.

Gómez, Á., Bélanger, J. J., Chinchilla, J., Vázquez, A., Schumpe, B. M., Nisa, C. F., and Chiclana, S. (2021). Admiration for Islamist groups encourages self-sacrifice through identity fusion. *Humanities and Social Sciences Communications* 8(1), 54.

Goodall, J. (2005). Primate spirituality. In B. Taylor (ed.), *The Encyclopedia of Religion and Nature*. New York: Thoemmes Continuum.

Gray, Jesse G. (1959). *The Warriors*. Lincoln, NE: University of Nebraska Press.

Handwerk, Brian (2003). Snake handlers hang on in Appalachian churches. *National Geographic News*, 7 April.

Harrod, J. B. (2014). The case for chimpanzee religion. *Journal for the Study of Religion, Nature and Culture* 8(1), 16–25.

Harvey, Larry (2016). *Burning Man 2017: Radical Ritual*. https://

journal.burningman.org/2016/12/black-rock-city/participate-in-brc/burning-man-2017-radical-ritual/ [accessed on 20 September 2020].

Henrich, Joseph (2009). The evolution of costly displays, cooperation and religion. *Evolution and Human Behavior* 30(4), 244–260.

Henrich, Joseph (2015). *The Secret of Our Success: How Culture Is Driving Human Evolution, Domesticating Our Species, and Making Us Smarter*. Princeton, NJ: Princeton University Press.

Henrich, N. S., and Henrich, J. (2007). *Why Humans Cooperate: A Cultural and Evolutionary Explanation*. Oxford: Oxford University Press.

Henslin, J. (1967). Craps and magic. *American Journal of Sociology* 73, 316–330.

Herrmann, P. A., Legare, C. H., Harris, P. L., and Whitehouse, H. (2013). Stick to the script: The effect of witnessing multiple actors on children's imitation. *Cognition* 129(3), 536–543.

Hockey, G. R. J. (1997). Compensatory control in the regulation of human performance under stress and high workload: A cognitive–energetical framework. *Biological Psychology* 45, 73–93.

Homans, G. C. (1941). Anxiety and ritual: The theories of Malinowski and Radcliffe-Brown. *American Anthropologist* 43(2), 164–172.

Horner, V., and Whiten, A. (2004). Causal knowledge and imitation/emulation switching in chimpanzees (*Pan troglodytes*) and children (*Homo sapiens*). *Animal Cognition* 8(3), 164–181.

Hove, M., and Risen, J. (2009). It's all in the timing: Interpersonal synchrony increases affiliation. *Social Cognition* 27(6).

Iannaccone, L. (1994). Why strict churches are strong. *American Journal of Sociology* 99(5), 1180–1211.

Inglehart, R. F. (2020). Giving up on God: The global decline of religion. *Foreign Affairs* 99, 110.

Inzlicht, M., Shenhav, A., and Olivola, C. Y. (2018). The effort paradox: Effort is both costly and valued. *Trends in Cognitive Sciences* 22(4), 337–349.

Jaubert, J., Verheyden, S., Genty, D., Soulier, M., Cheng, H., Blamart, D., Burlet, C., Camus, H., Delaby, S., Deldicque, D., Edwards, R. L., Ferrier, C., Lacrampe-Cuyaubère, F., Lévêque, F., Maksud, F., Mora, P., Muth, X., Régnier, É., Rouzaud, J.-N., and Santos, F. (2016). Early Neanderthal constructions deep in Bruniquel Cave in southwestern France. *Nature* 534(7605), 111–114.

Jonaitis, A. (1991). *Chiefly Feasts: The Enduring Kwakiutl Potlatch*. Seattle, WA: University of Washington Press.

Joukhador, J., Blaszczynski, A., and Maccallum, F. (2004). Superstitious beliefs in gambling among problem and non-problem gamblers: Preliminary data. *Journal of Gambling Studies* 20(2), 171–180.

Kapitány, R., and Nielsen, M. (2015). Adopting the ritual stance: The role of opacity and context in ritual and everyday actions. *Cognition* 145, 13–29.

Keinan, G. (1994). Effects of stress and tolerance of ambiguity on magical thinking. *Journal of Personality and Social Psychology* 67, 48–55.

Keinan, G. (2002). The effects of stress and desire for control on superstitious behavior. *Personality and Social Psychology Bulletin* 28(1), 102–108.

Kelley, Dean M. (1972). *Why Conservative Churches Are Growing: A Study in Sociology of Religion*. New York: Harper & Row.

Kim, T., et al. (2021). Work group rituals enhance the meaning of work. *Organizational Behaviour and Human Decision Processes* 165, 197–212.

Kjaer T. W., Bertelsen, C., Piccini, P., Brooks, D., Alving, J., and Lou, H. C. (2002). Increased dopamine tone during meditation-induced change of consciousness. *Cognitive Brain Research* 13(2), 255–259.

Klavir, R., and Leiser, D. (2002). When astronomy, biology, and culture converge: Children's conceptions about birthdays. *The Journal of Genetic Psychology* 163(2), 239–253.

Klement, Kathryn R., Lee, Ellen M. Ambler, James K., Hanson, Sarah A., Comber, Evelyn, Wietting, David, Wagner, Michael F., et al. (2017). Extreme rituals in a BDSM context: The physiological and psychological effects of the 'dance of souls'. *Culture, Health & Sexuality* 19(4), 453–469.

Knight, C. (1994). Ritual and the origins of language. In C. Knight and C. Power (eds), *Ritual and the Origins of Symbolism.* London: University of East London Sociology Department.

Konvalinka, I., Xygalatas, D., Bulbulia, J., Schjødt, U., Jegindø, E., Wallot, S., Van Orden, G., and Roepstorff, A. (2011). Synchronized arousal between performers and related spectators in a fire-walking ritual. *Proceedings of the National Academy of Sciences (PNAS)* 108(20), 8514–8519.

Kühl, H. S., Kalan, A. K., Arandjelovic, M., Aubert, F., D'Auvergne, L., Goedmakers, A., Jones, S., Kehoe, L., Regnaut, S., Tickle, A., Ton, E., Schijndel, J. van, Abwe, E. E., Angedakin, S., Agbor, A., Ayimisin, E. A., Bailey, E., Bessone, M., Bonnet, M., and Boesch, C. (2016). Chimpanzee accumulative stone throwing. *Scientific Reports* 6(1), 22219.

Lang, M., Kratky, J., Shaver, J. H., Jerotijević, D., and Xygalatas, D. (2015). Effects of anxiety on spontaneous ritualized behavior. *Current Biology* 25(14), 1892–1897.

Lang, M., Bahna, V., Shaver, J., Reddish, P., and Xygalatas, D. (2017). Sync to link: Endorphin-Mediated synchrony effects on cooperation. *Biological Psychology* 127, 191–197.

Lang, M., Krátký, J., Shaver, J., Jerotijević, D., and Xygalatas, D. (2019). Is ritual behavior a response to anxiety? In J. Slone and W. McCorkle, *The Cognitive Science of Religion: A Methodological Introduction to Key Empirical Studies.* London: Bloomsbury.

Lang, M., Krátký, J., and Xygalatas, D. (2020). The role of ritual behaviour in anxiety reduction: An investigation of Marathi religious practices in Mauritius. *Philosophical Transactions of the Royal Society B (Biological Sciences)* 375, 20190431.

Larsen, C. S. (2006). The agricultural revolution as environmental catastrophe: Implications for health and lifestyle in the Holocene. *Quaternary International* 150(1), 12–20.

Legare, C. H., and Souza, A. L. (2012). Evaluating ritual efficacy: Evidence from the supernatural. *Cognition* 124(1), 1–15.

Legare, C. H., and Souza, A. L. (2013). Searching for control: Priming randomness increases the evaluation of ritual efficacy. *Cognitive Science* 38(1), 152–161.

Legare, C. H., and Nielsen, M. (2015). Imitation and innovation: The dual engines of cultural learning. *Trends in Cognitive Sciences* 19(11), 688–699.

Legare, C. H., Wen, N. J., Herrmann, P. A., and Whitehouse, H. (2015). Imitative flexibility and the development of cultural learning. *Cognition* 142, 351–361.

Lester, D. (2009). Voodoo death. *OMEGA Journal of Death and Dying* 59, 1–18.

Liberman, Z., Woodward, A. L., Sullivan, K. R., and Kinzler, K. D. (2016). Early emerging system for reasoning about the social nature of food. *Proceedings of the National Academy of Sciences* 113(34), 9480–9485.

Liberman, Z., Kinzler, K. D., and Woodward, A. L. (2018). The early social significance of shared ritual actions. *Cognition* 171, 42–51.

Liu, L., Gou, Z., and Zuo, J. (2014). Social support mediates loneliness and depression in elderly people. *Journal of Health Psychology* 21(5), 750–758.

Lyons, D. E., Damrosch, D. H., Lin, J. K., Macris, D. M., and Keil, F. C. (2011). The scope and limits of overimitation in the transmission of artefact culture. *Philosophical Transactions of the Royal Society B: Biological Sciences* 366(1567), 1158–1167.

Madden, J. R. (2008). Do bowerbirds exhibit cultures? *Animal Cognition* 11(1), 1–12.

Malinowski, Bronislaw (1922). *Argonauts of the Western Pacific.* London: Routledge.

Malinowski, Bronislaw (1948). *Magic, Science and Religion and Other Essays 1948.* Boston, MA: Beacon Press.

Maltz, Maxwell (1960). *Psycho-Cybernetics.* New York: Simon & Schuster.

Mauss, M. (1990 [1922]). *The Gift: Forms and Functions of Exchange in Archaic Societies.* London: Routledge.

McCarty, K., Darwin, H., Cornelissen, P., Saxton, T., Tovée, M., Caplan, N., and Neave, N. (2017). Optimal asymmetry and other motion parameters that characterise high-quality female dance. *Scientific Reports* 7(1), 42435.

McCauley, Robert N., and Lawson, Thomas (2002). *Bringing Ritual to Mind: Psychological Foundations of Cultural Forms.* Cambridge: Cambridge University Press.

McClenon, J. (1997). Shamanic healing, human evolution, and the origin of religion. *Journal for the Scientific Study of Religion* 36(3), 345.

McCormick, A. (2010). Infant mortality and child-naming: A genealogical exploration of American trends. *Journal of Public and Professional Sociology* 3(1).

McCullough, M. E., Hoyt, W. T., Larson, D. B., Koenig, H. G., and Thoresen, C. (2000). Religious involvement and mortality: A meta-analytic review. *Health Psychology* 19(3), 211–222.

McCullough, M. E., and Willoughby, B. L. B. (2009). Religion, self-regulation, and self-control: Associations, explanations, and implications. *Psychological Bulletin* 135, 69–93.

McElreath, R., Boyd, R., and Richerson, P. J. (2003). Shared norms and the evolution of ethnic markers. *Current Anthropology* 44, 122–130.

McGuigan, N., Makinson, J., and Whiten, A. (2011). From over-imitation to super-copying: Adults imitate causally irrelevant aspects of tool use with higher fidelity than young children. *British Journal of Psychology* 102(1), 1–18.

Meggitt, M. J. (1966). Gadjari among the Walbiri aborigines of central Australia. *Oceania* 36, 283–315.

Memish, Z. A., Stephens, G. M., Steffen, R., and Ahmed, Q. A. (2012). Emergence of medicine for mass gatherings: Lessons from the hajj. *Lancet Infectious Diseases* 12(1), 56–65.

Meredith, M. (2004). *Elephant Destiny: Biography of an Endangered Species in Africa*. Canada: PublicAffairs.

Miller, L., Rozin, P., and Fiske, A. P. (1998). Food sharing and feeding another person suggest intimacy: Two studies of American college students. *European Journal of Social Psychology* 28, 423–436.

Montepare, J. M., and Zebrowitz, L. A. (1993). A cross-cultural comparison of impressions created by age-related variations in gait. *Journal of Nonverbal Behavior* 17, 55–68.

Nadal, R., and Carlin, J. (2011). *Rafa: My Story*. London: Sphere.

Neave, N., McCarty, K., Freynik, J., Caplan, N., Hönekopp, J., and Fink, B. (2010). Male dance moves that catch a woman's eye. *Biology Letters* 7(2), 221–224.

Nemeroff, C., and Rozin, P. (1994). The contagion concept in adult thinking in the United States: Transmission of germs and interpersonal influence. *Ethos* 22, 158–186.

Newberg, A., and Waldman, M. R. (2010). *How God Changes Your Brain*. New York: Ballantine Books.

Newson, M., Bortolini, T., Buhrmester, M., da Silva, S. R., da Aquino, J. N. Q., and Whitehouse, H. (2018). Brazil's football warriors: Social bonding and inter-group violence. *Evolution and Human Behavior* 39(6), 675–683.

Nielbo, K. L., and Sørensen, J. (2011). Spontaneous processing of functional and non-functional action sequences. *Religion, Brain & Behavior* 1(1), 18–30.

Nielbo, K. L., Schjoedt, U., and Sørensen, J. (2012). Hierarchical organization of segmentation in non-functional action sequences. *Journal for the Cognitive Science of Religion* 1, 71–97.

Nielbo, K. L., Michal, F., Mort, J. Zamir, R., and Eilam, D. (2017). Structural differences among individuals, genders and generations as the key for ritual transmission, stereotypy and flexibility. *Behaviour* 154, 93–114.

Nielsen, M. (2018). The social glue of cumulative culture and ritual behavior. *Child Development Perspectives* 12, 264–268.

Nielsen, M., Kapitány, R., and Elkins, R. (2015). The perpetuation of ritualistic actions as revealed by young children's transmission of normative behavior. *Evolution and Human Behavior* 36(3), 191–198.

Nielsen, M., Tomaselli, K., and Kapitány, R. (2018). The influence of goal demotion on children's reproduction of ritual behavior. *Evolution and Human Behavior* 39, 343–348.

Norenzayan, Ara (2013). *Big Gods: How Religion Transformed Cooperation and Conflict.* Princeton, NJ: Princeton University Press.

Norton, M. I., and Gino, F. (2014). Rituals alleviate grieving for loved ones, lovers, and lotteries. *Journal of Experimental Psychology: General* 143(1), 266–272.

OECD (2020). *Hours Worked (Indicator).* doi: 10.1787/47be1c78-en [accessed on 13 September 2020].

Over, H., and Carpenter, M. (2009). Priming third-party ostracism increases affiliative imitation in children. *Developmental Science* 12, F1–F8.

Over, H., and Carpenter, M. (2012). Putting the social into social learning: Explaining both selectivity and fidelity in children's copying behavior. *Journal of Comparative Psychology*, 126(2), 182.

Ozbay, F., Johnson, D., Dimoulas, E., Morgan, C., Charney, D., and Southwick, S. (2007). Social support and resilience to stress: From neurobiology to clinical practice. *Psychiatry* 4(5), 35–40.

Ozenc, F., and Hagan, Margaret (2017). Ritual design: Crafting team rituals for meaningful organizational change. *Advances in Intelligent Systems and Computing: Proceedings of the Applied*

Human Factors and Ergonomics International Conference.
New York: Springer Press.

Park, J. H., Schaller, M., and Vugt, M. V. (2007). Psychology of
human kin recognition: Heuristic cues, erroneous inferences,
and their implications. *Review of General Psychology* 12,
215–235.

Pawlina, W., Hammer, R. R., Strauss, J. D., Heath, S. G., Zhao, K.
D., Sahota, S., Regnier, T. D., et al. (2011). The hand that gives
the rose. *Mayo Clinic Proceedings* 86(2), 139–144.

Perrot, C., et al. (2016). Sexual display complexity varies non-
linearly with age and predicts breeding status in greater
flamingos. *Nature Scientific Reports* 6, 36242.

Poole, J. (1996). *Coming of Age with Elephants*. Chicago, IL:
Trafalgar Square.

Power, E. A. (2017a). Discerning devotion: Testing the signaling
theory of religion. *Evolution and Human Behavior* 38(1),
82–91.

Power, E. A. (2017b). Social support networks and religiosity in
rural South India. *Nature Human Behaviour* 1(3), 1–6.

Power, E. (2018). Collective ritual and social support networks
in rural South India. *Proceedings of the Royal Society B
(Biological Sciences)* 285, 20180023.

Rakoczy, H., Warneken, F., and Tomasello, M. (2008). The sources
of normativity: Young children's awareness of the normative
structure of games. *Developmental Psychology* 44(3), 875–881.

Rappaport, Roy (1999). *Ritual and Religion in the Making of
Humanity*, Cambridge: Cambridge University Press.

Reddish, P., Fischer, R., and Bulbulia, J. (2013). Let's dance
together: Synchrony, shared intentionality and cooperation.
PLOS ONE 8(8), e71182.

Reggente, M. A. L., Alves, F., Nicolau, C., Freitas, L., Cagnazzi, D.,
Baird, R. W., and Galli, P. (2016). Nurturant behavior toward
dead conspecifics in free-ranging mammals: New records for

odontocetes and a general review. *Journal of Mammalogy* 97(5), 1428–1434.

Rielly, R. J. (2000). Confronting the tiger: Small unit cohesion in battle. *Military Review* 80, 61–65.

Rossano, M. J. (2006). The religious mind and the evolution of religion. *Review of General Psychology* 10(4), 346–364.

Rossano, Matt J. (2010). *Supernatural Selection: How Religion Evolved*. Oxford: Oxford University Press.

Ruffle, B., and Sosis, R. (2007). Does it pay to pray? Costly ritual and cooperation. *The B. E. Journal of Economic Analysis & Policy* 7(1), article 18.

Sahlins, M. D. (1963). Poor man, rich man, big-man, chief: Political types in Melanesia and Polynesia. *Comparative Studies in Society and History* 5(3), 285–303.

Sahlins, M. (1968). Notes on the original affluent society. In R. B. Lee and I. DeVore (eds), *Man the Hunter*. New York: Routledge.

Sahlins, Marshall (1972). *Stone Age Economics*. Chicago, IL: Aldine.

Schachner, A., and Carey, S. (2013). Reasoning about 'irrational' actions: When intentional movements cannot be explained, the movements themselves are seen as the goal. *Cognition* 129(2), 309–327.

Schippers, M. C., and Van Lange, P. A. M. (2006). The psychological benefits of superstitious rituals in top sport: A study among top sportspersons. *Journal of Applied Social Psychology* 36(10), 2532–2553.

Schmidt, Justin O. (2016). *The Sting of the Wild*. Baltimore, MD: Johns Hopkins University Press.

Scott, James. (2017). *Against the Grain: A Deep History of the Earliest States*. New Haven, CT, and London: Yale University Press.

Shaver, J. H., Lang, M., Krátký, J., Klocová, E. K., Kundt, R., and Xygalatas, D. (2018). The boundaries of trust: Cross-religious and cross-ethnic field experiments in Mauritius. *Evolutionary Psychology* 16(4), 1474704918817644.

Shev, A. B., DeVaul, D. L., Beaulieu-Prévost, D., Heller, S. M., and the 2019 Census Lab. (2020). *Black Rock City Census: 2013–2019 Population Analysis*. Black Rock, NE: Black Rock City Census.

Singh, P., Tewari, S., Kesberg, R., Karl, J., Bulbulia, J., and Fischer, R. (2020). Time investments in rituals are associated with social bonding, affect and subjective health: A longitudinal study of Diwali in two Indian communities. *Philosophical Transactions of the Royal Society B: Biological Sciences* 375(1805), 20190430.

Skinner, B. F. (1948). 'Superstition' in the pigeon. *Journal of Experimental Psychology* 121(3), 273–274.

Slone, J. (2008). The attraction of religion: A sexual selectionist account. In J. Bulbulia, R. Sosis, E. Harris, R. Genet, C. Genet and K. Wyman (eds), *The Evolution of Religion*. Santa Margarita, CA: Collins Foundation Press.

Snodgrass, J., Most, D., and Upadhyay, C. (2017). Religious ritual is good medicine for indigenous Indian conservation refugees: Implications for global mental health. *Current Anthropology* 58(2), 257–284.

Soler, M. (2012). Costly signaling, ritual and cooperation: Evidence from Candomblé, an Afro-Brazilian religion. *Evolution and Human Behavior* 33(4), 346–356.

Sosis, R. (2007). Psalms for safety. *Current Anthropology* 48(6), 903–911.

Sosis, R., and Bressler, E. (2003). Cooperation and commune longevity: A test of the costly signaling theory of religion. *Cross-Cultural Research* 37(2), 211–239.

Sosis, R., Kress, H., and Boster, J. (2007). Scars for war: Evaluating alternative signaling explanations for cross-cultural variance in ritual costs. *Evolution and Human Behavior* 28, 234–247.

Sosis, R., and Handwerker, P. (2011). Psalms and coping with uncertainty. *American Anthropologist* 113(1), 40–55.

Stein, D., Schroeder, J., Hobson, N., Gino, F., and Norton, M. I. (2021). When alterations are violations: Moral outrage and punishment in response to (even minor) alterations to rituals. *Journal of Personality and Social Psychology.* doi: 10.1037/pspi0000352.

Štrkalj, Goran, and Pather, Nalini (eds) (2017). *Commemorations and Memorials: Exploring the Human Face of Anatomy,* Singapore: World Scientific Publishing Co.

Swann, W. B., Gómez, A., Seyle, D. C., Morales, J. F., and Huici, C. (2009). Identity fusion: The interplay of personal and social identities in extreme group behavior. *Journal of Personality and Social Psychology* 96(5), 995–1011.

Swann, W. B., Gómez, A., Huici, C., Morales, J. F., and Hixon, J. G. (2010). Identity fusion and self-sacrifice: Arousal as a catalyst of pro-group fighting, dying, and helping behavior. *Journal of Personality and Social Psychology* 99(5), 824–841.

Tajfel, H. (1970). Experiments in intergroup discrimination. *Scientific American* 223, 96–102.

Tewari, S., Khan, S., Hopkins, N., Srinivasan, N., and Reicher, S. (2012). Participation in mass gatherings can benefit well-being: Longitudinal and control data from a North Indian Hindu pilgrimage event. *PLOS ONE* 7(10), e47291.

Tian, A. D., Schroeder, J., Häubl, G., Risen, J. L., Norton, M. I., and Gino, F. (2018). Enacting rituals to improve self-control. *Journal of Personality and Social Psychology* 114, 851–876.

Todd, M., and Brown, C. (2003). Characteristics associated with superstitious behavior in track and field athletes: Are there NCAA divisional level differences? *Journal of Sport Behavior* 26(2), 168–187.

Udupa, K., Sathyaprabha, T. N., Thirthalli, J., Kishore, K. R.,

Lavekar, G. S., Raju, T. R., and Gangadhar, B. N. (2007). Alteration of cardiac autonomic functions in patients with major depression: A study using heart rate variability measures. *Journal of Affective Disorders* 100, 137–141.

van Leeuwen, E. J. C., Cronin, K. A., Haun, D. B. M., Mundry, R., and Bodamer, M. D. (2012). Neighbouring chimpanzee communities show different preferences in social grooming behaviour. *Proceedings of the Royal Society B: Biological Sciences* 279(1746), 4362–4367.

Veblen, Thorstein (1899). *The Theory of the Leisure Class: An Economic Study in the Evolution of Institutions*. London: George Allen.

Wagner, G. A., and Morris, E. K. (1987). 'Superstitious' behavior in children. *The Psychological Record* 37 (4), 471–488.

Walker, C. J. (2010). Experiencing flow: Is doing it together better than doing it alone? *The Journal of Positive Psychology* 5(1), 3–11.

Watson, T. (2016). Whales mourn their dead, just like us. *National Geographic*, 18 July.

Watson-Jones, R., Whitehouse, H., and Legare, C. (2015). In-Group ostracism increases high-fidelity imitation in early childhood. *Psychological Science* 27(1), 34–42.

Wayne, H. (1985). Bronislaw Malinowski: The influence of various women on his life and works. *American Ethnologist* 12(3), 529–540.

Wen, N., Herrmann, P., and Legare, C. (2016). Ritual increases children's affiliation with in-group members. *Evolution and Human Behaviour* 37(1), 54–60.

Wen, N. J., Willard, A. K., Caughy, M., and Legare, C. H. (2020). Watch me, watch you: Ritual participation increases in-group displays and out-group monitoring in children. *Philosophical Transactions of the Royal Society B (Biological Sciences)* 375(1805), 20190437.

Whitehouse, H. (1996). Rites of terror: Emotion, metaphor and memory in Melanesian initiation cults. *The Journal of the Royal Anthropological Institute* 2, 703–715.

Whitehouse, H. (2004). *Modes of Religiosity*. Walnut Creek, CA: Altamira.

Whitehouse, H. (2018). Dying for the group: Towards a general theory of extreme self-sacrifice. *Behavioral and Brain Sciences* 41, e192.

Whitehouse, H., and Lanman, J. A. (2014). The ties that bind us. *Current Anthropology* 55(6), 674–695.

Whitson, J. A., and Galinsky, A. D. (2008). Lacking control increases illusory pattern perception. *Science* 322(5898), 115–117.

Wilks, M., Kapitány, R., and Nielsen, M. (2016). Preschool children's learning proclivities: When the ritual stance trumps the instrumental stance. *British Journal of Developmental Psychology* 34(3), 402–414.

Wiltermuth, S., and Heath, C. (2009). Synchrony and cooperation. *Psychological Science* 20(1), 1–5.

Wood, C. (2016). Ritual well-being: Toward a social signaling model of religion and mental health. *Religion, Brain & Behavior* 7(3), 262–265.

Woolley, J. D., and Rhoads, A. M. (2017). Now I'm 3: Young children's concepts of age, aging, and birthdays. *Imagination, Cognition and Personality* 38(3), 268–289.

Woolley, K., and Fishbach, A. (2017). A recipe for friendship: Similar food consumption promotes trust and cooperation. *Journal of Consumer Psychology* 27, 1–10.

Woolley, K., and Fishbach, A. (2018). Shared plates, shared minds: Consuming from a shared plate promotes cooperation. *Psychological Science* 30(4), 541–552.

Wright, P. B., and Erdal, K. J. (2008). Sport superstition as a function of skill level and task difficulty. *Journal of Sport Behavior* 31(2), 187–199.

Xygalatas, D. (2007). *Firewalking in Northern Greece: A cognitive approach to high-arousal rituals*. Doctoral dissertation. Queen's University Belfast.

Xygalatas, D. (2012). *The Burning Saints: Cognition and Culture in the Fire-walking Rituals of the Anastenaria*. London: Routledge.

Xygalatas, D. (2014). The biosocial basis of collective effervescence: An experimental anthropological study of a fire-walking ritual. *Fieldwork in Religion* 9(1), 53–67.

Xygalatas, D., Konvalinka, I., Roepstorff, A., and Bulbulia, J. (2011). Quantifying collective effervescence: Heart-rate dynamics at a fire-walking ritual. *Communicative & Integrative Biology* 4(6), 735–738.

Xygalatas, D., Schjødt, U., Bulbulia, J., Konvalinka, I., Jegindø, E., Reddish, P., Geertz, A. W., and Roepstorff, A. (2013a). Autobiographical memory in a fire-walking ritual. *Journal of Cognition and Culture* 13(1–2), 1–16.

Xygalatas, D., Mitkidis, P, Fischer, R., Reddish, P., Skewes, J., Geertz, A. W., Roepstorff, A., and Bulbulia, J. (2013b). Extreme rituals promote prosociality. *Psychological Science* 24(8), 1602–1605.

Xygalatas, D., and Lang, M. (2016). Prosociality and religion. In N. Kasumi Clements (ed.), *Mental Religion*. New York: Macmillan, 119–133.

Xygalatas, D., Kotherová, S., Maňo, P., Kundt, R., Cigán, J., Kundtová Klocová, E., and Lang, M. (2017). Big gods in small places: The random allocation game in Mauritius. *Religion, Brain and Behavior* 8(2), 243–261.

Xygalatas, D., Khan, S., Lang, M., Kundt, R., Kundtová-Klocová, E., Kratky, J., and Shaver, J. (2019). Effects of extreme ritual practices on health and well-being. *Current Anthropology* 60(5), 699–707.

Xygalatas, D., Maňo, P., and Baranowski Pinto, Gabriela (2021a). Ritualization increases the perceived efficacy of instrumental actions. *Cognition* 215, 104823.

Xygalatas, D., Mano, P., Bahna, V., Kundt, R., Kundtová-Klocová, E., and Shaver, J. (2021b). Social inequality and signaling in a costly ritual. *Evolution and Human Behavior* 42, 524–533.

Xygalatas, D., and Mano, P. (forthcoming). Ritual exegesis among Mauritian Hindus.

Yerkes, R. M., and Dodson, J. D. (1908). The relation of strength of stimulus to rapidity of habit-formation. *Journal of Comparative Neurology and Psychology* 18, 459–482.

Young, F. (1965). *Initiation Ceremonies: A Cross-Cultural Study of Status Dramatization*. Indianapolis, IN: Bobbs-Merrill.

Young, Sharon M., and Benyshek, Daniel C. (2010). In search of human placentophagy: A cross-cultural survey of human placenta consumption, disposal practices, and cultural beliefs. *Ecology of Food and Nutrition* 49(6), 467–484.

Zacks, J. M., and Tversky, B. (2001). Event structure in perception and conception. *Psychological Bulletin* 127(1), 3–21.

Zahavi, Amotz (1975). Mate selection: A selection for a handicap. *Journal of Theoretical Biology* 53(1), 205–214.

Zahran, S., Snodgrass, J., Maranon, D., Upadhyay, C., Granger, D., and Bailey, S. (2015). Stress and telomere shortening among central Indian conservation refugees. *Proceedings of the National Academy of Sciences of the United States of America* 112(9), E928–936.

Zak, Paul J. (2012). *The Moral Molecule: The Source of Love and Prosperity*. Boston, MA: Dutton.

Zaugg, M. K. (1980). Superstitious Beliefs of Basketball Players. Graduate thesis. University of Montana.

Zeitlyn, D. (1990). Mambila Traditional Religion: Sua in Somie. Doctoral thesis, University of Cambridge.

Zohar, A., and Felz, L. (2001). Ritualistic behaviour in young children. *Journal of Abnormal Child Psychology* 29(2), 121–128.

ACKNOWLEDGEMENTS

Like all things in life, this book is the result of a long series of circumstances that expand far beyond the act of creating it. I have been extremely fortunate to meet many brilliant, kind and generous people, who influenced my thought and inspired my research. Any attempt to list them all here would run the risk of important omissions. Besides, scientific knowledge is a collective endeavour. It really does take a village. I therefore tend to think of those influences in terms of particular contexts and groups of people rather than individuals.

Having said that, there were three individuals whose influence has been truly catalytic. At the Aristotle University of Thessaloniki, Professor Panayotis Pachis was the one who sparked my interest in the scientific study of religion. As a student in Greece, I was a late bloomer. During my first couple of years in college I struggled to find motivation and was seriously considering dropping out. Through his teaching, mentorship and friendship, Panayotis allowed me to find my passion and set me on a path that led me to a wonderful journey.

In the course of that journey I had the good luck to become part of the right groups of people at the right times. Those groups include: the Interacting Minds Centre and the Religion, Cognition and Culture research unit at Aarhus University in Denmark, where I was first as a student and later as faculty; the Institute of Cognition and Culture at the Anthropology Department of Queen's University Belfast in Northern Ireland, where I got my doctoral degree; and the Seeger Center for Hellenic Studies, at Princeton University, New Jersey, where I served as a postdoctoral fellow. These settings were pivotal in my scholarly development by offering me the kind of guidance, support and freedom that any young researcher dreams of.

During my time as Director of the LEVYNA Laboratory for the Experimental Research of Religion at Masaryk University in the Czech Republic, I had the pleasure of interacting with an amazing group of people, many of whom became some of my most trusted collaborators, and even more of whom became my good friends.

More recently, at the University of Connecticut, my colleagues and students in the Department of Anthropology, the Department of Psychological Sciences, the Cognitive Science Program and the Humanities Institute have been a constant source of intellectual stimulation and inspiration. The latter was particularly instrumental in the making of this book: without a fellowship from the Humanities Institute I might never have had the time to embark on this project.

The research presented in this book would not have been possible without the help of my many collaborators and co-authors: the students who worked in my Experimental Anthropology Lab in Connecticut and the numerous Mauritian research assistants who helped me with my fieldwork. And, of course, it would not have been possible without the help and generosity of the various local communities I engaged with in the course of that fieldwork. I consider the years I spent living among those communities to be the best education I have ever received.

Moreover, I owe gratitude to the literary agency Science Factory, to my UK publisher, Profile Books, and to my US publisher, Little, Brown Spark. Their staff, leadership and collaborators guided me through the exciting but painstaking process of communicating scholarly ideas to a broader audience, and it is thanks to their input, trust and vision for this book that the project has come to fruition.

Finally, the two most influential individuals have been my parents. Although they never had the means or the opportunity to pursue any advanced education, they always drilled the importance of learning into their offspring. My own trajectory only became possible thanks to their many sacrifices, and for this reason this book is dedicated to them.

INDEX